THE GOSPEL OF WEALTH IN THE
AMERICAN NOVEL

THE GOSPEL OF WEALTH IN THE AMERICAN NOVEL

the Rhetoric of Dreiser and
Some of his Contemporaries

ARUN MUKHERJEE

CROOM HELM
London & Sydney

Croom Helm Ltd, Provident House, Burrell Row,
Beckenham, Kent, BR3 1AT

Croom Helm Australia, 44-50 Waterloo Road,
North Ryde, 2113, New South Wales

British Library Cataloguing in Publication Data

Mukherjee, Arun
    The gospel of wealth in the American novel:
    the rhetoric of Dreiser and some of his
    contemporaries.
    1. American literature — 20th century —
    History and criticism
    I. Title
    813'.52'09 PS223

ISBN 0-7099-4649-X

Printed and bound in Great Britain
by Billing & Sons Limited, Worcester.

CONTENTS

To My Mother

If you would praise God, and in terms that happen also to sanction one system of material property rather than another, you have forced Rhetorical considerations upon us.

Kenneth Burke
A Rhetoric of Motives

PREFACE

As an outsider born and brought up in the Third World, the United States of America and its self-images have always fascinated me. This fascination increased after my arrival in Canada when I sensed a contradiction between the images with which I had grown up and the images that I received from the south of the border through American television, print media and popular literature.

This book was born in the process of my struggle to resolve and understand that contradiction which I perceived between the images and the reality. It is the product of a joint effort for which I am grateful to several friends and colleagues: to Professor Peter Morgan, who has been a pillar of support all along, providing me with practical and moral support; to Patrick Taylor, scholar, friend and neighbour, who has been closely involved in the writing of this book and has given many valuable suggestions; to Professor Eric Domville, who introduced me to these authors; to Gail Posen, friend and educator, who has provided immeasurable support and sympathy, specially in those final weeks and days when the struggle to get to the end became most acute; and to my husband, Alok, without whose constant help and encouragement I would never have written this book.

Needless to say, the interpretations and conclusions contained in the book are my own.

I have made a few innovations in documentation within the text for the sake of readability. End note numbers are given within round brackets while page references from the novels that have been discussed in detail are given within square brackets.

I also need to explain my decision not to use

Preface

the Pennsylvania edition of <u>Sister Carrie</u>. I have serious disagreements with the methods used by the editors in preparing this so-called "authoritative" text. I have, therefore, used the Norton edition of the novel.

Arun P. Mukherjee
Toronto, Canada

Chapter One

INTRODUCTION

Business and the businessman have had a central place in American society ever since the inception of the nation. The way of life which the British landed gentry had always looked down upon and considered culturally and spiritually deficient, not only found its justification on the American soil but its champions, in turn, aggressively attacked the cultural hegemony of the landed aristocracy and successfully replaced it with their own, at least in America.

Though a few studies of American business ideology could be mentioned, few scholars have undertaken to study the culture and ideology of American business. Max Weber's The Protestant Ethic and the Spirit of Capitalism was, of course, the pioneering study to explain this way of life. In addition, Richard Hofstadter traced its historical development and late nineteenth century flowering in his Social Darwinism in American Thought.

Of course, there is no dearth of studies on American capitalism. However, these studies fail to take into consideration the cultural peculiarities of American capitalism, such as its "rags-to-riches" parables and its rhetoric of individual freedom that retain a transcendent appeal for Americans. By not taking the language employed by American business into account, such studies fail to grasp how ideology becomes concrete as symbol and rhetoric and gets expressed as a way of life.

It is not surprising, then, that literary critics have also turned their backs upon the businessman and the artists who were perceptive enough to understand the central place of the businessman in American life. While the

businessman continues to reign supreme in the seats
of power, the American literary establishment has
expelled him from the literary arena. It has done
so by two means: first, by creating a canon that
excludes the works of social realists, valorizing
Hawthorne, Melville, Dickinson, James, Eliot, Frost
and Pound at the expense of Howells, Dreiser,
Herrick, Lewis, Sinclair, Sandberg and Masters, not
to speak of the Black and other minority writers,
and secondly, by stressing the formal autonomy of
the literary text while disregarding its historical
context.

This ideological innocence on the part of the
mainstream American critic has resulted in a
particularistic, reductive and ahistorical
criticism. It celebrates the formal beauties of
the text in an aesthetic accessible only to an
elite. When it concerns itself with making value
judgements, it does so in words like sin, guilt,
soul, love and loss of self, and never in terms of
race and class conflicts, social power, democratic
rights and justice. As Edward Said puts it, "It is
not too much to say that American or even European
literary theory now explicitly accepts the
principle of non-interference, and that its
peculiar mode of approaching its subject matter . .
. is _not_ to appropriate anything that is worldly,
circumstantial, or socially contaminated."(1)

The result of this "non-interference" has been
a total disregard of, not only the relationship
between texts and their historical contexts, but
also of the relationship between the language of
the text and that of the social environment in
which it was created. Though much is written these
days about discourse, I have yet to see a work that
undertakes to bring out the subtle interconnections
between literary and social discourses. The
dominant method of literary criticism tells us more
about a writer's private symbolism, patterns of
this and that, esoteric allusions, textual
paradoxes and ambiguities than about how literary
texts appropriate the discourse employed by the
social powers of their time.

I believe that without this context, which is
not simply a knowledge of historical events but a
knowledge of the words they were put and presented
in, we not only grotesquely misread the texts - I
strongly disagree with the reader-response critics
who claim that multiple and contradictory readings
are inevitable - we also remain unaware of the role

literature plays as a social institution which
interacts with other institutions in adversarial or
hegemonic ways.

In this book, I have attempted to demonstrate
how literary texts become subversive, or
supportive, by appropriating the language used by
those who wield social power. When a literary text
subtly mimics and contradicts the received myths
and ideologies of the ruling class, it undermines
their authority by making us laugh at them. On the
other hand, the ruling class always manage to
attract some creative artists who provide the
legitimation that the former seek. Literature and
art, thus, are as much divided according to
ideological and class lines as the rest of the
society, a fact which is consistently ignored by
many literary critics.

Thus, I am not interested in a simple
historical account of how American novelists have
treated the American businessman. Nor is it my
intention to rate American novelists, as Emily
Watts has in a recent study, according to their
allegiance to what she calls "the positive values
of American capitalism".(2) I wish to explore the
way American novelists respond rhetorically to the
discourse of the American businessman and his
apologists. The pronouncements of the nineteenth
century American businessmen provide a sub-text
that is encoded in the fictional works of the turn
of the century. Thus, these texts are in a
dialogical relationship with the contemporary
business discourse and their irony, as well as
their formal strategies, can only be understood in
the context of this discourse.

This rhetorical model of reading literary
texts brings us back to the world that the
formalist critic had so contemptuously abandoned.
When a literary text is seen as rhetoric, it
becomes communication, a mediator of relationships
between different sections of society. The
literary critic who sees literature as
communication provides us with insights into what
prior utterances and actions provided the impetus
for the literary text and how they are woven into
the web of the text. The text, according to this
approach, is not an "icon" or an "urn" but an
utterance, and thus is encased in a context which
can only be torn apart at the risk of making the
utterance meaningless.

An accidental discovery has led me to this

approach. While going through an early twentieth century business textbook, I came upon a passage that was replete with the imagery of knight-errantry as analogies for the exploits of the modern businessman. The passage led me to ask whether the imagery of knight-errantry I had found in the turn of the century business fiction was parodic, a mimicry by the artist of the pretensions of the heroic businessman. This was, indeed, the first time that I had discovered the rhetorical uses of imagery.

To seek an answer to the question I went back to the business spokesmen of the period. Not only did I find extensive use of the imagery of knight-errantry, I also began to identify some other recurrent image patterns that were common to both literary and non-literary texts. When I turned again to the literary texts, I perceived rhetorical sallies, parodies, satire and irony that I had not encountered earlier. Other critics had not noticed these either.

This discovery has radically affected my own critical practice. Academic training had led me to believe that the creative artist used a special language. Imagery, I had been taught, was the special language of the artist. He was unique in his ability to unify disparate realms, make abstractions concrete, and connect thought and feeling through the power of metaphor. Other, non-literary, users of language supposedly did not do these.

I have come to believe that literary language is not only not different from the language of social intercourse, it deliberately appropriates the ideologically-charged language of the people in control of social power in order to subvert and challenge their legitimizing activities. Secondly, I believe that literature also contributes to the language of social intercourse by giving us the terminology with which we can explain ourselves to ourselves and to others. For example, the figures of the knight, the pilgrim and the superman that the businessman has incorporated into his own vocabulary were the contributions of creative artists. Finally, I hold that the struggle to appropriate socially honorific language is the key to social intercourse in a divided society. For example, both Ronald Reagan and Michael Harrington seek to appropriate for themselves John Winthrop's metaphor of "city on a hill."

Language, thus, can be seen as an arena of
social warfare where different social institutions
try to capture power through ownership of the
sacred vocabulary of a society. Literature
participates in that warfare, either through
creating heroes or undercutting them. It is my
belief that we cannot study literary texts by
removing them from the din and turmoil of this
battlefield and locking them in a soundproof
environment where the voices of social discourse
cannot be heard.

My analysis is indebted to the work of Kenneth
Burke and Hugh Dalziel Duncan who consider
linguistic symbols to be the key to understanding
social order. Burke's concept of "transcendence"
helped me to understand how the dominant group of a
society tends to legitimize its power by linking it
to a higher principle, through the appropriation of
the sacred vocabulary of religion or other
important social institutions. In this particular
case, Burke's analysis of rhetorical motives made
me realize that the American businessman
transformed his life in the marketplace by clothing
it in a religious vocabulary which portrays man's
life in the world in metaphors of wayfaring and
warfaring. Burke's notion of "symbolic bridges"
was equally illuminating. It showed me how the
business discourse of the period under discussion
here blended the metaphors of a knightly quest and,
later, of a social Darwinian jungle, with the
metaphors of pilgrimage from an earlier age. For
however disconnected they may seem on the surface,
all of them paint the world as a hostile
wilderness, a backdrop which is equally suitable
for the "trials" of the pilgrim, the jousts of the
knight, and the struggle of the "fit" and the
"unfit" of the social Darwinian. As Burke and
Duncan have demonstrated, a literary text is, first
of all, a rhetorical utterance. It is, says Burke,
a deliberate and structured "answer" to someone:

> Let us suppose that I ask you: "What did the
> man say?" And that you answer: "He said
> 'yes'." You still do not know what the man
> said. You would not know unless you knew more
> about the situation, and about the remarks
> that preceded his answer. Critical and
> imaginative works are answers to questions
> posed by the situations in which they arose.
> They are not merely answers, they are

strategic answers, stylized answers.(3)

Thus Burke taught me to read figurative language for its rhetorical motives. His analysis of symbolic devices as "eulogistic coverings" on the part of the dominant elite has provided me with a very valuable insight into both the social order and the literary text. He has shown me that literary texts, like other human utterances, are written with a rhetorical motive, whether it be to flatter a patron, to incite one's fellow beings to revolution, or to assuage one's own guilt.

In this book I have chosen to analyse the works as addresses to the reader who is expected to place them in the context of other addresses. I see these works as "strategic" and "stylized" answers to the dominant discourse of the period. Although I sense that this approach has some similarity to the currently popular semiotic approach, I find that Burke's terminology is much less cluttered with technicalities and is much more political.

While the major portion of the book is devoted to the work of Dreiser, the writer most sensitive to the ideology of business, I have discussed four of his contemporaries in some detail in order to establish the validity of my point about the socially shared nature of language. All these writers participate in, and contribute to, the rhetoric common to their time.

Chapter Two examines the historical shift in attitudes towards business and the accumulation of wealth in the light of the pioneering studies of Max Weber and R. H. Tawney. I have considered the statements of business and religious leaders for their rhetorical implications. I have proposed that the changed attitude to wealth is brought about through a symbolic shift. What had previously been associated with disease and darkness is now symbolized as a religious quest. Similarly, censorious terms such as greed, rapacity and avarice are replaced by honorific ones like thrift, virtue, prudence and diligence. I have compared this rhetoric with that employed by two writers of the period, namely Hawthorne and Frances Hodgson Burnett, to demonstrate how literary texts interact with the dominant discourse of the period.

The following three chapters deal with Dreiser's response to the rhetoric of business. Chapter Three analyses Dreiser's autobiographical writings from the viewpoint of examining his youthful allegiance to, and later disillusionment with, the dominant ideology of his society. Chapter Four looks at the Cowperwood trilogy and proposes that Dreiser, instead of being an unabashed extoller of the superman of business, was a harsh critic who satirized his heroic pretensions by employing the mock-heroic mode. I propose that his irony has not been noticed by his critics because the discourse that he parodied has been disregarded by them. Chapter Five examines three other works by Dreiser in order to look at his portrayal of the overall effect of the "symbolic environment" created by this "heroic" businessman. Thus, in his Sister Carrie, The "Genius" and An American Tragedy, Dreiser probes the impact of business ideology on the lives of ordinary men and women who must perforce live in the jungle world created by the businessman's metaphors. The lives of Carrie, Eugene and Clyde are determined by their acceptance of the heroic world as truth on the one hand, and their inability to live up to its demands on the other.

Chapter Six compares Dreiser's response to the heroic metaphors of business with those of some of his contemporaries. The Rise of Silas Lapham by William Dean Howells, Letters from a Self-Made Merchant to His Son by George Horace Lorimer, The Pit by Frank Norris and A Life for a Life by Robert Herrick give an indication of the prevailing climate of opinion. While Howells and Herrick are critical of the businessman's appropriation of an exalted vocabulary, Lorimer and Norris approve of it and use it in their own novels. Whatever may be the difference in their attitudes, however, all these novelists employ the prevalent metaphors, whether to mock or to exalt them.

My endeavour, thus, is admittedly ambitious. I have laid claim to analysing literary texts with the purpose of uncovering the ideological underpinnings of American society. My emphasis, therefore, falls on those areas of the texts that are referential and communicative. I have supplied verifiable historical evidence which allows us to go back and forth between literary and non-literary texts to see their interconnectedness. And I have sought to speak in a much more rigorous language than that of critics who vaguely speak of "materialistic values of American society" and the

"search for the self".
 In <u>Literature as Social Discourse</u>, Roger Fowler remarks that "there has so far been little detailed linguistic research into sociologically and ideologically interesting language."(4) I feel that this study is a modest effort in that direction.

NOTES

 1. Edward Said, <u>The World, the Text, and the Critic</u> (Harvard University Press, Cambridge, Mass., 1983) 3.
 2. Emily Stipes Watts, <u>The Businessman in American Literature</u> (University of Georgia Press, Athens, 1982) 151.
 3. Kenneth Burke, <u>The Philosophy of Literary Form</u>: <u>Studies in Symbolic Action</u>, 2nd edn. (Louisiana State University Press, Baton Rouge, 1967) 1.
 4. Roger Fowler, <u>Literature as Social Discourse</u> (Batsford Academic and Educational Ltd., London, 1981) 27.

Chapter Two

KNIGHTS AND PILGRIMS: BUSINESSMAN'S SELF-IMAGES

The usual place assigned to seekers of wealth in
literary typology has been the darkness of the
bottomless pit. Working within the Judaeo-
Christian framework, Western literature has
generally associated wealth with a state of mental
and spiritual sickness. The descriptive terms
assigned to its pursuit have been as a rule
negative and censorious: greed, avarice, rapacity,
covetousness and cupidity, for example. And avid
seekers of wealth like Shakespeare's Shylock,
Jonson's Volpone, Massinger's Sir Giles Overreach,
Dickens' Ralph Nickleby, Hawthorne's Judge
Pyncheon, James' Gilbert Osmond and Lawrence's
Gerald Crich are all characters of darkness,
corrupted by the taint of the devil. As in the
legend of King Midas, wealth in literature has been
symbolic of death, social as well as personal. Not
only does it petrify the affected person, his sin
also causes violent disruptions in the social
fabric.
        In their suspicion of wealth, writers have
been faithful to the tenets of Christianity. The
Bible had declared that it was easier for a camel
to pass through the eye of a needle than for a rich
man to enter heaven. "The love of money is the
root of all evil", Paul declared. "Ye cannot serve
God and Mammon", preached Matthew. Trade,
according to the mediaeval doctrine, was dangerous
to the soul "since, regarded in itself, it serves
the lust of gain."(1) Honest labour in a craft
was the approved religious conduct. However, the
craftsman was enjoined to earn only as much as was
necessary to provide for his bodily wants.
        Early Christianity discouraged economic
initiative and generation of capital. Though Paul
had declared that "if any one would not work,

neither should he eat", one was to earn no more than the amount needed to satisfy one's corporeal needs. Weber explains that for Aquinas and Paul, work, by itself, had no transcendental sanction. For them, "labour is only necessary <u>naturali ratione</u> for the maintenance of individual and community." Activity in the world is merely a thing of the flesh, as necessary as eating or drinking but amoral in itself. What really counted as spiritual activity for them was contemplation: "the highest form of monastic productivity lay in the increase of the <u>Thesaurus ecclesiae</u> through prayer and chant."(2)

However, the religious revolution in the sixteenth century stood this traditional scheme of morals on its head. The pursuit of wealth which had so far been regarded as the deadliest of perils to the spirit became, under the new dispensation, "not merely an advantage, but a duty". Tawney has traced the change in linguistic usage thus:

> What is significant, in short, is not the strength of the motive of economic self-interest, which is the commonplace of all ages and demands no explanation. It is the change of moral standards which converted a natural frailty into an ornament of the spirit, and canonized as the economic virtues habits which in earlier ages had been denounced as vices. . . . Baptized in the bracing, if icy, waters of Calvinist theology, the life of business, once regarded as perilous to the soul - <u>summa periculosa est emptionis et venditionis negotiatio</u> - acquires a new sanctity. Labour is not merely an economic means: it is a spiritual end. Covetousness, if a danger to the soul, is a less formidable menace than sloth. So far from poverty being meritorious, it is a duty to choose the more profitable occupation. So far from there being an inevitable conflict between money-making and piety, they are natural allies, for the virtues incumbent on the elect - diligence, thrift, sobriety, prudence - are the most reliable passport to commercial prosperity. Thus the pursuit of riches, which once had been feared as the enemy of religion, was now welcomed as its ally.(3)

What transformed wealth from its designation as the deadliest of sins to the ornament of the saints was the new interpretation of "the calling". The word, according to Weber, had meant "the purely religious idea of the call through the Gospel taught by the apostle", carrying "no suggestion of a specifically religious valuation of secular labour in a calling".(4)   After the Reformation, the word signified a meaningful secular activity performed as a command of the Divine will. A Christian was no longer required to shun the world as the friars and monks of the Catholic church had done.   Their abandonment of the world was utterly reprehensible to the Puritan:

> The begging friars and such monks as live only to themselves and to their formal devotion, but do employ themselves in no one thing to further their own subsistence or the good of mankind . . . yet have the confidence to boast of this their course as a state of perfection; which in very deed, as to the worthiness of it, falls short of the poorest cobbler, for his is a calling of God, and theirs is none.(5)

A Christian was to participate in worldly activity with the same fervour as he showed in prayer: "Be wholly taken up in diligent business of your lawful callings, when you are not exercised in the more immediate service of God."(6)   It was incumbent upon every believer to enhance the glory of God's creation by the utmost possible contribution of his labour.   "It is for action that God maintaineth us and our activities; work is the moral as well as the natural end of power. . . . It is action that God is most served and honoured by . . .", wrote Richard Baxter.(7)   Faith without works was not enough.   John Bunyan stated: "At the day of Doom men shall be judged according to their fruits. It will not be said then, Did you believe? but, Were you doers or talkers only?"(8)

Work, even when performed as a fulfillment of God's command, necessarily results in pecuniary rewards.   As Weber and Tawney demonstrate, the Puritans did very well in the marketplace. And they saw their success as a sign of God's favour. According to Tawney, "success in business is in itself almost a sign of spiritual grace, for it is proof that a man has labored faithfully in his

11

vocation, and that 'God has blessed his trade.'"(9)
Consequently, men were divided as the "elect" and
the "damned" according to their success in
business. Lack of prosperity was a sure sign of
being unregenerate. Since wealth was no longer a
means but an end, the proof of one's industry, one
was forbidden to stop at the point of having
satisfied one's corporeal needs. Wesley, though
troubled by the consequences of riches on moral
character, wrote nevertheless: "we must exhort all
Christians to gain all they can, and to save all
they can; that is, in effect, to grow rich."(10)
That is to say, "the conscientious discharge of the
duties of business" had been exalted from the
secular to the spiritual realm, to become "the
loftiest of religious and moral virtues".(11) A
Scottish divine lamented in 1709 that trade had
been "put in the room of religion".(12)

Sociologists, following Max Weber, have noted
that human beings tend to resort to honorific
symbols of authority when they need to justify
their actions:

> Those in authority within institutions and
> social structures attempt to justify their
> rule by linking it, as if it were a necessary
> consequence, with moral symbols, sacred
> emblems, or legal formulae which are widely
> believed and deeply internalized. These
> central conceptions may refer to a god or
> gods, the "votes of the majority," the "will
> of the people," the "aristocracy of talents or
> wealth," to the "divine right of kings," or to
> the allegedly extraordinary endowment of the
> person of the ruler himself.(13)

As Hugh Dalziel Duncan states, "When in power, we
must create a magic, a poetry, and, finally, a
divinity about the symbols we use to legitimize our
position. We do this generally by usurping symbols
already charged with sacred power." Such symbols,
he goes on to say, "are charismatic vessels of
hierarchy. They glow and have radiance. They move
us because they identify us with a higher order and
thus produce within us a feeling of sublimity."(14)
The Puritans, in their attempt to place their
business activities within the aegis of religion,
were motivated by this desire for legitimation.
William James says: "we are saved from the
[sense] of wrongness by making proper connection

with the higher powers."(15) Similarly, Kenneth Burke points out the need within the individual for "pleasant imagery" in order to "favorably identify his cause or unfavorably identify the cause of an opponent."(16) The prosperous Puritan consequently saw his life clothed in the prominent symbols of his religion. Since wealth was being sought not for itself but under Divine injunction, he could symbolize his life in pursuit of wealth as a drama of salvation, as the quest of the soul for its heavenly home. Not only did he anoint himself, he proscribed all other approaches to God. As Weber says, the search for the "Kingdom of God" became "exclusive," to be undertaken "only through the fulfilment of duty in the calling. . . ."(17) This symbolic transubstantiation of the life of the prosperous businessman becomes apparent in the following passage from John Preston:

> Even those common actions are steppes that lead to the Journey; Even as you see; take a servant that is set to worke or to goe a Journey, that is to mowe or to drive a Cart; even the whetting of the Sithe is a part of his worke as well as his mowing of the grasse; the provendring of his horse is a dispatching of his Journey, a going on in it, as well as when he rides, and so the oyling of the wheele is a drawing on, as well as every steppe he takes.(18)

Like Preston, Cotton Mather also used the image of the journey to convey the connection between business activity and religion:

> A Christian at his Two Callings, is a man in a Boat, Rowing for Heaven; the House which our Heavenly Father hath intended for us. If he mind but one of his Callings, be it which it will, he pulls the Oar, but on one side of the Boat, and will make but a poor dispatch to the Shoar of Eternal Blessedness. . . . Yea, a Calling is not only our Duty, but also our Safety. Men will ordinarily fall into horrible Snares, and infinite Sins, if they have not a Calling, to be their preservative. . . . The temptations of the Devil, are best Resisted by those that are least at Liesure

> [sic] to Receive them. An <u>Occupation</u> is an
> <u>Ordinance</u> of God for our safeguard against the
> <u>Temptations</u> of the Devil. A Bird on the <u>Wing</u>
> is not so soon catch'd by the <u>Hellish Fowler</u>.
> A man is upon the Wing, when he is at the
> <u>Work</u>, which God hath set him to do. . . .(19)

All religious symbolism, specially that of
Judaism and Christianity, frequently portrays man's
life as a pilgrimage towards his heavenly home.
Northrop Frye considers the quest myth as "the
central myth of literature".(20) Georg Roppen and
Richard Sommer, in their encyclopaedic study of the
quest metaphor, write that the quest motif is
perhaps "the most complex and capacious in the
history of the conventions of literature":

> Because of the way in which these three
> elements [destination, landscape, the True
> Way] correspond to the three fundamental human
> concerns - (1) the intrinsic nature of man and
> inanimate substance; (2) society and ethical
> organization; and (3) the final purposes of
> existence and consciousness - it will be small
> occasion for wonder that the metaphor has lent
> itself well to great and comprehensive
> formulations of religious belief in
> literature; has, indeed, been almost
> exclusively employed to this end in Pagan and
> Christian worlds alike. Depending upon the age
> and upon our own tolerance of vision, the
> Journey to Life, Empire, or God - as they are
> respectively viewed by Homer, Virgil and Dante
> - is the projection of a single disposition of
> man: his adjustment to the unknown, the
> unrealized, and untamed.(21)

What is intriguing, then, is not the metaphor
but the particular context in which it is applied
by John Preston or Cotton Mather. Quest for us has
a serious import. It symbolizes matters of the
spirit. The knights adventured for the Holy Grail
in their most exalted literary incarnations. The
heroes of myths went on the seas or underground to
be initiated into the meaning of life. In the
hands of such modern writers as Conrad and Herman
Hesse quest came to symbolize a search for
identity.
In the light of its literary past, its
equation with the production of wealth is certainly

novel and thought-provoking. It can only mean that economic activity has been sanctified by being joined to a transcendent order. Having become a religious activity, it can justifiably be clad in the symbols associated with it. Since the businessman in his counting house is active in the service of God, he, like a good Puritan, is an earnest Pilgrim. For, as Haller tells us, the Puritan pulpits were obsessed with the metaphors of "wayfaring and warfaring". The symbolism of the nativity and passion meant nothing to them. They told the individual that "his soul was a traveler through a strange country and a soldier in battle. He was a traveler who, fleeing from destruction, must adhere through peril and hardship to the way that leads home."(22)   Other historical evidence also substantiates that Puritans saw themselves as travelling through a wilderness in which darkness reigned supreme. They were soldiers of God fighting Satan. According to Haller, Bunyan's allegory is not unique, but an expression of the general bent of the Puritan mind: "His great allegories were but single items coming from a single practitioner - though a genius - in a vast literature, only a portion of which has been preserved and the forms and conditions of which have been almost completely overpast and forgotten."(23)

What is being suggested here, on the basis of the above evidence, is that the Puritan businessman defined his life in the dominant symbols of his belief. His pastors assured him that the profit on his ledger was a sign of his having been a brave fighter in the war against the Devil. As Richard Huber says, "The successful man was the ascetic who bent down and finally triumphed over his own worst tendencies."(24)   The journey towards wealth, according to this philosophy, was a moral journey, from vice to virtue, from the snares of the Devil to the arms of God. Wealth, these pious men claimed, was symbolic. It was simply the sign of God's favour, a reward of their having been steadfast in virtue. John D. Rockefeller, Sr., discoursing on the way to wealth, warned the young aspirant "to avoid the temptations which beset him, to select carefully his associates and give attention at once to his spiritual side as well as to his mental and material sides."(25)   One must presume that he followed this course himself for he

firmly believed that his wealth was the sign of his
election. "The good Lord gave me the money. . . ."
"I believe the power to make money is a gift of
God", "to be developed and used to the best of our
ability for the good of mankind. Having been
endowed with the gift I possess, I believe it is my
duty to make money and still more money, and to use
the money I make for the good of my fellow man
according to the dictates of my conscience."(26)

Money is seen here as a transcendent value,
finding its justification by being identified with
God's will. Its value for the pious and prosperous
businessmen like Rockefeller is totally symbolic:
it stands for their virtuous behaviour which in its
turn was symbolized in the imagery of the quest.
Wilbur F. Crafts, who wrote his Successful Men of
Today on the basis of a questionnaire sent out to
prominent businessmen, writes: "One of the most
respected of Brooklyn's citizens quotes, as powers
in his life, two verses of Scripture: 'Seek ye
first the kingdom of God and His righteousness. . . .'" "Yet other business mottoes are: 'Be
a whole man.' 'Not slothful in business, fervent
in spirit, serving the Lord.' 'Commit thy way unto
the Lord, and he shall direct thy paths.' 'Do
justly, love mercy, and walk humbly with thy
God.'"(27) One also comes across very frequent
references to exalting passages from the Bible,
Shakespeare, Longfellow and other contemporary
poets while reading the success literature of the
period. Usually these passages are on the theme of
the difficulties of the journey of life. The
Reverend William Lawrence's imagery is
illuminating: "And when a man has reached this
point [success in business activity], he has indeed
reached one of the high plateaus of character: from
this rise the higher mountain peaks of Christian
graces, but here he is on the standing-ground of
the higher civilization."(28)

In other words, the pious businessman in his
shop or office was not just making a living in
order to satisfy his material wants or his vanity
but was on his way to God. As A. Whitney Griswold
noted, "We are not surprised to find Puritan
merchants mentioning God prominently in their
invoices - thanking Him for profit gained, or
ascribing losses to His greater glory."(29) The
prosperous ones sincerely felt that by paying
vigorous attention to their trade, they were
ascending heavenward. As the social histories of

the period show, the wealthy men of America were
fervently religious. Not only did they make large
monetary donations to the church, they were very
active members of the congregation. Many of them
taught Sunday school, dutifully impressing upon the
younger generation the rewards of following the
straight and narrow path. Their pastors reinforced
their self-confidence by proclaiming that
"Godliness is in league with riches."(30)

The metaphoric landscape of Christianity was
thus completely transformed. The social hierarchy
was said to be a reflection of divine Providence.
The wealthy were the people of light, the stewards
of the Lord, whereas the poor were the people of
darkness. Russell H. Conwell was expressing a
familiar sentiment in his famous Acres of Diamonds
when he said that "the number of poor who are to be
sympathized with is very small. To sympathize with
a man whom God has punished for his sins, thus to
help him when God would still continue a just
punishment, is to do wrong, no doubt about it, and
we do that more than we help those who are
deserving."(31) A famous businessman told the
students of Syracuse University: "Why is there
still so much poverty? One reason is because
nature or the devil has made some men weak and
imbecile and others lazy and worthless, and neither
man nor God can do much for one who will do nothing
for himself."(32)

The process of social mobility, according to
this view, becomes the drama of the soul's
salvation. The journey from rags to riches is not
merely a Cinderella story in America. Beginning
with Benjamin Franklin's Autobiography, it has
been clothed in a religious cast and surrounded by
metaphors of a spiritual ascent. Since poverty is
the realm of the Devil, and wealth that of the
Divine, the journey from one state to another takes
the lineaments of a Dantesque quest. This is how
it was cast in the massive body of success
literature, a good deal of which was written by
Protestant clergymen. The biographies of prominent
businessmen trumpeted how they had triumphed
against their poor backgrounds by sheer will and
faith in God. Young men were exhorted to follow
their example and promised the blessings of wealth
if they led Christian lives. The pursuit of wealth
was a process of moral and spiritual growth which
had its beginnings in pain and anguish and which
ultimately led to a state of bliss.

The rags-to-riches theme did not stay confined to the sermon and the biography but became the prominent literary motif of the age. The popular novels for the adolescents were about a mythic hero who begins his life in depressed circumstances, journeys through various adventures on the way and finally reaches his desired goal. All this, of course, takes place under the aegis of Christian symbolism. The adventures of the hero are depicted as temptations planted by the Devil and struggles with evil characters. When the hero has successfully proved himself through the various trials, he is amply rewarded. The prosperous businessmen act as father figures, helping the virtuous hero in his hour of need and providing the wider framework of a moral social order.

How close the alliance between the pursuit of wealth and the perilous matter of salvation was for these novelists becomes clear from a novel written by Frances Hodgson Burnett. <u>Two Little Pilgrims'</u> <u>Progress</u> traces the fortunes of two siblings on the road to success, whose mileposts are described in terms borrowed from Bunyan's book. Money in this book is a transcendent symbol, allied to the highest spiritual concerns. The feeling one gets after reading the novel is that of a happy harmony between the temporal and the eternal. All contradictions are smoothed out by irradiating the earthly with the heavenly. Meg and Robin live with their Aunt on a farm which seems "hideous and exasperating and sordid" to them.(33) Though not explicitly cruel, Aunt Matilda is, none the less, incapable of feeling any emotions and the children feel deprived of affection. Robin and Meg, as a result, keep close to each other and live in a private world of their own, symbolized by the "Straw Parlour" at the top of the barn. Robin has made up his mind that "he would not be poor like his father, but would be very rich" [16]. He saves every penny he gets though he is generous enough to buy a gift for his sister at Christmas. The two, true to the stereotype, are thrifty and industrious. They read <u>Pilgrim's Progress</u> in their spare time.

She was a child with an imagination, and she used to invent new adventures for Christian as he toiled up the Hill of Difficulty. . . . But her great addition to the story was her description of the City on the Hill, which she

> always followed Christian into, and which she
> called the City Beautiful. . . . In it there
> were all the things she and Robin wanted and
> all the joys they yearned for. Their father
> and mother were there, and she and Robin lived
> with them in a sort of fairy palace, which it
> was her delight to add to the plan and
> contents of, every time she told the story and
> they wanted a new possession. [17-8]

The Celestial City of Bunyan has been transformed
here to a cornucopia, brimming with the fullness of
attractive material objects. However, the two
realms stay wedded together by a discreet
integration of imagery. The City Beautiful is also
abundant in natural beauty and is bathed in a
particular glory.

The imaginary City Beautiful is "millions of
miles" [20] away from the sordid reality that
surrounds the children. However, just when the
intensity of imagination makes Meg acutely aware of
her present narrow state, they come to hear of
"a City Beautiful - a real one - on this earth and
only two hundred miles away" [21]. The city is
Chicago and all the people are talking about the
World Fair at its shore. The children decide to
run away from the farm and start planning their
journey. The second chapter is subtitled "The
Bottom of the Hill of Difficulty". Chapter III,
"The First Step Up", and Chapter IV, "A Step
Higher", narrate the hard manual labour the
children undertake to save their fare. Chapter VI
is subtitled "'Burdens Don't Fall Off by
Themselves'" and recapitulates the progress of the
journey.

> "And I know I was thinking about it when I
> said, 'We are not going to stay here
> always. That is the first step up the Hill of
> Difficulty.'"
> "And that day when you said you would not let
> it go by you," Meg would answer, "that was
> the day we reached the Wicket Gate." [62]

As Kenneth Burke reminds us, symbols do not just
effect a merger between the natural and the human
but also between the disparate realms of human
action.(34) They create identifications between
the secular and the spiritual, wealth and virtue,
property and natural law, self-interest and public

good, and might and right. The ethereal City on the Hill which the human imagination had kept so assiduously separate from the material is dragged down to the level of the Cinderella story here.

Burnett spells out every parallelism in great detail with direct quotations from Pilgrim's Progress lest her readers miss the meaning. And, with the help of exalted symbols of the celestial sphere, she transforms the grimy, industrial city of Chicago into a vision of the sublime. How exaggerated this picture is becomes clear from the contemporary portraits of the city by Henry Blake Fuller and Robert Herrick who were not so impressed by the World Fair and who made it a point to draw out the contrast between the reality and the dream presented in the Exposition.

In Burnett's world, however, there are no uneasy conflicts between the vision and the reality, between "the world we live in and the world we want to live in".(35) The merger is symbolized by the fact that the children keep their copy of the Pilgrim's Progress near "the treasure", the little hoard that is being accumulated to take them to Chicago. It is also spelt out in words.

> "Robin," said Meg suddenly, shutting the book and giving it a little thump on the back, "it's not only Christian's city that is like our city. We are like Christian. We are pilgrims, and our way to that place is our Pilgrim's Progress." [70-1]

The remaining details of the pilgrimage of these fortune seekers do not require recounting. The parallels from Bunyan are deliberately piled up at every step in their journey. In Chapter X they reach the "golden gates" and are admitted to the "holy ground" of the Exposition. The next five chapters are devoted to the Exposition which is described in details as sensuous as "The Eve of St. Agnes". However, the children must remain spectators as yet, not having any money to indulge their fantasies. Yet, it is all for the best, for the reader knows that a bereaved wealthy man has been so taken by their looks that he follows them wherever they go. He takes charge in Chapter XV and like the Aladdin's lamp, fulfills their wildest desires.

They are taken to eat in "a dining place for

creatures of another world. It was so brilliant
with light, so decorated, so gorgeous" [179]. In a
luxurious hotel room they "slept the sleep of Eden
and dreamed the dreams of Paradise" [184]. The
businessman does the thing to be expected of him:
by the end of the penultimate chapter he adopts
them. As Meg says, "Oh, dear John Holt. We have
got into the City Beautiful, and you are going to
let us live there always" [205].

The plot comes full circle when we find out
that John Holt is one of the "Self-made Western
men" [210] who started "as lonely and poor as we
are when he was twelve" [199]. He has spent his
life in "work and bold ventures" and has amassed
an "unlimited fortune". Robin's life, we are led to
expect, will follow a similar pattern: "in his
small boyish body was imprisoned the force and
ability which in manhood build great schemes, and
not only build but carry them out. In him was
imprisoned one of the great business men, inventors
or political powers of the new century" [28].

The novel creates a world where the id and the
ego live in perfect harmony, where gratification
causes no guilt, where the body and the soul are no
longer at war. True to the spirit of the times,
"Godliness is in league with riches" here. The
journey from rags to riches, instead of being
merely a secular adventure, has become a spiritual
quest. The life of wealth and luxury which caused
so much anguish for early Christianity, and many
other religions, has finally been justified. This
has been done with the help of the same symbols
that had at first cast it out in the darkness.

Utterances outside literature are but
fragmented metaphors. The statements of a Carnegie
or a Rockefeller can only be understood through the
help of the complex symbolic acts enacted in the
works of literature affirmative of the values of a
society. Burnett's novel, as well as those of
Horatio Alger, Frank Munsey, Harold Bell Wright, E.
P. Roe and Gene Stratton Porter provide the reader
with a glimpse into the metaphoric landscape of
American culture. In this literature, the journey
from rags to riches is a symbolic journey of
self-affirmation, a test of manhood, a kind of
initiation ritual every male American must go
through if he is to achieve self-identity. And
because religion was the most important institution
of the nineteenth century American society, the
journey is decked out in symbols borrowed from the

religious sphere. The uniqueness of this
configuration becomes apparent when compared to the
rags-to-riches journeys of Dickens' waifs. Oliver
Twist and David Copperfield are entirely dependent
on the benevolence of prosperous elders. Their
ordeal does not have any religious significance.

Also significant is the dearth of merchant
heroes in British fiction. Its heroes are usually
men of independent means or, else, they make their
living as sailors, army men, lawyers, journalists
etc. One can only interpret this phenomenon as an
indication that the Puritan values of hard work and
self-reliance did not get a free field in Britain
in the way they did in the United States. In
Britain, as Martin Green points out, the heroes of
popular fiction came from the "aristomilitary
caste".(36) The era of colonial expansion created
a different mood and different heroes in that
country. Also, the factor of class in the older
countries worked against the parvenu or nouveau
riche.
This is not to say that the self-made man did
not encounter any opposition in America. "Serious"
writers have consistently displayed a hostile
attitude towards the pretensions of the self-made
man. When he insisted on his piety, the American
writer exposed him by pointing out the
inconsistencies in his casuistry. The usual
response of serious literature has been to
challenge his use of the sacred symbols for
partisan purposes. When the prospering businessman
presented himself as a pilgrim, these writers
pointed out the falsity of his claim by realigning
the appropriated symbols to their traditional
sphere.

The process becomes very clear in a tale by
Hawthorne. Written in 1843, "The Celestial
Railroad" comments upon the devaluation of the
spiritual symbols of Puritan life. Drawing upon
Bunyan's Pilgrim's Progress for its structure,
the tale forces the reader to notice the gap
between the ideal of Puritan conduct and the
falsehood which goes under its name. Hawthorne
places a railroad in the metaphoric landscape of
Bunyan. The wealthy citizens of the City of
Destruction, a "populous and flourishing town", are
its passengers, "setting forth towards the
Celestial City as cheerfully as if the pilgrimage
were merely a summer tour." All the difficulties
of the passage have been overcome. The Slough of

Despond has been bridged, the Hill of Difficulty tunnelled, the Valley of Humiliation filled up by the debris of excavation and the Valley of the Shadow of Death lit by gaslight. The "enormous burdens" are not carried on the pilgrims' shoulders but "snugly deposited in the baggage car".(37) Appollyon has been hired as the engineer whereas Mr. Greatheart has been relieved from service. The City of Vanity with its Vanity Fair is a commercial capital and "there is no longer the want of harmony between the town's-people and pilgrims". "On the contrary, as the new railroad brings with it great trade and a constant influx of strangers, the lord of Vanity Fair is its chief patron, and the capitalists of the city are among the largest stockholders."(38) However, as expected, the celestial railroad takes the pilgrims only as far as the river where they climb into a ferry boat which will take them to their everlasting destruction.

It is noteworthy here that Hawthorne resorted to the same imagery as was commonly being used for the exaltation of a social group. It points out the intricate connection between social experience and literary forms. In the first place, the dominant class had appropriated Bunyan's metaphors to justify its way of life to itself as well as to others. In Hawthorne, this social act provides the parodic form. His allegory derives its power from his ability to turn the tables upon his opponents. The same process can be seen at work in The Rise of Silas Lapham and the novels of Dreiser. Their structuring principle is the parody of the popular literary modes which uphold the values and beliefs of the self-made man. While the quest in these works takes the protagonist in an upward direction, after the required ordeals of the road, the serious novelists underplay the difficulties of the road while questioning its ultimate destination. As Northrop Frye points out, the novel thrives on the parody of romance which is usually "kidnapped" by the powerful section of a society.(39) It thus provides a balancing influence in social affairs. According to Kenneth Burke, art prevents society from becoming totally dogmatic by its irreverence for the people in power. "An art may be of value purely through preventing a society from becoming too assertively, too hopelessly, itself."(40) However, as Burke himself suggests, the transforming power of art may remain muffled due to several reasons. "[A] 'good' rhetoric neglected by the press obviously cannot be so 'communicative' as a poor rhetoric backed nation-wide by headlines. And often we must think of rhetoric not in terms of some one particular address, but as a general <u>body of identifications</u> that owe their convincingness much more to trivial repetition and dull daily reinforcement than to exceptional rhetorical skill."(41) The fact remains that the canonization of the businessman, though challenged by these writers, went on unhampered. The Protestant churches were on his side and their pastors did their utmost to present him as the model of Christian virtue, going so far as to condemn all poverty as sinful and all strikes as unlawful. Moreover, the American cultural values of self-help and egalitarianism were favourable to his image. He appealed to the popular imagination as the promise incarnate of American democracy. No wonder that Horatio Alger, George Horace Lorimer, Russell Conwell, Elbert Hubbard and Norman Vincent Peale were more influential than the highbrow writers. The power of the self-made businessman lay in his symbolic appeal to the American imagination. As Burke demonstrates, the social classes appeal to each other through the rhetoric of "courtship".(42) The self-made businessman identified himself with the poor lads and promised them the same glorious future if only they could stay on the straight and narrow path. Poverty, as Carnegie and others like him insisted, was good for building character. Moral growth was possible only through undergoing hardships. The closeness of this ideal to the Puritanic injunction for self-control and the actual possibility of making it contributed to the high prestige of the self-made man.

The symbols derived from the religious sphere were, in this sense, essentially democratic. What they emphasized was the millionaire's similarity with the common man and their equal status in the presence of God. The straight and narrow path, though difficult, was considered to be open for every one. Though the battle was a hard one, it was not against external enemies but against the evil within one's own self. Even though poverty was considered a self-inflicted malady in this scheme of things, the sons and daughters of the poor could escape it. In the course of time, however, some new symbols were created and appropriated which were not so democratic. They

24

created a halo around the self-made man by presenting his achievements as superhuman and hence inaccessible to ordinary human beings.

Contemporary literature provided a rich quarry of role models which the elite eagerly adapted to their own use. Literature, as Joan Rockwell, along with other literary sociologists, points out, is not just a reflection of society, "but it also 'produces' society, because it has a normative effect on its members, perhaps especially in childhood."(43) Rockwell says that "literary characters personify social norms and values, they . . . set patterns for imitation which are very much wanted in times when society is being unmade and reassembled in new and strange ways."(44) The literature to which American plutocracy turned for its new symbols was the romance novel which flourished since the early nineteenth century under the impetus of Sir Walter Scott. It created an ideal world of brave and courteous knights and beautiful damsels. "Like a collective Miniver Cheevy, great parts of the American reading public loved the days of old when swords were bright and steeds were prancing, cursed the commonplace, and sighed for what was not."(45) W. P. Trent complained, "Almost every day a new historical romance comes to my table - now the scene is laid in the Italy of the fourteenth century, now in the France of the thirteenth, now it is in Wales, now in the Faroe Islands. Nearly always the story is told by the chief actor, who has hairbreadth escapes in plenty. . . ."(46) Harry Thurston Peck, another reviewer, condemned Howells because his blood did not stir at the "splendid pictures of chivalry".(47) Howells and Twain considered romance to be anti-democratic and responded to it as bitterly as modern intellectuals do to violence on the television. Walter Scott, lamented Twain, had set the world "in love with dreams and phantoms; . . . with silliness and emptinesses, sham grandeurs, sham gauds, and sham chivalries of a brainless and worthless long-vanished society." (48)

For the readers, however, the heroes of romance were irresistible. Women, specially, were captivated by the ideals of knighthood. Laura Jadwin in Frank Norris' The Pit has obviously been fed on these romances: "A man ought to love a woman more than she loves him. It ought to be enough for him if she lets him give her everything she wants in the world. He ought to serve her like the old knights - give up his whole life to satisfy some whim of hers; and it's her part, if she likes, to be cold and distant."(49) The knight she marries is the millionaire Curtis Jadwin whose trading in futures in the commodity exchange is transformed through her active imagination into the mighty deeds of knight-errantry. Similarly, Miss Bradley in Henry Blake Fuller's The Cliff Dwellers puzzles the realtor by applying heroic metaphors to describe his business:

> "What was it she said, now? Oh, yes; all this down-town racket came to her like the music of a battle-hymn. Our hustling, it seems, resembles a hand-to-hand combat from street to street - she lugged in mediaeval France. And to finish up with, she told me I was like a gladiator stripped for the fray."(50)

Hugh Dalziel Duncan notes that it was the women novelists of Chicago who gave business the heroic note.(51) Belonging to the mercantile households, they saw their men as epic heroes and provided their deeds with a poetic veneer the men themselves might not have cared for.

However, it was not long before these metaphors were applied in all seriousness by the men themselves. Elbert Hubbard, one of the darlings of big business, wrote:

> We do business now according to Marquis of Queensbery rules, where formerly London rules governed the contest. Our fight is with six-ounce gloves. Horseshoes and railroad-spikes are barred. There was a time when we fought with bared knuckles. But business is not yet a ladies' lunch - a suave and innocuous, harmless, tabby Four o'Clock. It is a struggle for supremacy. And it is a fight to a finish. And it is just as full of romance as were the knightly jousts of old.(52)

He proclaimed, "There is a romance of business, and a heroism of business, that literature will yet take note of."(53) Henry James, one remembers, had made the same demand from American novelists. Many novelists answered to these demands though they were divided on the issue of whether to paint this

26

new hero as Lancelot and Galahad or as their ironic counterpart Don Quixote. The enduring names, however, made the latter choice.

Yet, in their time, their voices were a cry in the wilderness, a frantic note against the crescendo of encomiums. The dominant media - the pulpit, the press and the popular novel - set the tone. Here, John Dewey says, "business was ordained as the great romantic adventure", and "the economic man" made into "a hero of romance".(54) It became a glorious vocation, a means of status honour, something it had never succeeded in becoming in the Old World.

However, this new aristocracy looked back to the Old World to supply it with radiant symbols which would provide it with a more glamorous identity. To quote a business executive:

> Business is today the profession. It offers something of the glory that in the past was given to the crusader, the soldier, the courtier, the explorer, and sometimes to the martyr - the test of wits, of brain, of quick thinking, the spirit of adventure, and especially the glory of personal achievement. Making money is not the chief spur to such men as Dupont, Chrysler, Durant, Filene, Hoover, Heinz, Eastman, Curtis, Gary, Ford, Grace. Money to them is no more than the guerdon. They engage in business, and in the business they engage in, because there are no longer any long, slimy, green dragons holding captive maidens in durance vile; no holy sepulchres to be reft from the infidel, no Pacifics to be viewed for the first time. Business is today the Field of the Cloth of Gold.(55)

Money-making, when allied to the symbols of the heroic past, becomes a glorious adventure. Now it can be viewed as the latest sport, a new test of manliness, and all disturbing questions of ethics and morality can be brushed aside. The feudal symbols perform two services for the modern businessman. On the one hand, they provide him with a desired identification, on the other, they allow him to avoid the unpleasant by sidetracking the entire issue. Society is no longer divided between the rich and the poor, the privileged and the underdogs. The metaphors of the game or the joust neutralize the moral issues.

27

The identification with the mediaeval aristocracy did not remain confined to verbal metaphors. The plutocracy made the same statement through its architectural designs. "From Fifth Avenue to Nob Hill the silhouettes of cities were altered by the building of vast residences incorporating in a single fantastic design the turrets of French chateaux, the spires and crenelations of Rhenish castles, and the gables of English manor houses, all encrusted with cast-iron ornamentation and florid jigsaw ruching."(56) The rich married their daughters to the European aristocrats. They also invested in elaborate genealogies in order to prove their royal lineage and coats of arms were on display everywhere. This craze is reflected in the contemporary media through illustrations and cartoons which frequently painted business conquests in the pictorial symbols of knight-errantry.

The vogue of the heroic metaphors did not do away with the earlier, religious symbolism entirely. Elbert Hubbard, for example, speaks of business as "calling" and as "romance" in the same breath. Moreover, they <u>are</u> intrinsically connected. Both see the world as a wilderness to be conquered at the peril of one's life. Both landscapes are peopled by demonic figures, and a war must be waged by the pilgrim as well as the knight. The connection between the two is apparent from the fact that Bunyan's imagination had been shaped largely by his reading of the mediaeval romances. If the pilgrim and the knight came together in nineteenth century America, the reason must be looked for in the role of literature as a social institution.

Though these metaphors were primarily used to provide what Bentham calls "eulogistic coverings"(57) for the motives of the business class, they also served to determine the way the Americans saw the world around them. For human beings, as many social scientists have noticed, live in a symbolic environment created by words. Duncan, perhaps, states the issue most clearly: "the environment of man is a symbolic environment. He acts <u>in</u> and <u>through</u> symbolization of his physical and biological environment, and the environmental 'laws' which affect him are symbolic as well as physical and biological, for when man communicates about his environment, he is acting in the realm of symbols, not only in 'nature,' 'environment,' or 'force,' and the 'laws' he must seek to understand are the laws of symbols as well as of nature."(58) In a phrase that has become a truism, Walter Lippman stated that the actions of human beings are determined by "the pictures in our heads": "We shall assume that what each man does is based not on direct and certain knowledge, but on pictures made by himself or given to him."(59)

The symbolic environment created by the metaphors of pilgrimage as well as the heroic quest was a bleak one. The world the questers inhabit is the polar opposite of the harmonious, gentle world we see in the literature of the pastoral tradition. If the pastoral spirit makes a cosy home in this world, providing solace and joy to the human heart, the landscape painted by the Puritans is that of a hostile country. Tawney describes it vividly: "The fire of the spirit burns brightly on the hearth; but through the windows of his soul the Puritan, unless a poet or a saint, looks on a landscape touched by no breath of Spring. What he sees is a forbidding and frost-bound wilderness, rolling its snow-clad leagues towards the grave -- a wilderness to be subdued with aching limbs beneath solitary stars. Through it he must take his way, alone." (60)

If social Darwinism found a ready acceptance in America, the reason perhaps lies in its symbolic appeal to the Puritan mind. As Richard Hofstadter noted, there are quite a few similarities between Calvinism and the new theory.(61) How closely allied they were in spirit becomes clear from this excerpt from the Christian Advocate of March 20, 1879:

> What is heaven but the company of the fittest? Only a few of the best men reach that promised land. The very laws of salvation in the universe work together, that the man of God may survive. He is the fittest on earth to survive. He triumphs over enemies without and within, even death itself. . . . How wise to let those of weak digestion from gluttony die, and the temperate live. What benevolence to let the lawless perish, and the prudent survive. . . . Halleluiah to our God, who makes and keeps the better and separates the worse!(62)

Metaphors, thus, are not only used to name

29

reality, but they also determine the way we relate
to it. The businessman transforms the hitherto
unglamorous commercial life to exalt his own
self-image and in the process of doing that creates
a model of society that determines how other people
are going to live. As Duncan says, "it is the
images used in daily communication that control us,
and whoever controls the creation and communication
of these controls society."(63)

The American society became a desolate
wilderness when the businessman decided to clothe
himself in the metaphors of the quest. The
pastoral vision of a nurturing community which had
been invoked by the Founding Fathers was given up
in favour of the individualistic, predatory jungle
in which the brave fought glorious battles and the
weak went under as a matter of course.

Turn of the century America painted the
achievements of the self-made man as being truly
superhuman. It exhorted its young men to emulate
them at the risk of failure. It was cowardice, the
philosophers of success preached, to be satisfied
with a modest goal. Dreiser derided them for
saying that "We are lazy Napoleons, idle Hannibals,
wasteful and indifferent John D. Rockefellers". As
to their advice to young men to "'Take it!' - 'It'
meaning 'the world!'" Dreiser thought it was
equivalent to sending them forth "to breast the
ocean in a cockleshell".(64) Dreiser's, however,
was not the predominant view, which had other,
exalted names for the pursuit of wealth. "Honorable
names", Duncan states, "give power because they
endow actions with dignity, radiance, and
glory."(65) By the same token, all other
occupations were somehow mean and puerile because
they were accorded names decidedly insulting. The
writers and painters were "sissies" or
"ink-slingers", while the academics were
"canned-culture boys". As a result, few young men
could achieve a sense of self-affirmation outside
the "real" world of business.

Serious American writers have reflected their
concerns about this world-view in forms that make
articulate the mythic nature of the quest for
wealth and the impact of this experience on the
American psyche. In their separate ways they have
spoken for the establishment of true democratic
values of equality and dignity. Man, they have
unequivocally insisted, can find happiness only
through leading a life hedged by kindness and

fellow-feeling and not through unbridled individualism. In the following pages I have analyzed some of these literary responses to the American quest for wealth. Dreiser is the main focus of this study as he, more than any other American novelist, made it the central motif of his work. Four novels of his contemporaries are analyzed to provide a perspective. There is a common bond that unites their work even when they seem to be on opposite sides. They illuminate each other's work in a way that volumes of close textual reading could not do. The commonality of their concerns provides a new interpretation of the creative process, not as something totally private but a product of the writer's response to the socio-political reality. The similarity of their themes, structures and symbolic patterns points out how far the private self is determined by the social structure and suggests that a critic disregards the social reality only at the risk of distorting the writer's meaning. The following pages, I believe, will substantiate these statements.

NOTES

1. Aquinas, quoted in R. H. Tawney, Religion and the Rise of Capitalism: A Historical Study (1926; New American Library, New York, 1954) 38.
2. Max Weber, The Protestant Ethic and the Spirit of Capitalism, trans. Talcott Parsons, foreword R. H. Tawney (Charles Scribner's Sons, New York, 1958) 159.
3. Tawney, foreword, Weber, The Protestant Ethic and the Spirit of Capitalism, 2-3.
4. Weber, 208, fn.3.
5. Richard Steele, quoted in Tawney, Religion and the Rise of Capitalism, 200.
6. Richard Baxter, quoted in Tawney, 201.
7. Quoted in Weber, 260, fn.9.
8. Bunyan, quoted in Tawney, 199.
9. Tawney, 204.
10. Quoted in Weber, 175.
11. Tawney, 200.
12. Rev. Robert Woodrow, quoted in Tawney, 198.
13. Hans Gerth and C. Wright Mills, Character and Social Structure: The Psychology of Social Institutions (1953; Harcourt, Brace &

World, Inc., New York, 1964) 277.

14.   Hugh Dalziel Duncan, *Language and Literature in Society: a Sociological Essay in Theory and Method in the Interpretation of Linguistic Symbols With a Bibliographical Guide to the Sociology of Literature* (The University of Chicago Press, Chicago, 1953) 131-2.

15.   Quoted in Duncan, *Language and Literature in Society*, 130-1.

16.   Burke, *A Rhetoric of Motives* (1950; University of California Press, Berkeley and Los Angeles, 1969), 38.

17.   Weber, 178.

18.   Quoted in William Haller, *The Rise of Puritanism; Or The Way to the New Jerusalem as Set Forth in Pulpit and Press from Thomas Cartwright to John Lilburne and John Milton, 1570-1643* (1938; Harper & Brothers, New York, 1957) 147.

19.   Cotton Mather, "A Christian at His Calling," Moses Rischin, ed., *The American Gospel of Success: Individualism and Beyond* (Quadrangle Books, Chicago, 1965) 24-5.

20.   Northrop Frye, *Fables of Identity: Studies in Poetic Mythology* (Harcourt, Brace & World, Inc., New York, 1963) 18.

21.   Georg Roppen and Richard Sommer, *Strangers and Pilgrims: An Essay on the Metaphors of Journey* (Norwegian University Press, Oslo, 1964) 12.

22.   Haller, 142.

23.   Haller, 150.

24.   Richard M. Huber, *The American Idea of Success* (McGraw-Hill Book Company, New York, 1971) 72.

25.   John D. Rockefeller, Sr., quoted in Huber, 76.

26.   Rockefeller, Sr., quoted in Huber, 77.

27.   Wilbur F. Crafts, *Successful Men of Today and What They Say of Success* (1883; Arno Press, New York, 1973) 67, 74.

28.   William Lawrence, "The Relation of Wealth to Morals," *The World's Work* 1 (January 1901); rptd. in Conrad Cherry, ed., *God's New Israel: Religious Interpretations of American Destiny* (Prentice-Hall, Inc., Englewood Cliffs, N. J., 1971) 249.

29.   A. Whitney Griswold, "Three Puritans on Prosperity," *New England Quarterly* 7 (September 1934) 478.

30.   Lawrence, "The Relation of Wealth to

Morals," 246.
31. Russell H. Conwell, <u>Acres of Diamonds</u> (Harper & Brothers Publishers, New York, 1915) 21.
32. Mr. Dodd, quoted in W. J. Ghent, <u>Our Benevolent Feudalism</u> (The Macmillan Company, New York, 1902) 29.
33. Frances Hodgson Burnett, <u>Two Little Pilgrims' Progress: A Story of the City Beautiful</u> (Frederick Warne and Co., London, 1895) 10.
34. Burke, <u>Language as Symbolic Action: Essays on Life, Literature, and Method</u> (1966; University of California Press, Berkeley, 1973) 187.
35. Frye, <u>The Educated Imagination</u> (Indiana University Press, Bloomington, 1964) 151.
36. Martin Green, <u>Dreams of Adventure, Deeds of Empire</u> (Basic Books, New York, 1979) 220.
37. Nathaniel Hawthorne, "The Celestial Railroad," <u>Nathaniel Hawthorne: Representative Selections, with Introduction, Bibliography, and Notes</u>, ed. Austin Warren (American Book Company, New York, 1934) 68, 70.
38. Hawthorne, 78.
39. Frye, <u>The Secular Scripture: A Study of the Structure of Romance</u> (Harvard University Press, Cambridge, Mass., 1976) 57.
40. Burke, <u>Counter-Statement</u>, 2nd ed. (University of California Press, Berkeley, 1968) 105.
41. Burke, <u>A Rhetoric of Motives</u> (1950; University of California Press, Berkeley, 1969) 25-6.
42. Burke, <u>A Rhetoric of Motives</u>, 208-12.
43. Joan Rockwell, <u>Fact in Fiction: The Use of Literature in the Systematic Study of Society</u> (Routledge & Kegan Paul, London, 1974) viii.
44. Rockwell, 65.
45. James D. Hart, <u>The Popular Book: A History of America's Literary Taste</u> (Oxford University Press, New York, 1950) 199.
46. W. P. Trent, "Mr. Howells and Romanticism," <u>The Authority of Criticism and Other Essays</u> (1899); rptd. in Edwin H. Cady and David L. Frazier, ed., <u>The War of the Critics over William Dean Howells</u> (Row, Peterson and Company, Evanston, Illinois, 1962) 82.
47. Harry Thurston Peck, "Living Critics, XII-William Dean Howells," <u>Bookman</u> 4 (February

1897); rptd. in Cady and Frazier, 78.
48.	Quoted in Perry Miller, "The Romance and
the Novel," Nature's Nation (Harvard University
Press, Cambridge, Mass., 1967) 273.
49.	Frank Norris, The Pit, introduced by
James D. Hart, Charles E. Merrill Standard Editions
(1903; Charles E. Merrill Publishing Company,
Columbus, 1970) 168.
50.	Henry B. Fuller, The Cliff Dwellers
(Harper & Brothers Publishers, New York, 1893) 49.
51.	Duncan, The Rise of Chicago as a
Literary Center from 1885 to 1920: A
Sociological Essay in American Culture (The
Bedminster Press, Totowa, N. J., 1964) 2.
52.	Elbert Hubbard, The Book of Business
(The Roycrofters, East Aurora, N. Y., 1913) 31.
53.	Hubbard, 144.
54.	John Dewey, "The Collapse of a Romance,"
The New Republic 70 (April 27 1932); rptd. in
Daniel Aaron and Robert Bendiner, ed., The
Strenuous Decade: A Social and Intellectual
Record of the 1930's (Doubleday & Company, Inc.,
Garden City, New York, 1970) 13, 14.
55.	Ernest Elmo Calkins, Business the
Civilizer (Little Brown & Co., n.p., 1928) 232.
Quoted in James H. S. Bossard and J. Frederic
Dewhurst, University Education for Business: A
Study of Existing Needs and Practices (University
of Pennsylvania Press, Philadelphia, 1931) 7.
56.	Hart, The Popular Book, 182.
57.	Quoted in Burke, A Rhetoric of Motives,
100.
58.	Duncan, Symbols in Society (1968;
Oxford University Press, New York, 1972) 70-1.
59.	Walter Lippman, Public Opinion (1922;
Penguin Books, New York, 1946) 17.
60.	Tawney, 90.
61.	Richard Hofstadter, Social Darwinism in
American Thought, rev. ed. (George Braziller, New
York, 1965) 51.
62.	Anonymous, "Survival of the Most Fit,"
Christian Advocate 20 March 1879; rptd. in Arthur
J. Bettini and Cecile M. Copsey, ed., The American
Response: Readings in Social and Political
History (Boyd & Fraser Publishing Company, San
Francisco, Calif., 1974) 143-4.
63.	Duncan, Symbols in Society, 33.
64.	Theodore Dreiser, "Hey, Rub-A-Dub-Dub!"
Hey Rub-A-Dub-Dub: A Book of the Mystery and
Wonder and Terror of Life (Boni and Liveright, New

York, 1920) 6.
    65.   Duncan,   Symbols in Society, 21.

Chapter Three

THE BUSINESS CULTURE: DREISER'S EXPLORATION OF A MYTH

Dreiser has left a massive record of his own self as well as of his times in <u>Dawn</u> and <u>A Book About Myself</u>. Though it is customary among his critics to use these books for information on his fictional characters as well as for pointing out his so-called yearning for material success, the works themselves have not received the critical attention due to them. The neglect is unfortunate since, as works indissolubly connected with his fiction in terms of similar symbolic and structural strategies, they provide a valuable insight into the symbolic environment of Dreiser's age. Biography, as David Brion Davis points out, is an indispensable tool for understanding "the way cultural symbols and metaphors have been assimilated and used by specific individuals." It provides "a concreteness and sense of temporal development that most studies of culture lack. And by showing how cultural tensions and contradictions may be internalized, struggled with, and resolved within actual individuals, it offers a promising key to the synthesis of culture and history."(1) It is this aspect of biography that interests me most in Dreiser's case. His autobiographies show, above all, how, as a child and a youth, he perceived his society and how, as a mature individual, he came to reject its received myths.

Chapter Three of <u>Dawn</u> relates some very significant memories of the child Dreiser. They show that individuals born in a poor, deprived environment become conscious of the power of money rather early. "I remember", Dreiser writes, "dreaming of beautiful red, green, blue, and yellow marbles floating about in the air, and of nickels, dimes and quarters lying everywhere on the ground! What disappointment, what despair, to wake at morn

and find that a seeming reality was not!"(2) How
well the child knew the connection between money
and the desirable objects of the world is apparent
from another experience he narrates of the death of
a watchman who used to give him candy when going
past his home on the way to work. The child was
taken to have a last look at his old friend: "He
was waxy and still, his features quite as I had
known them, but, most interesting of all to my
childish mind, there were five-cent pieces on his
eyelids!" [20]. Dreiser relates that by this time
he knew his "nickels", even though he did not yet
know death, and could not resist the temptation to
pick them up, a temptation which, of course, was
instantly thwarted.

Another very revealing account is that of a
house. "I am passing the residence of a rich man.
On a green sward before the house stands a giant
iron stag, its horns spreading enormously. My face
is pressed between two iron pickets of the fence,
to see" [18]. The phrase, "the residence of a rich
man" is extremely significant for me. Another
writer might have just described the great animal
standing in the garden. However, in Dreiser's
mind, money and the desirable became connected very
early in life. And this connection had important
consequences for the creative artist. The rich
man's house appears as a symbolic centre in all his
novels, a stimulus arousing desire and unhappiness
and thereby a motivation for action. Indeed the
rich man's house became an obsession with Dreiser.
As Dawn and A Book About Myself describe, in
his youthful days of reporting, when he wandered
from city to city - Chicago, St. Louis, Toledo,
Buffalo, Pittsburgh and New York - one of his
favourite pastimes was wandering outside the
mansions of the great. And he attributed the same
characteristics to a number of his characters. The
mansions arouse painful desires in the hearts of
his characters who feel that they would be "happy"
if they could only be allowed to live in them. The
action in a Dreiser novel stems from this
particular desire. As Matthiessen puts it, "The
theme of the outsider . . . is the most recurrent
in Dreiser's work. He knew what it meant from his
earliest memories, from when he had hung around the
railroad tracks in Terre Haute, helping his older
brothers and sisters pick up the scattered bits of
coal that were desperately needed for the family
fire. He was the poor boy staring hungrily into

the bright windows of the rich."(3)

Stuart P. Sherman, in his famous diatribe against Dreiser, remarked: "Read one of these novels, and you have read them all."(4) There certainly is some truth to the statement. Money and the desire for it are the two prime movers of his plots. His characters rob, steal, prostitute themselves and even murder in order to get it. Indeed, Dreiser can be justly charged with limiting himself to a very narrow field of human endeavour "from which the obligations of parenthood, marriage, chivalry, and citizenship have been quite withdrawn or locked in a twilight sleep".(5) However, Dreiser was not alone in thinking that wealth had become the sole preoccupation of the American mind, overshadowing all the above-mentioned roles. A number of other people thought so too. Even as far back as 1842, Reverend Caleb Stetson was commenting on it from his pulpit: "An overweening estimate of money, and an excessive and unscrupulous eagerness to acquire it", he felt, had become "national characteristics". "The basis of our civilization", Stetson complained, "is wealth The love of money is almost the universal passion."(6) Charles Francis Adams wrote in a similar vein: "The present evil has its root deep down in the social organization, and springs from a diseased public opinion. Failure seems to be regarded as the one unpardonable crime, success as the all-redeeming virtue, the acquisition of wealth as the single worthy aim of life."(7)

Thus, by the time Dreiser was born in 1871, the stage had already been set. The Jeffersonian ideal of an agrarian country with independent, contented, more or less equal free-holders had already faded. As Dreiser remarks in Dawn, what he knew of that past came from his mother:

The world of her rearing must have been a pleasant one, for often I have heard her speak of her parents' prosperity as farmers, of orchard and meadow and great fields of grain, and of some of the primitive conditions and devices of pioneer life that still affected them - neighbors borrowing fire, Indians coming to the door to beg or be sociable, the spinning of wool and cotton on hand looms, the home manufacture of soap, shoes, and furniture. [4]

The life Dreiser knew at first hand was not
that of an agrarian community living in harmony and
brotherhood. It was a life divided by sharp social
contrasts and he felt them extremely keenly, having
been born among the have-nots. His first contacts
with his social superiors filled him with envious
longings. One of the boarders in the house had a
daughter whom Dreiser described thus, once again
with reference to her economic worth:

> In connection with the girl I remember a blue
> velvet dress she wore; also that none of us
> could afford so fine a thing. Besides, the
> contents of the room, or rooms, they occupied
> must have been superior according to the
> standards I then had to go by, for looking
> through the door at a dresser ornamented with
> silver-backed toilet articles, I remember
> wishing that I might live in such a room. [21]

Dreiser knew the have-nots' agony of yearning
for things, rich, colourful, pretty things like the
blue velvet dress, and also the agony of life in
shabby and colourless surroundings. The poor,
however, do not appear in his novels in isolation,
as they do, for example, in those of Upton
Sinclair, Stephen Crane and Frank Norris. The
world of Dreiser's novels is a world of contrasts.
Its two extremes are the mansions of the rich and
the tenements of the poor. Dreiser takes extreme
care to place his characters accurately in the
geographical space of the city. The hierarchy of
the city is explained to the last detail. The
mansions and the tenements, divided spatially,
constitute the "two nations" of Dreiser, his heaven
and hell. The movement of his novels is the
movement of people between these two physical
spaces. This movement is described in the familiar
imagery of journeys: those of pilgrimage and of
knightly quests. Often Dreiser uses a mediaeval
landscape in which the quester struggles through a
stiff upward climb to get to "a city with a wall
about it".(8)
The rhetorical nature of this imagery can be
appreciated only when it is seen side by side with
the imagery provided by the gospel of success.
Unlike the highbrow American writers who had
"derived from something very like an aristocracy -
old rooted families, conscious of having made the
country what it was and of the right to set its

spiritual tone from the pulpit, the rostrum, the academy, and the press",(9) Dreiser had inherited very little of the idealistic past of America. Before he came across such writers as Emerson, Thoreau and Irving, he had spent his time reading Horatio Alger. Unlike Henry James, who grew up distrusting the prevailing values of his society, Dreiser was inculcated with the dreams and aspirations of millions of young boys. One of the very first books he read was Hill's Manual of Etiquette and Social and Commercial Forms. The book was forced on his mother by an itinerant salesman. Apart from describing the complexities of manners and style, the book also contained "pictures of cities and great buildings and of men who began as nothing in this great sad world but rose by honesty and industry and thrift and kind thoughts and deeds to be great: such men as George Washington and Thomas Jefferson and Benjamin Franklin and Thomas Paine and Christopher Columbus! Heigh Ho!" He says in Dawn that the book opened up new vistas to his imagination: "Ah, how poetry and romance, ambition and achievement, burst upon me as realities and possibilities from the pages of that book! . . . I devoured it page by page, holding it on my knees or spread out on the grass in the shade at the side or back or front of the house, my mind mounting upon the wings of fancy, my body upon the magic carpet of Sulieman" [105].

Before he had reached his eleventh year, he was regularly reading The Family Story Paper, The Fireside Companion and The New York Weekly. These were soon followed by Horatio Alger with his Diamond Dick, Brave and Bold, Pluck and Luck and Work and Win. As to their effect on his mind, he says in Dawn: "It was a colorful world which they presented, impossible from a practical point of view and yet suggesting that freedom of action which we so often experience in dreams." They made him "intensely dissatisfied with the life I was living" and filled him with a desire to run away. However, there were the problems of money and the necessity of parting from the family. "So instead I went along tamely enough, to school and church, and contented myself with baseball or fishing or reading of the deeds and adventures of newer and even grander heroes" [125-6].

Ralph D. Gardner relates that Horatio Alger was a major influence on American consciousness from the Civil War to the Great Depression in the

Thirties. "Parents approved, ministers recommended them and, judging from teachers' presentation inscriptions, Algers led all the rest as prizes for penmanship, punctuality and Sunday school excellence. It is safe to assume that, during this era of America's transcontinental expansion, industrial growth and the arrival of wave upon wave of immigrants from distant lands, virtually every boy and many girls read Alger."(10) As Dreiser's experience testifies, Alger's stories about the Great City made the poor boy's world a world of tremendous possibilities: all one had to do to become rich was to go to the city and something would happen. For Alger's heroes, contrary to his constant harping on thrift and virtue, do not rise in the world like Benjamin Franklin, with slow, tedious labour. Instead, like Dickens' orphans, they always happen to find the right patron. The Horatio Alger world is thus a dream world and wish fulfillment its governing principle. However, he wrote of it with such convincing realism that the realization of the readers' dreams seemed an imminent possibility. The perusal of such literature, as is apparent in Dreiser's case, filled the reader with vague longings and dissatisfactions: "In short", he notes in _Dawn_, "my budding personal attitude was that of an ambitious but pleasure-loving _parvenu_. Instead of taking to heart the emphasis in our home and elsewhere on the need of energy, study of a practical character, ambition, self-denial and some other things in order that one might properly prepare oneself for the battle of life, I was for mooning about and dreaming of how delightful it would be to do this and that, have this and that - without effort - by luck or birth, as it were" [197]. Carrie is similarly vague about the ways of getting money though her dreams are full of it. The reader is told early in the novel: "She would get in one of the great shops and do well enough until - well, until something happened. Neither of them knew exactly what. They did not figure on promotion. They did not exactly count on marriage. Things would go on, though, in a dim kind of way until the better thing would eventuate, and Carrie would be rewarded for coming and toiling in the city" [11].

Braced with his readings of Horatio Alger and Samuel Smiles - the latter recommended to him by his teacher - Dreiser decided to migrate to the city.   One fine day, Dreiser says in <u>Dawn</u>, he decided to leave home.   The immediate motivation came from a Sunday newspaper account of activities on Halstead Street in Chicago.   And then there was the example of so many of his friends who were leaving in droves.   In a dramatic passage Dreiser describes his dialogue with his mother that must have been repeated in scores of other American homes of the time:

> "Ma, I am going to Chicago!"
> "Why, what do you mean? When?" she asked, astonished.
> "To-day!"
> "What for?"
> "I want to get work, if I can. I'm tired of Warsaw. If you'll give me my fare and three dollars, I'll go to-day. I can get something. I know I can. I see lots of places advertised in the papers." [294]

Though the Industrial Revolution arrived in England first, the peasantry moved to the cities only reluctantly, and with no illusions about bettering their lot.   Late nineteenth century America, however, was teeming with visions of opportunities created by the breakneck speed of industrialization.   And as the writers of success manuals proclaimed, the race was free for all. As Wyllie explains:

> On the eve of the Civil War this rags-to-riches theme had already captured the imagination of young men living close to the centers of business enterprise. . . . This was the appealing dream, born of the opportunities of the urban frontier and nourished by a rising army of self-help propagandists.   In the days before Sumter the counting room clerk and the bobbin boy dreamed more of private fortune than of military glory.   And though the Civil War imposed military values on the nation, it did so only temporarily.   Out of the war came rich new opportunities for acquisition, a new generation of self-made men, and a well-ordered gospel of business success.(11)

When Dreiser decided to leave Warsaw with three dollars and a paper bag lunch, he was motivated by these legends of the times. And if he saw the city as the right place to be, he was not alone. Wyllie quotes from the current self-help handbooks: "A boy at home seldom has a chance", said one. "No man can expect to become distinguished in any sphere unless he has the amplest field for the exercise of his powers", said another. "A. T. Stewart", declared one writer, "located anywhere out of New York City, would not be where he is, and many a clergyman or lawyer, fixed in a small village, would not have reached the eminence which the world freely accords them."(12)

Thus the young Dreiser, or for that matter, Carrie and Eugene Witla, embarking on the train Chicago-bound, are reenacting a drama which was being played on the national stage. When they leave home, with a pang of regret for all that home had represented but eager, according to Dawn, "to reconnoiter this fairyland alone, to wander about and get work" [206], they become representative figures, shedding light on a complex period of American history. Hugh Dalziel Duncan has recorded the mythic nature of this experience:

> The great American story of conquering the city (the story that was to be told over and over again of the boy or girl who leaves village, farm and native land to test fate in the city) is born in the Chicago literature of the years after the Civil War. Dennis Fleet in 1872, Daniel Trentworthy in 1887, Carrie Meeber in 1900 are only three among many young rural heroes whose symbolic voyage from farm to city and from a lower to a higher class within the city, was so much a part of all American life from 1880 to 1900. Unlike the affected sophisticates of Chatfield-Taylor, the mild skeptics of Fuller, or the censorious New England heroes of Herrick, the Carrie Meebers of Chicago literature saw in Chicago a modern Baghdad, a city of a thousand wonders where each day brought forth fresh marvels.(13)

Though the city is a "fairyland" in one sense, the applicant must cross a dangerous territory before he can gain admittance. As Duncan's account shows, the experience was frequently described in martial imagery. Dreiser, too, went to the city in a fighting mood, just as Carrie, Eugene and Cowperwood would go later. His mood, as he described that train ride, was not that of a stoic philosopher who has no illusions but that of a young warrior confident of victory:

> That ride to Chicago was one of the most intense and wonderful of my life. For to me it was of the very substance of adventure. . . . I was not afraid; rather, I was pleased and assured. . . . Stepping out of the train, it was as though I were ready to conquer the world. Neither fear nor loneliness possessed me; rather, if anything, there was something determined and even aggressive in my attitude. [296]

Chicago, to Dreiser at sixteen, is like "a young giant" [296], a suitable rival whom it would be glorious to subdue. The similarity of this language with that of the courtly romance is unmistakeable. "The world of knightly proving", says Auerbach, "is a world of adventure. . . . Nothing is found in it which is not either accessory or preparatory to an adventure. It is a world specifically created and designed to give the knight opportunity to prove himself."(14)

The cities of late nineteenth century America as the Americans saw them were the venues of such a self-assessment. As Andrew Carnegie, that self-proclaimed spokesman of his age, phrased it so succinctly: "They [the poor youth of the rural areas] appear upon the stage, athletes trained for the contest, with sinews braced, indomitable wills, resolved to do or die. Such boys always have marched, and always will march, straight to the front and lead the world; they are the epoch-makers."(15)

When critics puzzle over the reference to "the little half-equipped knight" in Sister Carrie and find it trite, they only show how distance in time obliterates the referential aspects of a text. For Carrie, above all, is a representative figure, "a soldier of fortune", reenacting the national dream in words that must have rung a bell in the contemporary reader's mind. Dreiser's military image is in keeping with the mood of the time.

However, while Carnegie and other apostles of success never commented on the obverse side of the heroic quest, Dreiser always presented it in a defamiliarizing setting. As his tone in Dawn and A Book About Myself indicates, the fantasies of the young man are tempered by the older Dreiser's commentaries. Similarly, in the novels a mature and detached narrator criticizes the extravagant desires of his characters. The world of dreams is surrounded by the world of grim reality and the reader is forced to alternate between them. Thus, though Dreiser takes off from popular literature and popular values, he ends up deconstructing them.

Nevertheless, Dreiser has been charged with many sins: of identifying with the success values of his characters, of glorifying wealthy businessmen, of writing sentimentally and without self-consciousness. His autobiographies, instead of being seen as the record of a phase of American consciousness, have been used indiscriminately to prove either Dreiser's own cultural deficiencies, or his sympathetic identification with characters he meant to crticize. Lehan's approach is quite representative: "Dreiser was merely revealing his own sense of self when he took flight into fancy and identified himself with Yerkes. He had, after all, written in A Book About Myself that 'To be president or vice-president or something, some great thrashing business of some kind. Great God, how sublime it seemed!'"(16) It happens again and again. Instead of seeing Dreiser's confessions as motivated by his desire to portray his society's general aspirations, they are seen as his personal weaknesses. The fact is that Dreiser was reenacting the great American Dream, the dream that obsessed millions in his time. Many a sixteen year old dreamed that he "could rise from the streets of New York, Boston or Philadelphia to the splendid mansions which were beginning to line the avenues of those cities". The dream, as John Tebbel insists, was "not political, but commercial".(17)

Dreiser expressed himself with total frankness. His ludicrous fantasies, his exaggerated ambitions, his cruelty to other human beings: he did not hide anything that concerned himself. If Carrie sold herself for a suit of clothes, Dreiser had chosen sweethearts for their monetary status. These facts have been taken as evidence against him. But there is another way of reading them. I have chosen to read them for their self-consciousness. They are a careful analysis of the way late nineteenth century Americans apprehended themselves and their world.

As the evidence presented so far has shown, it was a world of heroic proportions. Democratic America visualized itself in images borrowed from the battlefield. Though martial and Darwinian imagery can be found even today in the business section of the daily newspapers and in the pronouncements of conservative politicians, it is no longer as ubiquitous as it was in the turn of the century America. Then, the young man was exhorted to go into the battle of life in extended analogies of the pilgrimage on the one hand and the battlefield on the other. The advance notice of one of Horatio Alger's novels described it thus: "Suddenly thrown on the world to make his own way in life, Rodney Ropes develops a pluck and courage that cannot fail to inspire admiration and a strong desire to follow his fortunes as he leaves school to battle for his daily bread."(18)

In Dreiser's case, however, Dawn describes how the exuberant self-confidence was usually followed by a "sudden sinking of heart, disconcerting flashes of failure . . ." [300]. "I think that at times the vastness of the city was almost too much for my by now almost rural brain." It "had a reducing effect on me, so much so that I was not sure of myself in any way" [302]. The sight of the defeated evoked visions of terror in Dreiser. This terror, quintessentially presented in the decline of Hurstwood, is a leitmotif of Dreiser's work as well as his life:

> [T]he wretchedness of men weighed on me and I would ponder by the hour over the suffering and the hunger in New York alone, the crowded tenements, the sick babies, the people sweating under undue loads this very summer day and the women sewing, sewing, way late into the night.(19)

This fear of failure, however, was not a permanent state. The success-seeker habitually alternated between the two moods: "Outside of every store of any size, the great wholesale houses in particular, I stood viewing a land of promise. In one of these, surely, was my future. . . . I saw myself, a great roll-top desk before me, a large enclosed office around me, myself dictating to whom? And about what? Great matters and affairs, of course" [335].

Exploration of a Myth

The one year Dreiser spent at Indiana University through the generous financial help of his high school teacher did not bring any basic changes to his apprehension of life. He says in Dawn that the distance that separated him from the more fortunate was all that he took note of. "I wanted", he wrote, "a profession and money and a good family such as other people could boast of. . . . Not only that, but for the time being I wanted to swagger about the world like Levitt or O'Connor, to show off (me!), have good clothes, smart friends, and this and that. I can only smile indulgently concerning myself as I was then, think not too drastically of that boy whose heir and, in part, creation I am. For, in part at least, is he not still here and thinking on his own follies?" [442].

When he finished the year at college, he was "more courageous, more ambitious". Once again, he drew vigour from the monuments of others' achievements. Chicago seemed even more promising than it had before. "As for Chicago, it seemed stronger, brisker, more colorful even than before. . . . I liked it much, for here one sensed vigorous, definite projects under way, great dreams and great achievements, and behind them strong, definite-minded, if not so terrifically visionful, men at work. It was more money, money, money, and the fame of the same, the great fortune idea. . . . I remember thinking, as I made my way home that everything was before everybody in Chicago, if they but thought so, and that in spite of all my doubts, I would find work and joy somewhere here [466].

While he drove a laundry wagon at eight dollars a week, "my mind naturally skipped all intermediate labor" and conceived of the future when he would be "wealthy, happy, famous, with some radiantly beautiful woman to share my happiness" [539]. Like Clyde, he thought of short cuts to success. "Ah, to succeed financially by marriage with some beautiful and wealthy girl, or otherwise attain to some such atmosphere as this! All my thoughts were of luxury such as I saw here - a petty and wholly material viewpoint, as I see it now. But so it was. And when I thought of Nellie MacPherson - I am sorry to have to confess this - she seemed a mere trifle. How quickly I would leave her for something better!" [542]. So much for Horatio Alger's pious virtues! Obviously, he had to compete with the glossy representations of

47

the gossip columns. At any rate, his readers seem
to have imbibed only a love for the pleasures of
riches and not his advice as to the straight and
narrow path. Dreiser sensed this contradiction at
the heart of the dream. Long before he
immortalized the murder of Roberta Alden, he had
been obsessed with the cold-blooded murderer whose
sole motive was money. He recorded fifteen such
murders in a manuscript called "American
Tragedies". His interest in this type of murder
continued even after An American Tragedy had been
written. In 1935 he wrote a series of articles on
Robert Edwards entitled "I Find the Real American
Tragedy".(20) On a trip to Indianapolis he went to
visit the grave of John Dillinger, a bank robber
and murderer of sixteen, a visit made fun of by
Dreiser's biographer, Swanberg, who finds it
difficult to understand Dreiser's view "that
Dillinger was a victim of American social
inequities".(21) Mencken also found this trait of
Dreiser quite amusing. "The truth is", he wrote to
Dreiser, "that society is probably fundamentally
wise in putting its Edwardses to death. After all,
they are decidedly abnormal, and when they live
their careers are commonly very costly to the rest
of us."(22)

Dreiser, however, stuck to his belief that
such tragedies occurred because of "the shabbiest
and most degrading doctrine"(23) that was impressed
upon Americans from their childhood. For hadn't he
used Nellie MacPherson and Alice in a similar
shabby way? Driven by his "ridiculous youthful
goal" of luxury, had not he looked at the mansions
of the rich and wished for a rich girl to fall in
love with him? At eighteen, all he could think of
was how to make it come about: "my brain was fairly
bubbling with ideas of still greater grandeur to
come; in short, how I might climb and climb until
even the best hotels would not be beyond me and I
could walk unashamed and untroubled in the best
theatres, etc., money in my pocket, a sense of real
ability and fitness to live enfolding me as a
cloak" [581]. This sentence in Dawn pulls in all
the strands of the theme: the perilous journey, the
re-birth of the self and the symbolic garb to
confirm its new image. The word "fitness" also
indicates the social Darwinistic cast of the
"gospel of wealth".

The picture postcard mansions, made as
imitations of the houses of European nobility, are

desired goals of Dreiser's characters who equate
the possession of them with happiness. Carrie goes
on a ride to Euclid Avenue and returns home greatly
unhappy. In almost every novel Dreiser sends his
characters to ogle at the houses of the rich. These
houses and business offices are equated with fairy
palaces in his novels. The analogies are symbolic
in two ways. They symbolize, on the one hand, the
power and achievements of their builders, and on
the other, hope to the outsider. They almost shout
aloud to the hopeful that their present owner had
once been an outsider, for Wyllie tells us that "an
American who knew nothing of the careers of Amos
and Abbott Lawrence, Samuel Appleton, John Jacob
Astor, Peter Cooper, Cornelius Vanderbilt, Stephen
Girard, or George Peabody was considered hopelessly
uninformed."(24)

To the young in heart and body, these mansions
spoke of a glorious future. So long as one was
young and just entering the world, one could
reconcile such disparate activities as driving a
laundry wagon and thinking of millionaires. The
young Dreiser's experience was similar: "My eyes
were constantly fixed on people in positions far
above my own. Those who interested me most were
bankers, millionaires, artists, executives,
leaders, the real rulers of the world."(25) Dreiser
says in A Book About Myself that at nineteen he
felt the world was just opening before him: "I was
like some bird poised on a high twig, teetering and
fluttering and ready for flight. . . . Joy was
ever before me, the sense of some great adventure
lurking just around the corner" [19]. "No common
man am I", Dreiser kept repeating to himself. In
an image in this work, one which recurs repeatedly
in his fiction, Dreiser gives a hint about the way
his mind saw the world at this time: "I wanted to
shake off the garments of the commonplace in which
I seemed swathed and step forth into the public
arena, where I should be seen and understood for
what I was" [34].

As Duncan points out, Dreiser's fiction
abounds in "the hierarchal imagery of clothes".(26)
Changes of clothes symbolize the progress - or
backsliding - of his characters in their quest for
wealth. Carrie, for example, compares Drouet and
Hurstwood in terms of their apparel and finds
Drouet wanting. This also gives an indication to
the reader as to how far she herself has come from
the stage when Drouet symbolized the romance and

enchantment of Chicago in her eyes.

At twenty one, the externalities occupied Carrie's creator with a similar passion. He says in <u>A Book About Myself</u> that the rich men and women in their "sunny prosperity", "disporting themselves about the lawns and within the open-windowed chambers of the houses" could not but be envied. "To me in my life-hungry, love-hungry state, this new-rich prosperity with its ease, its pretty women and its effort at refinement was quite too much. It set me to riotous dreaming and longing made me ache to lounge and pose after this same fashion" [44-5].

In the book, Dreiser also tells of other people - well-meaning and intelligent in all other respects - who were similarly swayed by these dreams. Richard Wood, his illustrator friend at the <u>Globe-Democrat</u>, came from an identical background and harboured identical aspirations:

> He had much the same desire as I had at the time: to share in the splendors of marble halls and palaces and high places generally; and, like myself, he had but little chance. Fresh from Bloomington, Illinois, a commonplace American town, he was obsessed by the commonplace dream of marrying rich and coming into the imaginary splendors of that west end life of St. Louis which was so interesting to both of us. Far more than myself, I am sure, he seemed to be seething with an inward rebellion against the fact that he was poor, not included in the exclusive pleasures of the rich. At the same time he was glowing with a desire to make other people imagine that he was or soon would be of them. What airs! What shades of manner! He, like myself, was forever dreaming of some gorgeous maiden, rich, beautiful, socially elect, who was to solve all his troubles for him. [122]

The flames of these desires were not only fed by the visible objects of the external world which symbolized riches, but the popular theatre was also responsible for adding fuel to them. Dreiser had fallen under its spell during his first visit to Chicago at the age of seventeen. He loved seeing such extravaganzas as <u>Ali Baba and the Forty Thieves</u> and <u>The Crystal Slipper</u>, which were the usual fare at the great ten-story Chicago Opera

House.   He was still under their spell when, at
twenty one, he became the drama critic for the
Globe-Democrat.   Looking back in 1931, Dreiser
wrote,   "The spirit of these plays captivated my
fancy at that time and elevated me into a world of
unreality which unfortunately fell in with the
wildest of my youthful imaginings. . . . To be
rich, elegant, exclusive, as in the world of
Frohman and Mr. Jones and Mr. Pinero!" In blaming
these dramatists for promoting a false view of
life, Dreiser, the social realist, sees a direct
link between art and life.   The world of these
plays was an escape from reality and not "life as
it is", which became Dreiser's credo as a novelist.
These plays, by their depiction of the world of
elegance and riches, filled the minds of the less
fortunate youth with restlessness and romantic
yearnings:

> The dreary humdrum of actual life was
> carefully shut out from these pieces; the
> simple delights of ordinary living, if they
> were used at all, were exaggerated beyond
> sensible belief.   And elsewhere - not here in
> St. Louis, but in the East, New York, London,
> Paris, Vienna, St. Petersburg - were all the
> things that were worthwhile.   If I really
> wanted to be happy I must eventually go to
> those places, of course. . . . [179-80]

Dreiser satirized such plays at great length
in Sister Carrie.   A visit to such a play, "one
of those drawing-room concoctions in which
charmingly over-dressed ladies and gentlemen suffer
the pangs of love and jealousy amid gilded
surroundings" [228], makes Carrie dissatisfied with
her modest, but comfortable New York flat. However,
despite Dreiser's contempt for the commercial
theatre, expressed in no uncertain terms in Sister
Carrie and elsewhere, his critics insist on seeing
Carrie's success on the stage as an artistic
flowering.   Thus, Sister Carrie becomes another
"portrait of an artist" type of work, and its
engagement with social reality becomes secondary.
  A Book About Myself categorically connects
the commercial theatre to the rags-to-riches myth.
Dreiser writes that these plays made him and his
journalist friends dream of a luxurious life which
could only be had in a big city like New York:

I began to dream more than ever of establishing some such perfect atmosphere for myself somehow, somewhere - but never in St. Louis, of course. That was too common, too Western, too far removed from the real wonders of the world. Love and mansions and travel and saccharine romance were the great things, but they were afar off, in New York. [181]

Dreiser confesses that his misery was the result of his temperament which was not that of the kind "which puts moderate place and position first and sets great store by the saving of money". Instead of these moderate aims, he wished for the impossible dream which the biographies of self-made men inspired in youths like him. "Life ought certainly to bring me something better, something truly splendid - and soon. I deserved it - everything, a great home, fine clothes, pretty women, the respect and companionship of famous men. Indeed all my pain and misery was caused by just such a lack or lacks as this" [182-3].

In A Book About Myself, he describes his feeling that St. Louis did not have much to satisfy his "driving desire to get on, to do something, to be more than I was and have all the pleasures I craved at once . . ." [337]. When his brother, Paul Dresser, the famous singer, visited St. Louis, he told him that New York was the place for him. "It was the city", according to Paul. "It was great, wonderful, marvelous, the size, the color, the tang, the beauty" [352]. He decided to leave St. Louis for the metropolis, packed his bags and started his journey eastwards, full of the dreams democratic America had inspired in the hearts of millions. Not wishing to leave any details of his material aspirations unsaid, he describes the ride to Grand Rapids, his first stop in the journey that would ultimately take him to the city of dreams:

I selected a table adjoining one at which sat two drummers who talked of journeys far and wide, of large sales of binders and reapers and the condition of trade. They seemed to me to be among the most fortunate of men, high up in the world as positions go, able to steer straight and profitable courses for themselves. Because they had half a broiled spring chicken, I had one, and coffee and rolls and French Fried potatoes, as did they,

52

feeling all the while that I was indulging in
limitless grandeur. At one station at which
the train stopped some poor-looking farmer
boys in jeans and "galluses" and wrinkled hats
looking up at me with interest as I ate, I
stared down at them, hoping that I should be
taken for a millionaire to whom this was
little more than a wearisome commonplace. I
felt fully capable of playing the part and so
gave the boys a cold and repressive glance, as
much as to say, Behold! I assured myself that
the way to establish my true worth was to make
every one else feel small by comparison. [362]

In passages like this, Dreiser showed the
other, less endearing side of the "gospel of
wealth". The wealthy were supposed to be the
epitome of all the Christian virtues in the
official version whereas the poor, when deserving,
were seen as the diligent workers who would be
there tomorrow. The rhetoric was all about
brotherhood and the need for virtuous conduct.
Dreiser, however, painted an unflattering reality
in which the rich and the poor were related on the
basis of the rich man's need to show himself off.
Dreiser pointed out this paradox of American life
many times: "Manufacturers and strong men generally
like large families. Where else would they get the
tools wherewith they work - the cheap labor - and
the amazing contrasts between poverty and wealth,
the contemplation of which gives them such a
satisfaction in their own worth and force?"(27)
Surprisingly, such unashamed recounting of his
youthful experiences and aspirations has not led
American critics to an examination of America's
cultural and economic arrangements. Instead, they
have called Dreiser a Babbit.(28) His bitter irony
was probably incomprehensible to his critics as
they judged the vulgarity of youthful Dreiser's
aims as personal failure. Certainly, no other
American writer before Dreiser had confessed to
such cultural deficiencies.
Consequently, if Dreiser had hoped for an
airing of the issues he had raised, that has not
occurred. While the so-called leftist critics have
held Dreiser's work in high esteem, the mainstream,
supposedly neutral critics, who have done detailed
studies of his novels, have concluded that he
worshipped wealth and the wealthy, avowed the
survival of the fittest and yet exhibited a genuine

concern for the downtrodden though claiming that
nothing could be done about them. And all these
pronouncements have been made in a most
condescending tone, making Dreiser into a naughty
boy who preached Communism while hankering after
money and fame in his personal life.

It is, hence, necessary that an attempt be
made to provide Dreiser's views about life and
society up to the time that he came to write
Sister Carrie. It is necessary because, to
this day, Dreiser's novels are being interpreted in
the light of his so-called social Darwinism, his
alleged admiration for the heroic businessman and
his supposed yearnings for grandeur. In the
remaining portion of this chapter, I shall present
a record of Dreiser's progress from being an ardent
believer in the gospel of success to a novelist who
exposed its contradictions in complex rhetorical
modes.

We find in Dawn and A Book About Myself
that the same Dreiser who seemed obsessed with fine
houses and fine clothes was also obsessed with
their exact opposite: the teeming slums and their
degrading poverty. His was not simply the sympathy
shown by an outsider. A constant fear of being
pulled back to the same dire strait dogged him all
through his life. Whatever other effects this fear
had on his personality, it made him extra-sensitive
to the miseries of the poor. Starting as a
newspaperman, full of ambition, he still could not
avert his eyes from the hovels that lay on his
route to the newspaper building. And though
sociologists like Sumner were writing scholarly
books about the inevitability of poverty, Dreiser
says in A Book About Myself that he could not
stop himself from asking some disturbing questions.
"Why didn't society do better by them? . . . Why
didn't they do better by themselves? Did God, who,
as had been drummed into me up to that hour was all
wise, all merciful, omnipresent and omnipotent make
people so or did they themselves have something to
do with it? Was government to blame, or they
themselves?" [65].

Dreiser continued to walk through tenements,
"much as a man may tread the poisonous paths of a
jungle, curious and yet fearsome" [65]. Whatever
the image of the financial jungle meant to the
self-made man, to Dreiser, as many essays in The
Color of a Great City show, it always meant the

wild growth of slums through which the perilous
path of success lay. As Clifton Fadiman noted,
"The fear of poverty is the central drive behind
his entire career as an artist."(29) The city of
Dreiser's experience was a place of stark contrasts
and the sight of poverty threw him into the utmost
depression. Living in a society where the social
contract was the only kind of relationship binding
men, Dreiser developed a deep neurotic fear of
being left helpless, a fear which ultimately gave
birth to the character of Hurstwood. The fear,
however, had ample basis. He saw many of his
fellow journalists fall on evil days and A Book
About Myself mentions four suicides among his
acquaintances. Dreiser recounts in great detail
the story of Clark, a fellow reporter on the
Republic. A bright and ambitious man to begin
with, Clark lost his hold on life due to his wife's
unfaithfulness and started drinking. One day,
after his absence from the paper for several weeks,
Dreiser met him on the street: "A short, matted,
dirty black beard concealed a face that bore no
resemblance to Clark. A hat that looked as though
it might have been lifted out of an ash-barrel was
pulled slouchily and defiantly over long uncombed
black hair. His face was filthy, as were his
clothes and shoes, slimy even. An old brown coat .
. . was marked by a greenish slime across the back
and shoulders, slime that could only have come from
a gutter" [224]. In a scene reminiscent of the
meeting between Hurstwood and Carrie, Dreiser
recalls giving his friend a dollar. Afterwards, "I
bustled out of that vicinity as fast as I could, I
was so startled and upset by this that I hurried
back to the lobby of the Southern Hotel (my
favorite cure for all despondent days), where all
was brisk, comfortable, gay. Here I purchased a
newspaper and sat down in a rocking-chair. Here at
least was no sign of poverty or want. In order to
be rid of that sense of failure and degradation
which had crept over me I took a drink or two
myself" [225]. Hurstwood, one may recall, resorts
to a similar tactic.

While looking for work on the New York papers,
with his meagre savings of two hundred forty
dollars fast slipping away, Dreiser succumbed to
similar moods. "About me on the benches of the
park", he recalls in A Book About Myself, "was,
even in this gray, chill December weather, that
large company of bums, loafers, tramps, idlers, the

flotsam and jetsam of the great city's whirl and strife to be seen there today. I presume I looked at them and then considered myself and these great offices, and it was then that the idea of Hurstwood was born" [463-4].

Dreiser is the first American novelist who succeeded in tapping the great fears that lurked within the hearts of men who were not strong enough to act according to the formula that explained life as a battle to the finish. What prevented him from accepting the popular equation between wealth and worth, vice and poverty, was an awareness of these fears and the havoc they could wreak upon a man's morale. He noticed them within his own character. In Dawn, A Book About Myself, as well as An Amateur Laborer, he recounts several experiences when he felt utterly incompetent and cowed by what he describes in A Book About Myself as "the hugeness and force and heartlessness of the great city, its startling contrasts of wealth and poverty, the air of ruthlessness and indifference and disillusion that everywhere prevailed" [479]. It made him realize - long before he came in contact with Freudian psychology through his friend Dr. Brill - that man was not entirely in control of himself. Walking through the abodes of misery, debating the problems of responsibility, he came to the conclusion that "man is the victim of forces over which he has no control" [65]. Thus Dreiser went against the prevailing philosophy of his times which blamed personal vice for poverty.

While I see Dreiser's psychological determinism as a retort to the gospel of success which blamed the individual for his economic failure in interchangeable terms of moral laxity or lack of fitness, it has given rise to interminable arguments among Dreiser's critics about freedom of the will. Thus, a recent book tells us that Dreiser wants to suggest that "Hurstwood has not done his best to turn the tide. . . . Such elements as environment and heredity are not to blame for his downfall; he himself is to blame."(30)

If Dreiser had tried to portray the heartlessness of social Darwinian America through Hurstwood's decline, that intention, and its implications in terms of social responsibility toward the sick, the old, the homeless, are totally lost in the endless discussion about the conflict in Dreiser's fiction between his philosophical determinism and the free will that he "unknowingly" grants his characters. We are exhorted to the Lawrentian dictum of believing the tale and not the teller.

Another widespread tendency among Dreiser's critics is to make his tragedies of the social system into tragedies of "fate". Dreiser, however, does not write of "man's tragic nature" in the same sense as Greek dramatists did. His primary interest in delineating characters stems from their economic life which overshadows other aspects of their personality, a fact Dreiser deplores. Be they ordinary country girls or boys, artists or financiers, what Dreiser explores in their personality is the nature of the impact society's economic life has had on them. Carrie and Witla, both artists of some kind, come to the city to satisfy their acquisitive dreams and not in pursuit of an aesthetic ideal.

As Dreiser wrote to Robert H. Elias, his emphasis had always been on man in relation to society: "Since I started in observing my world and writing about it, I have been interested in the effects of social systems on individuals."(31) He expressed a similar opinion in a letter to Dorothy Dudley:

In regard to my interest in economics, I have always been interested in economics and the social set-up in this country and all countries - humanity in general. I think that the text of my books shows that from the first to the last. My reason for troubling with the economic phase here is because conditions as they are now are certain to be addled and to make ridiculous literary achievements of almost all kinds other than economic. There is a social unbalance here which would not permit of any sane picture that did not clearly reflect social unbalance.(32)

However, many eminent critics of Dreiser fail to take notice of the economic underpinnings of his fiction. Alfred Kazin would have us believe that Dreiser had no interest in social reform, that the "basic mistake of all the literary critics was to think that he could ever see this world as something to be ameliorated."(33) In fact, all he wanted to do was to sing of "the beauty of the iron city" and contemplate it with "metaphysical

wonder."(34) Kazin proposes that Dreiser came to
see the American scene as a paradigm of reality:
"The cruelty and squalor of the life to which he
was born suggested the theme of existence; the
pattern of American life was identified as the
figure of destiny. It was life, it was immemorial,
it was as palpable as hunger or the caprice of God.
And Dreiser accepted it as the common victim of
life accepts it, because he knows no other, because
this one summons all his resources."(35)

The next step in this argument is that "Where
the other novelists of his time saw the evils of
capitalism in terms of political or economic
causation, Dreiser saw only the hand of fate.
Necessity was the sovereign principle."(36) Critics
like Robert Penn Warren, Richard Lehan, W. A.
Swanberg and Donald Pizer, along with many lesser
ones, suggest that Dreiser saw the social
Darwinistic world of nineteenth century America as
the "reality", and though he railed against it, he
considered it to be unchangeable. The subject
matter of the novels, according to this formula,
can be summed up by the phrase: "the essential
tragedy of life".(37) All that one can learn from
reading Dreiser is that "life is essentially
circular, that it moves in endless repetitive
patterns".(38)

The critics go on to talk about the
unfulfilled desires of Dreiser's characters, about
the move from illusion to disillusion, about the
inexorable destiny and the helpless human being, "a
poor blind fool".(39) They insist that "in his
novels his mind did remain inviolate and he saw his
American scene not as revealing any dialectical
process, or endorsing any moral or political
theory, but simply as being Life, wonderful,
terrible, very mysterious."(40)

One suspects that when life is capitalized as
Life, and problems of a certain period of human
history turned into problems of fate and destiny,
the critic is saved from committing himself to any
ethical, economic or political statements since
life is tragic for both rich and poor, Americans
and, let us say, Ethiopians. This, as Kenneth
Burke says, is the tactic employed by the rhetoric
of "courtship". One talks about matters such as
fate and destiny, death and disease, matters that
allow the rich to claim kinship with the poor in a
common human bond, as being the victims of a common
foe.

But Dreiser was interested in tracing "the effects of social systems on individuals" and that is rarely talked about. The American critic's "tragedy of life" approach equates the tragedy of a starving beggar on the streets of an Indian city to that of a man like Frank Cowperwood. What gets left out is a meaningful discussion of the social reality, the here and now out of which the novelist creates his art. As Raymond Williams states in a similar context:

And it is then astonishing that a whole school of criticism has succeeded in emptying The Heart of Darkness of its social and historical content, about which Conrad leaves us in no possible doubt. My quarrel with a whole tradition of criticism of fiction is about just this kind of endless reduction of deliberately created realities to analogues, symbolic circumstances, abstract situations. The Congo of Leopold follows the sea that Dombey and Son traded across, follows it into an endless substitution in which no object is itself, no social experience direct, but everything is translated into what can be called a metaphysical language - the river is Evil; the sea is Love or Death. Yet only called metaphysical, because there is not even that much guts in it. No profound and ordinary belief, only a perpetual and sophisticated evasion of these deliberately created, deliberately named, places and people, situations and experiences. . . . But of course you know the defence. The immediate situation, the local instance, is the Congo, but then what is developed is a "larger" reality. And since all good novels depend on this kind of extension, so that they are more than the truth about only that man, that place, that time, this way of putting it can appear convincing. But there is all the difference in the world between discovering a general truth in a particular situation and making an abstract truth out of a contingent situation. It is the difference between creative seriousness and a now fashionable game.(41)

The issue at stake is the total misinterpretation of Dreiser's meaning. For if

Dreiser is writing about helpless human beings
squirming in the grip of a blind fate, hostile
critics like Robert Shafer and Lionel Trilling are
quite right in the charge that he has attempted to
create "a literature as valueless and insignificant
as possible", that "he has nothing to tell us
except that there is nothing to tell about life
until it can be reduced even below the apparent
level of animal existence, to the point where it
becomes a meaningless chaos of blind energies."(42)
    Dreiser, however, thought that he was writing
his novels in order to communicate something
meaningful. He criticized those who are prone to
"a quiet acceptance of things as they are without
any regard to the well-being of the future". He
refused to believe with them that life was made of
"immutable forms" and that human effort was
meaningless.(43) How little applicable are words
like fate and destiny to his novels is apparent
from what Dreiser told Claude Bowers about An
American Tragedy: "I call it that because it
could not happen in any other country in the
world."(44) The remark shows that he did not think
that Clyde's tragedy was caused by a divine
dispensation.
    It is necessary here to resolve the difference
between the absolutist "man's tragic nature" type
of approach and the one that sees Dreiser as a
social realist. The former sees Dreiser's
characters as moths who are driven by that desire
for wealth which is in-built in man. The latter,
on the other hand, assesses Dreiser as a social
critic who emphasized the role of the environment.
Men followed certain goals, he believed, because
society held them up for admiration and emulation.
And social institutions, he believed, were not
"immutable" but part of a historic process and
subject to change.
    Though critics like Eliseo Vivas and Gerald
Willen have challenged the deterministic
interpretations of Dreiser's fiction and consider
humanistic values integral to it, they do so by
separating the artist from the philosopher. Vivas
proposes that we disregard what he calls "the
editorial bias" and concentrate on "the dramatic
picture" alone.(45) It is hard for me to see how
one can separate the "dramatic picture" from the
total verbal structure. The present study assumes
no such split between the novelist and the
philosopher and sees the novels as symbolic

representations of Dreiser's philosophy. The problem, as I see it, is not with Dreiser's philosophy but with the lack of attention it has received. The error made by his critics is that of confusing his views on the ultimate nature of reality with his ethics. It is true that Dreiser consistently denied man the ability to achieve ultimate knowledge and was personally tormented by this lack. It is also true that he refused to grant a special status to man as a being apart from nature. However, the fact that he considered man's mind an inadequate vehicle to arrive at the meaning of the riddle of the universe does not necessarily mean that he denied it the ability to discriminate ethically.

Even under the immediate impact of the writings of Spencer, Tyndall and Huxley, when he felt "blown to bits", Dreiser believed that mechanical determinism need not necessarily mean social determinism. He says in A Book About Myself that he hoped, even then, that "since nature would not or could not do anything for man, he must, if he could, do something for himself" [459]. In other words, Dreiser saw that ethics, being entirely a human creation, need not be subject to the vast forces that operated in the universe. Though nature remains indifferent to man, there could be "a man-made series of rules governing the game here and not elsewhere. . . ."(46) Dreiser advised man "to think of himself rather as a waif, an unloved orphan in space, who must nevertheless and by his own effort make his own pathetic way in the world."(47)

These sentiments clearly show that Dreiser believed that man, though limited, could keep his own house in order. The following passage presents Dreiser's view very clearly:

> [I]f it were possible in the face of the driving forces which seem wholly to manipulate him to reach man and by a suggestion aid him, it would be that in the face of so much confusion he no longer wastes time on theories wholly unrelated to himself or his own material welfare, his essential necessities here, but rather that he see to it first of all, and clearly, that his life here is something which is to be lived here and now to the utmost, in the best form for all - during seventy years, if not longer - here, and not

elsewhere. . . . For is it not high time that
we all realized how essential it is to make
life worth while for all here, knowing as we
now do that man is not a pet in Nature and
that if he makes anything of himself and his
social as well as his mental state here it
must be with the full understanding that he
can expect but little if any aid from Nature
or the forces directing him, certainly none
that would tend to ultimately enlarge his own
mental clarity and supremacy. . . .(48)

Dreiser told Dudley that the effect of reading
Spencer had been the unfolding of a vast,
mysterious universe, the contemplation of whose
mystery and beauty drew him away from his "blazing
and unchecked desire to get on". From now on "He
ceased thinking of himself as a creature who must
push up and on and at the top of the ladder would
receive rewards."(49)

It is important to remember the connection
between Dreiser's encounter with Spencer and the
subsequent loss of his desire to get on in the
world. The post-Spencer Dreiser felt that the
universe was beckoning man to explore its mystery,
to contemplate its beauty, whereas man wasted his
time in such petty pursuits as grabbing for more
and more dollars. For Dreiser, from now on, the
true "seekers" were philosophers and scientists.
They, not the businessmen, were the "men who go
forth to fight a battle, or who, courageous and yet
poorly equipped, venture into a strange and
difficult land in search of gold. . . ."(50) Here,
as elsewhere, Dreiser appropriates the favourite
battle imagery of the businessman to describe
another kind of hero. Dreiser felt that the
achievement of the philosopher, the scientist and
the artist had gone unrecognized in America. An
excessive devotion to commercial achievement had
turned Americans into lop-sided personalities.

Artistically, intellectually, philosophically
we are weaklings; financially and in all ways
commercial we are very powerful. So one-sided
has been our development that in this latter
respect we are almost giants. Strange, almost
fabulous creatures have been developed here by
this process, men so singularly devoid of a
rounded human nature that they have become
freaks in the matter of money-getting. I

refer to Rockefeller, Gould, Sage, Vanderbilt the first, H. H. Rogers, Carnegie, Frick.(51)

Dreiser refused to see the money giants as romantic figures, insisting that "even giants are but pygmies".(52) Despite the allegations of his critics, Dreiser consistently criticized the American financiers in his writings:

Unless one accepts the subtleties of Nature as one finds them, sees in all an inexplicable and yet biologic or universally constructive plan, and in these riant and lawless individuals a scheme of hers to achieve something quickly, there is nothing very admirable or even explicable about the dark goings to and fro of such types as the late J. P. Morgan, H. H. Rogers, Thomas F. Ryan, William C. Whitney, or any of a score of other large fortune- builders so recently in control of stupendous matters here and elsewhere. They are not explicable save as motivating forces in the hands or will of higher powers - good, bad or indifferent. Seen at close range they are more suggestive of sharks and we of sniveling blue-fish, and it is plainly to our best interests either to keep out of their way or unite firmly to oppose them in whatever way we can, unless we choose to be promptly eaten.(53)

Critics have not taken account of the fact that Dreiser counts himself among the bluefish rather than the sharks. If the Cowperwood trilogy were read from the point of view of a bluefish, it would yield an entirely different meaning.

Dreiser blamed the rich for being "individually and socially destructive".(54) He felt that their idealized portraits in the self-help books along with their exhortation to less fortunate fellow Americans to follow suit were most misguiding. He felt that "Mr. Smiles and most of the others who have written on the subject of self help failed in, or perhaps avoided, emphasizing the basic need for ability and ingenuity, as well as real opportunity somewhere."(55) Those who had already made it seemed to Dreiser to be giving their personal qualities too much credit and none to their opportunities. Thus, even while writing for the

Success magazine whose format was to present people who "had gone out and captured what they went after - had shown pluck, were insistent, and stuck to what they were doing - literally, had torn success out of the stingy hands of opportunity", in short, "the glorious drama of poverty",(56) Dreiser took every opportunity to debunk the notion. The excerpt below from his interview with a prominent lawyer is illuminating, both in presenting popular rhetoric of the period as well as Dreiser's ironic response to it. Dreiser, the interviewer, asked:

"What do you consider to be the genuine battle of a youth to-day? - the struggle to bear poverty while working to conquer?"
"Not at all," came the quick answer. "Poor clothes and poor food and a poor place to dwell in are disagreeable things and must be made to give place to better, of course, but one can be partially indifferent to them. The real struggle is to hang on to every advantage, and strengthen the mind at every step. There are persons who have learned to endure poverty so well that they don't mind it any longer. The struggle comes in maintaining a purpose through poverty to the end. It is just as difficult to maintain a purpose through riches."
"Money is not an end, then, in your estimation."
"Never, and need is only an incentive. . . . That intense feeling that something has got to be done is the thing that works the doing. I never met a great man who was born rich."
This remark seemed rather striking in a way, because of the fact that Mr. Choate's parents were not poor in the accepted sense. . . . Mr. Choate was the youngest of four brothers, and, after receiving a [high] school education in Salem, was sent to Harvard, where he was graduated in 1852, and later from its law school in 1854. Influence procured him a position in a Boston law office. . . .
"Isn't it possible, Mr. Choate," I ventured, "that your having had little or no worrying over poverty in your youth might cause you to under-estimate the effect of it on another, and over-estimate the importance of sticking with determination to an idea

through wealth or deprivation?"(57)

To convince ordinary people that they are "lazy Napoleons, idle Hannibals, wasteful and indifferent John D. Rockefellers", who would attain success only if they tried hard enough was, to Dreiser, an act of cruelty. The majority of people, he believed, are "weak and limited, exceedingly so . . . and to fill their humble brains with notions of an impossible supremacy, if it could be done, would be to send them forth to breast the ocean in a cockleshell." However, the "editors, authors, social reformers, et cetera" go on spreading this erroneous belief at the cost of inestimable misery and heartbreak. "And, yet, here on my table, borrowed from the local library for purposes of idle or critical examination, is a silly book entitled 'Take It!' - 'It' meaning 'the world!'; and another 'It's Yours!' - the 'It' in this case meaning that same great world! All you have to do is to decide so to do - and to try! Am I a fool to smile at this very stout doctrine, to doubt whether you can get more than four quarts out of any four-quart measure, if so much?"(58)

As a result of this doctrine, Dreiser felt that "almost every young person was possessed of an ingrowing ambition to be somebody financially and socially. . . . This ambition did not imply merely the attainment of comfort and the wherewithal to make happy one's friends, but rather the accumulation of wealth implying power, social superiority, even social domination." Dreiser found this race for financial and social superiority opposed to the stated equalitarian principles of the American Constitution. "It struck me as anomalous, in a supposedly Christian Democracy dedicated to the principle of brotherly love." He complained that "it was the rare American heart that was set, for instance, on being a great scientist, discoverer, religionist, philosopher, or benefactor to mankind in any form. True enough, a man might start out to be a doctor, a lawyer, a merchant, an inventor, perhaps even a scientist, but his private obsession, due to the national obsession which I have just described, was that the quick and sure way to do this was to get money."(59)

Dreiser came to the conclusion that while this single-minded race for wealth may have proved fruitful in some instances, in the case of the

65

average American it had been nothing short of
disaster. When it did not lead him to the electric
chair, it deprived his mind of the ability to
attain "normal satisfaction in normal wants". On
the contrary, "not only is the whole energy of our
lives turned into a miserable struggle for the
unattainable, namely, the uninterrupted and
complete gratification of our desires, but our
hearts are soured and our natures warped by the
grimness of the struggle. Life is made bitter. The
natural hunger of the heart for righteous
relationships is stifled. We become harsh, cold,
indifferent." The Dreiser who says, "We cannot
forever crowd into cities and forget man for
mammon",(60) is hardly a neutral spectator or a
social Darwinist. In fact, throughout his career,
Dreiser remained deeply concerned with the issues
of his times and wrote about them with an
impressive consistency.
Dreiser took a stand against the predominant ideals
of his times which equated the accumulation of
wealth with the heroic ordeal. His novels are a
protest against the prevailing "gospel of wealth"
and its attendant metaphors of the heroic quest. He
punctures these metaphors to drain them of their
honorific content and to show how inadequate the
heroic myth actually is as a way of apprehending
reality or as a guide to meaningful conduct.

NOTES

1.   David Brion Davis, "Cultural History and
the American Identity," Wilton S. Dillon, ed., The
Cultural Drama: Modern Identities and Social
Ferment,(Smithsonian Institution Press, City of
Washington, 1974) 155.
2.   Dreiser, Dawn (Horace Liveright, Inc.,
New York, 1931) 17-8.
3.   F. O. Matthiessen, Theodore Dreiser,
The American Men of Letters Series (William Sloane
Associates, New York, 1951) 4.
4.   Stuart P. Sherman, "The Barbaric
Naturalism of Mr. Dreiser," The Nation 101
(December 2 1915):648-50; rptd.in John Lydenberg,
ed., Dreiser: A Collection of Critical Essays,
Twentieth Century Views Series (Prentice-Hall,

Inc., Englewood Cliffs, N. J., 1971) 71.
    5.   Sherman, 69.
    6.   Caleb Stetson, quoted in Fred Somkin,
Unquiet Eagle: Memory and Desire in the Idea of
American Freedom, 1815-1860 (Cornell University
Press, Ithaca, N. Y., 1967) 21.
    7.   Charles Francis Adams, Jr., quoted in
George Wheeler, Pierpont Morgan and Friends:
The Anatomy of a Myth (Prentice-Hall, Inc.,
Englewood Cliffs, N. J., 1973) 101.
    8.   Dreiser, Sister Carrie: An
Authoritative Text, Backgrounds, Sources, Criticism
ed. Donald Pizer (W. W. Norton, New York, 1970)
241.
    9.   Ellen Moers, Two Dreisers (The Viking
Press, New York, 1969) xiv.
    10.   Ralph D. Gardner, foreword, Horatio
Alger, Jr., Cast Upon the Breakers (Doubleday &
Company, Inc., Garden City, N. Y., 1974) 12-3.
    11.   Irving G. Wyllie, The Self-Made Man in
America: The Myth of Rags to Riches (Rutgers
University Press, New Brunswick, N. J., 1954)
19-20.
    12.   Quoted in Wyllie, 28, 29.
    13.   Duncan, The Rise of Chicago as a
Literary Center, 8.
    14.   Erich Auerbach, Mimesis: The
Representation of Reality in Western Literature,
trans. Willard R. Trask (1946; Princeton University
Press, Princeton, N. J., 1953) 136.
    15.   Andrew Carnegie, The Gospel of Wealth
and Other Timely Essays (1886; The Century Co.,
New York, 1901) 64.
    16.   Richard Lehan, Theodore Dreiser: His
World and His Novels (Southern Illinois University
Press, Carbondale, 1969) 100.
    17.   John Tebbel, From Rags to Riches:
Horatio Alger, Jr., and the American Dream (The
Macmillan Company, New York, 1963) 5.
    18.   Gardner, foreword, Horatio Alger, Jr.,
Cast Upon the Breakers, 11.
    19.   Dreiser, An Amateur Laborer, ed. with
an introduction by Richard W. Dowell et al.
(University of Pennsylvania Press, Philadelphia,
1983) 85.
    20.   Dreiser, "I Find the Real American
Tragedy," Donald Pizer, ed., Theodore Dreiser:
A Selection of Uncollected Prose (Wayne State
University Press, Detroit, 1977) 291-9.
    21.   W. A. Swanberg, Dreiser (Charles

Scribner's Sons, New York, 1965) 481.
22.   Quoted in Swanberg, 426.
23.   Dreiser, "The Toilers of the Tenements,"
The Color of a Great City (Boni and Liveright, New
York, 1923) 99.
24.   Wyllie, 16.
25.   Dreiser, A Book About Myself (1922;
Boni and Liveright, New York, 1927) 33.
26.   Duncan, Communication and Social Order,
365.
27.   Dreiser, A Hoosier Holiday (John Lane
Company, New York, 1916) 391.
28.   Lehan, 40.
29.   Quoted in R. N. Mookerjee, Theodore
Dreiser: His Thought and Social Criticism
(National Publishing House, Delhi, 1974) 11.
30.   Yoshinobu Hakutani, Young Dreiser: A
Critical Study (Fairleigh Dickinson University
Press, Rutherford, 1980) 188.
31.   Dreiser, Letters of Theodore Dreiser:
A Selection, ed. Robert H. Elias, 3 vols.
(University of Pennsylvania Press, Philadelphia,
1959) 3: 784.
32.   Dreiser, Letters, 2: 583.
33.   Alfred Kazin, introduction, Alfred Kazin
and Charles Shapiro, ed., The Stature of Theodore
Dreiser: A Critical Survey of the Man and His
Work (Indiana University Press, Bloomington, 1955)
10.
34.   Kazin, introduction, The Stature of
Theodore Dreiser, 11.
35.   Kazin, On Native Grounds: An
Interpretation of Modern American Prose Literature
(Reynal and Hitchcock, New York, 1942) 83.
36.   Kazin, On Native Grounds, 86.
37.   Pizer, preface, Sister Carrie, ix.
38.   Pizer, The Novels of Theodore Dreiser:
A Critical Study (University of Minnesota Press,
Minneapolis, 1976) 25.
39.   Kazin, On Native Grounds, 84.
40.   John Lydenberg, "Theodore Dreiser:
Ishmael in the Jungle," Dreiser: A Collection
of Critical Essays, 31.
41.   Raymond Williams, The English Novel:
From Dickens to Lawrence (1970; Paladin, Frogmore,
Herts, 1974) 118-9.
42.   Robert Shafer, "An American Tragedy:
A Humanistic Demurrer," Norman Foerster, ed.,
Humanism and America, (Farrar and Rinehart, New
York, 1920); rptd. in The Stature of Theodore

Dreiser, 124.
43.   Dreiser, "True Art Speaks Plainly,"
Booklover's Magazine 1 (February 1903): 129; rptd.
in Sister Carrie, 473.
44.   Claude Bowers, My Life (New York, 1962)
156; quoted in Mookerjee, 93.
45.   Eliseo Vivas, "Dreiser, An Inconsistent
Mechanist," Ethics (July 1938); rev. and rptd. in
The Stature of Theodore Dreiser, 243.
46.   Dreiser, "What I Believe," Forum 82
(November 1929) 279-81, 317-20; Theodore Dreiser
: A Selection of Uncollected Prose, 251.
47.   Dreiser, "A Counsel to Perfection," Hey
Rub-A-Dub-Dub: A Book of the Mystery and Wonder
and Terror of Life, 123.
48.   Dreiser, "A Counsel to Perfection,"
120-1.
49.   Quoted in Dorothy Dudley, Dreiser and
the Land of the Free: A Novel of Facts (1932;
Wishart & Company, London, 1933) 119.
50.   Dreiser, "Woods Hole and the Marine
Biological Laboratory," Collecting Net 3 (July 21
1928) 1-2; rptd. in Theodore Dreiser: A
Selection of Uncollected Prose, 242.
51.   Dreiser, "Life, Art and America," Hey
Rub-A-Dub-Dub: A Book of the Mystery and Wonder
and Terror of Life, 266-7.
52.   Dreiser, The Titan (1914; The World
Publishing Company, Cleveland, New York, 1925) 551.
53.   Dreiser, "The American Financier," Hey
Rub-A-Dub-Dub: A Book of the Mystery and Wonder
and Terror of Life, 84.
54.   Dreiser, America is Worth Saving
(Modern Age Books, New York, 1941) 279.
55.   Dreiser, unpublished manuscript,
Theodore Dreiser: A Selection of Uncollected
Prose, 273.
56.   Dreiser, unpublished manuscript,
Theodore Dreiser: A Selection of Uncollected
Prose, 275.
57.   Dreiser, "A Talk with America's Leading
Lawyer: Or What Success Means," Success 2
(January 1898) 40-41; rptd.in Theodore Dreiser:
A Selection of Uncollected Prose, 121-2.
58.   Dreiser, "Hey, Rub-A-Dub-Dub!," Hey
Rub-A-Dub-Dub: A Book of the Mystery and Wonder
and Terror of Life, 5, 6.
59.   Dreiser, "I Find the Real American
Tragedy," Theodore Dreiser: A Selection of
Uncollected Prose, 291-2.

60.   Dreiser, "The Loneliness of the City,"
Tom Watson's Magazine 2 (October 1905) 474-5;
rptd. in Theodore Dreiser: A Selection of
Uncollected Prose, 157-8.

Chapter Four

THE COWPERWOOD TRILOGY AND THE HEROIC MYTH

Dreiser's turning away from the portraits of fallen
women of his own family to that of a magnate of
finance has been seen by some as "a drastic shift
of interest".(1) A close look, however, reveals
that essential thread of unity which runs through
Dreiser's entire fiction. It is his need to
scrutinize the motivating causes underlying human
action as they manifest themselves in the
individual's dreams and aspirations and ultimately
result in his actions that joins such apparently
dissimilar works as Sister Carrie, Jennie
Gerhardt, the Cowperwood Trilogy, The "Genius"
and An American Tragedy. However, when these
novels are studied in isolation from one another it
does become hard to explain the "drastic" shifts
except in terms of dubious, far-fetched
autobiographical similarities. When read in this
manner, Sister Carrie and The "Genius" become
rather unsatisfactory Künstlerromans, while the
Cowperwood trilogy appears to be an "awestruck"
paean to the businessman-superman, and An American
Tragedy is simply the penance of a man who became
disillusioned after losing heavily in stocks during
the Depression. A close scrutiny of the texts,
however, leads to the conclusion that almost all of
Dreiser's novels could have been titled An
American Tragedy.
    When Dreiser chose to portray the
Cowperwood-Yerkes figure, it was not so much due to
its topical interest, or because Mencken was
goading American novelists to write the great
American novel on the businessman figure, as
because of Dreiser's conviction that Cowperwood's
dreams of grandeur were somehow stereotypical.
Cowperwood is not a Nietzschean Superman, as most
critics have considered him to be. Rather, he is a

representative figure, a microcosm that reflects
the macrocosm of American society. The symbolic
environment he has created for himself has striking
similarities to that of Drouet, Carrie, the young
Dreiser of Dawn and A Book About Myself, and
Clyde. According to Dreiser, the America of his
youth was dreaming the same dreams en masse:

> The spirit of America at that time was so
> remarkable. It was just entering on that
> vast, splendid, most lawless and most savage
> period in which the great financiers, now
> nearly all dead, were plotting and conniving
> the enslavement of the people and belaboring
> each other for power. Those crude and parvenu
> dynasties which now sit enthroned in our
> democracy, threatening its very life with
> their pretensions and assumptions, were just
> in the beginning. . . . Giants were plotting,
> fighting, dreaming on every hand, and in this
> city [Buffalo], as in every other American
> city I then visited, there was a singing,
> illusioned spirit. Actually, the average
> American then believed that the possession of
> money would certainly solve all his earthly
> ills. You could see it in the faces of the
> people, in their step and manner. Power,
> power, power, - every one was seeking power in
> the land of the free and the home of the
> brave.(2)

Sister Carrie was Dreiser's first attempt to
fictionalize this "singing, illusioned spirit" that
lured hundreds of thousands from their rural
retreats to the fast growing urban centres. The
American city inspired the wildest hopes and dreams
in people like Carrie, Cowperwood, Eugene and
Clyde, not to mention the hundreds of minor
characters in Dreiser's novels who are carbon
copies of the protagonists. Jennie Gerhardt is
perhaps an exception among Dreiser's young people
and seems to have been created as a contrast to
Carrie. In a sense, she is the only major
character in Dreiser's world who acts primarily due
to necessity rather than desire. Unlike the
majority of his characters, she does not dream of
that "social supremacy" - a favourite phrase of
Dreiser's - which drives Carrie, Cowperwood and
Eugene. Jennie, therefore, is an exception to the
spirit of the times as Dreiser saw it. The nation

72

as a whole, he perceived, was imaginatively gripped by the self-made man, the man who was deemed to have made the long, heroic journey from rags to riches, thereby proving that in American democracy birth was no hindrance to success. The editors, the writers, the clergymen were exhorting the populace in the name of the self-made man and few there were who did not want to embark on that journey. One may well wonder whether the trouble Dreiser had in completing <u>Jennie Gerhardt</u> had something to do with this spirit of the age.

The links that bind "The Trilogy of Desire" with the other stories of desire Dreiser wrote have been largely ignored by his critics. That Cowperwood bears striking resemblance to Carrie and Clyde has not been noticed by critics because they have insisted on seeing the trilogy as the product of Dreiser's awestruck admiration for the big capitalist, whom he is supposed to have seen as "a maker and shaper" of modern America.(3) The fact is that there is no debate. It is generally agreed that Dreiser admires and exonerates Cowperwood. As proof, critics quote passages from the autobiographical volumes without realizing that these books record Dreiser's youth in the ironic light of his present knowledge. As Dreiser wrote, "The love and tragedy of eighteen and twenty is the butt and the jest of the sophistication of forty; looking back on the first state as an illusion and an utter folly and the second as the equivalent of peace and a reasonable amount of mental and physical comfort."(4)

The irony arising from this double vision, however, has gone unnoticed. Instead, the Cowperwood trilogy is taken to be a straight-faced glorification of the superman by a writer who harboured such ambitions of his own and identified unashamedly with his larger-than-life hero. A serious wrong is thus perpetrated on Dreiser. He is denied that self-consciousness, that "sophistication of forty" which all good writers are known to possess - a self-consciousness which allows them to grasp the vital aspects of their time and present them in symbolic forms. If Dreiser is not doing that in his novel, if he is merely reciting another saga of the might of the superman, he is obviously not doing something unique. It was a feat done over and over in his time. Moreover, there is also the fact that Dreiser denied that he was a Nietzschean.(5)

If we take his statement seriously, Dreiser
intended to do something more than just telling us
to admire the millionaire since he was a more
complex product of the evolutionary process. To
return to his own statement, through the character
of Cowperwood he wanted to explore the deeply
ingrained myths of his society - the myths that had
so powerfully moved him in youth and which he found
to be all-pervasive in their breadth and scope. At
least that is how he described his purpose:

> Some tales are too great to be told, or they
> need retelling. Certain I am of one thing,
> the age that produced at once the mechanical
> perfection of the world and its most colossal
> fortunes is classic. From that period
> certainly some Croesus, Lepidus and Maecenas
> is sure to show forth in fable, song, or
> story. In my limited search and with my
> selective tendencies none seemed of so great
> import, socially, sociologically, financially,
> philosophically as the individual whom I have
> selected.(6)

It was the representative aspect of
Cowperwood, rather than his super-human stature
that most appealed to Dreiser. As he told a
newspaper interviewer, "In The Financier I have
not taken a man so much as I have a condition,
although any one who follows the detailed study of
Cowperwood's life would fancy perhaps that it was
more a man than a condition that I was after."(7)
Cowperwood is then an allegorical figure who
represents a "condition" instead of being a
lifelike character in the mode of realistic writers
like George Eliot, William Dean Howells and Henry
James. Cowperwood is the essence of the spirit of
the age as Dreiser perceived it. He is the fantasy
of the average American blown to its utmost
exaggeration in order to expose its pathetic
meaninglessness and vulgarity.
The "business of the author", Dreiser
believed, was to "tell the truth", and "having said
as much, to abide the result with patience".
Instead of a "quiet acceptance of things", a true
writer worked towards the "well-being of the
future".(8) He held that the writer could bring
about social change by making people understand
their situation: "If life is to be made better or
more interesting, its condition must be understood.

No situation can be solved, no improvement can be effected, no evil remedied, unless the conditions which surround it are appreciated."(9) Thus, far from seeing life as a mere spectacle, as his critics have maintained, Dreiser saw life in the old-fashioned terms of writers with a vision. He wanted to persuade his readers that things needed to be changed.

When Dreiser told his interviewer that it was a "condition" he was after in the Cowperwood trilogy, he was adhering to his programme of understanding life in order to change it for the better. The Cowperwood trilogy is another attempt on his part to "tell the truth" so that his readers will be persuaded. The programme is the same as the one he had proposed in 1903: to picture "the wretched results of modern social conditions".(10) In another pertinent essay, he blamed the modern city for destroying "normal satisfaction in normal wants" by its "disturbing . . . show of pleasures and diversions we cannot obtain". The next paragraph of the essay summarizes the career of Cowperwood:

> Not only is the whole energy of our lives turned into a miserable struggle for the unattainable, namely, the uninterrupted and complete gratification of our desires, but our hearts are soured and our natures warped by the grimness of the struggle. Life is made bitter. The natural hunger of the heart for righteous relationship is stifled. We become harsh, cold, indifferent.(11)

Cowperwood is an embodiment of this "condition" of the soul. When Dreiser undertook to write about him, he hoped to show his readers how meaningless the supposedly ideal existence was. He showed Cowperwood, along with the numerous other businessmen in the trilogy, to have lost all trace of essential humanity. They are consistently portrayed as rats, pigs, dogs, wolves, leopards and tigers. Contrary to the popular interpretation, this animal imagery was not meant to condemn the whole human race to the unconscious, reasonless existence of beasts. Instead, it is reserved for the corrupt politico-business class whose predatory world Dreiser contrasted with a moral, intellectual and artistic world created by the human spirit which inspires the reader with hope for humanity.

Cowperwood, however, is not a dark villain of the typical anti-business novel of the period. When Dreiser said that he had presented his protagonist "unidealized and uncursed",(12) he had meant us to see Cowperwood in terms of the social forces which conditioned him. He neither idealized him as an invincible, suprasocial superman nor cursed him as an unregenerate devil. However, this stance has been taken to be a moral ambiguity on the part of Dreiser, a "mixed attitude" which is inferior to the "heartfelt denunciations of Upton Sinclair" on the one hand and to "the incisive critical judgment of Myers" on the other.(13) Unfortunately, Matthiessen is unable to see that Dreiser's stance has a close resemblance to that of Myers. In fact, Dreiser acknowledged his debt to Gustavus Myers who, like Dreiser, wanted to present his history of the great American fortunes without "prejudice" or "declamation" in order to "seek and eradicate the cause" of "an epidemic" from which, he felt, the society was suffering.(14) He, too, blamed the myths surrounding the businessmen which represented "their accumulations as the rewards of industry and ability", as "preeminent examples of thrift, enterprise and extraordinary ability".(15)

Cowperwood must be seen against the background of these prevalent myths that shape his identity. He is not one of the "monsters of commercial and political crime", one of those "especial creatures of infamy" that pervaded the writings of the muckrakers. Instead, Dreiser, like Myers, sees him as "the natural, logical outcome of a system".(16) Dreiser is interested in the texture of his dreams and their origins because they explain some fundamental truths about Dreiser's society. The trilogy is an attempt to answer the question he posed at the end of The Titan: "Who plans the steps that lead lives on to splendid glories, or twist them into gnarled sacrifices, or make of them dark, disdainful, contentious tragedies? The soul within? And whence comes it? Of God?"(17)

For the naturalist Dreiser, the "soul within", "the temperament", was the product of the social forces. That is why Cowperwood is not to be cursed but understood. By going back to his very beginnings Dreiser hoped to make us understand the causes underlying the nature of the state of affairs. Cowperwood's individual destiny has a public meaning in the sense that society itself is responsible for leading Cowperwood towards the socially and spiritually destructive path he has taken. In fact, Dreiser accused all of us of harbouring a secret admiration for Cowperwood and his likes.(18)

That Cowperwood's steps are planned by the universal aspirations of his society, Dreiser made amply clear through the allegorical nomenclature. It is no accident that his first and middle names, Frank and Algernon, recall the two famous figures associated with the theme of success, namely, Benjamin Franklin and Horatio Alger. It is also no accident that his last name is phonetically similar to copper. The last part of his name seems to point to the jungle-like world he inhabits. His mythic nature is made clear beyond doubt in The Stoic: "And now, here she [Berenice] was, planning on the morrow to visit his tomb again, the last material vestige of all the values that had seemed so vividly real and wonderful to her at the time, but which now, in comparison with all she had experienced in India, were no longer important to her."(19)

Indeed, the trilogy must be studied from the perspective of the popular myth as propagated by the success manuals, the media and the commissioned and uncommissioned biographies of the famous rich. Such works had two aims, often contradictory: to exalt the stature of the already rich and to exhort the reader to attempt emulation. They emphasized the heroic nature of the struggle. The ideal hero of these books was the Franklinian Poor Richard who rose to the top through courage, enterprise, hard work, intelligence and sheer determination. In short, it was all a question of one's mettle and daring. The rich in America fondly reminisced over their humble beginnings, and the more obscure and deprived the origin, the more glorious was their struggle considered.(20)

The qualities that align such works to a quest romance are thematic, metaphorical as well as structural. The pursuit of wealth in these works is exalted as a glorious mode of existence, worthy of a single-minded, exclusive form of devotion. These works deliberately underplay the exchange value of money in order to heighten its achievement value. The ostentations of the successful rich are never described or discussed. They are always seen in action: as generals and war-heroes or, better still, as knights of yore who perform difficult deeds as a sort of challenge. The personal

qualities that are emphasized are martial, to the
exclusion of all other modes of excellence, such as
literary, musical, philosophical or religious.
   Both the mediaeval quest romance and the
modern gospel of wealth romance view the external
world as an adversary to be subdued by personal
force, which almost seems to exist so that the
strength of the protagonist may show forth
brightly. Life, for both, is a battleground
devised with the sole purpose of exhibiting the
glory of the heroic contestants. The battle must
be fierce if it has to provide an appropriate
testimony to the prowess of the warriors. The
metaphor was invoked often and continues to be used
by business writers to this day.
   Both the romances proceed lineally through an
accumulation of details. The individual is
pictured marching on the perilous road towards
success, undeterred by all the obstacles which seem
to litter his path. At times he himself goes out
to meet them when they are not forthcoming
themselves, simply to enhance his heroic stature.
   The basic ingredients of this structure are
present in the Cowperwood trilogy. Dreiser uses
the hero's biography as a controlling form, with
due emphasis on his early childhood adventures. He
gives a detailed account of how Cowperwood went
about making his various conquests. True to the
popular mode, Dreiser structures his novel in terms
of the high points of Cowperwood's financial
career. Like a typical romance of business, it
even shows the hero at the nadir of his fortune,
only to show him overcome it with his own effort.
   The similarity, however, is superficial. The
Cowperwood trilogy uses this basic structure in
order to undercut it. Dreiser parodies the popular
mode in order to satirize the values of his
society. He uses a form which has been identified
with certain kinds of expectations with the sole
purpose of disappointing them so that the reader
can perceive the contrast between the ideal and the
actual. Like Fielding, for whom Dreiser professed
an admiration, he chooses the imitative form of
parody as the most appropriate vehicle for his
attack.
   However, this deliberate discrepancy between
form and content and the resultant satirical
overtones have been overlooked by the majority
critical opinion which sees the novel as a

straightforward "version of the American success story" with a "bare Horatio Alger pattern" showing oddly through. Cowperwood, according to this line of thought, is "Dreiser's version of 'the survival of the fittest,' intermingled with traits of Nietzsche's 'Superman.'" Alternately, it is claimed that "Cowperwood was the embodiment of so much that he himself had longed for and missed".(21) The result of this identification, it is alleged, is a "lack of final judgement" on Dreiser's part. Those who have espoused these opinions feel that Dreiser "shared, as the mass of people of his time shared, in being attracted to what might well destroy, in a curiously blurred dream that combined Horatio Alger with Darwin and Nietzsche."(22)

This point of view, which denies Dreiser any sense of discrimination, begins with Elias and Matthiessen and continues to be popular to the present day. The possibility that Cowperwood could be a parody of the superman rather than the superman himself is not at all acknowledged. It is common to see Cowperwood's interior monologue being quoted as Dreiser's definitive statement. It is also common to see other characters' opinions regarding Cowperwood being quoted as proof of Dreiser's approval of the hero without regard to the possibility that those characters might have been qualified by the narrator.

Obviously, Dreiser has not been given the close textual reading he deserves. His novelistic devices have been ignored in order to push across a point of view which does not stand the light of examination. If we turn our attention to the novels proper, we discover that Dreiser's intention was neither to "exalt his hero",(23) as Matthiessen and others claim, nor to make us "greatly dread him",(24) as Masters thought he ought to have done, but to present a portrait of a greatly puffed up man who had an unduly high estimate of himself and on whom reality never dawned. That the portrait is not wholly comic is due to the fact that Dreiser thought the "genus financier" too dangerous for social well-being. Nonetheless, he did find them comic: "In America, the history of our financiers is so full of thievery and selfishness as to appear comic were it not for the mass misery which so many of their deeds involved."(25) That Dreiser could write in a lighter vein about this species is clear from a character-sketch in Twelve Men.(26) In

---

---

fact, the semi-frivolous tone of the narrator, the nature of the main character and the incidental details are so similar to The Great Gatsby that the sketch has been considered to have provided Fitzgerald with the inspiration for his novel.(27) This character-sketch is ample evidence of the humorous attitude Dreiser took towards the financier's pretensions. He probably would have taken the same tone in the novel were it not for the fact that Cowperwood has far more social power than the unnamed character of the sketch. The tone Dreiser adopted for the trilogy tries to balance the comic with the serious. The financier is too dangerous to be treated entirely comically. Hence, in The Titan Cowperwood is described in the metaphors of disease: as a "virus" [124], a "condition" which can infect and destroy the whole body politic. However, the comic mood is not entirely absent from the trilogy.

In the second paragraph of the opening chapter of The Financier, the narrator gives the clue that makes the reader aware of the ironic tone. Henry Worthington Cowperwood, Cowperwood's father, we are told, "looked upon life as a business situation or deal, with everybody born as more or less capable machines to take part in it. It was surprising to him to see how many incapable or unsatisfactory machines there were; but, thank heaven, now that he was getting along fairly well, this was no affair of his."(28) This peculiar attitude towards life, however, is not unique to Henry Cowperwood. He is an eminent citizen of the Philadelphia commercial circle, lodged in Third Street, "center of all Philadelphia, and indeed almost, at that time, of all national finance" [3]. The other citizens to whom Dreiser introduces us are all from this small circle and behave exactly like Henry Cowperwood. They approve of him and are, in turn, approved of by him; they are all "capable machines". The people in this society value themselves and others in terms of money they possess and we are repeatedly told of their "worth".

It is this society with its hierarchy of money which deeply influences Cowperwood. As a child, he moves into three new houses as his father progresses from clerk to teller to vice-president, each house being one story higher than the other. With the upward progression also comes a different set of "connections" [10], the older set being discreetly dropped. "When his tellership arrived he was not so familiarly greeted, except by those who were much superior to him financially" [17].

Thus the world-view Cowperwood inherits from his family and the immediate social circle is that of a hierarchy which is not stationary like those of the past but mobile and opportunistic. All of its members are upwardly mobile, seeking greater wealth along with which go greater prestige and status. The acquisition of wealth is associated in their mind with actual physical progression which is both upward and lineal. The progression is socially declared by the change of residences as well as of one's acquaintances. The residences are not changed arbitrarily but in a certain direction - west in Cowperwood's case - in the direction of a city's "better" neighbourhoods. Thus, every such move is symbolic of the higher plane the upwardly mobile person deems himself to have arrived at.

We are told in The Financier that Cowperwood is liked by all because he displays the right kind of attitude. He makes and drops friends according to their "connections" and though he is "a good leader", he is also "a splendid second to those older than himself whom he sincerely admired" [5]. His role models are Steemberger and Francis J. Grund, whom the narrator describes as pig-like. Their methods are not exactly legitimate, but that does not bother this extremely pious society. On the contrary, their financial adventures are the talk of the town. "Young Frank listened to the story of these transactions with a greedy ear. They seemed wonderful to him; but this whole world of money was like a fairyland, full of delight. Why, in third street there was nothing but money, great piles of it" [20]. Thus begins Cowperwood's fascination with finance, even before he has reached thirteen.

At thirteen, Cowperwood drives his first bargain and dazzles his father and uncle. His interest in "money" is considered "a good trait" by his highly respected uncle [25]. By eighteen, others are taking note of him too. "That's a smart young fellow", says Tighe. "He'll make his mark", thinks Rivers [94].

The glorification of Cowperwood's character, thus, starts early. That this world of "capable machines" is less than perfect does not enter Cowperwood's mind. He swallows its assumptions wholesale without being the least aware of "those

silly fancies which might trouble the less rational
brains of this world" [2], those "emotions and
subtleties of life" which so appeal to poets [18].
This other world which the commercial society
cannot see was described even more explicitly in
Jennie Gerhardt which has many links with The
Financier since Dreiser alternated between the
two.

> That other world of flesh into which has been
> woven pride and greed looks askance at the
> idealist, the dreamer. If one says it is
> sweet to look at the clouds, the answer is a
> warning against idleness. If one seeks to give
> ear to the winds, it shall be well with his
> soul, but they will seize upon his
> possessions. If all the world of the
> so-called inanimate delay one, calling with
> tenderness in sounds that seem to be too
> perfect to be less than understanding, it
> shall be ill with the body.(29)

Another passage from Jennie Gerhardt gives
an even more important clue to Dreiser's estimate
of his hero and his society.

> The trouble with Lester was that, while
> blessed with a fine imagination and
> considerable insight, he lacked the ruthless,
> narrow-minded insistence on his individual
> superiority which is a necessary element in
> almost every great business success. To be a
> forceful figure in the business world means,
> as a rule, that you must be an individual of
> one idea, and that idea the God-given one that
> life has destined you for a tremendous future
> in the particular field you have chosen. It
> means that one thing, a cake of soap, a new
> can-opener, a safety razor, or speed-
> accelerator, must seize on your imagination
> with tremendous force, burn as a raging flame,
> and make itself the be-all and end-all of your
> existence. As a rule, a man needs poverty to
> help him to this enthusiasm, and youth. The
> thing he has discovered, and with which he is
> going to busy himself, must be the door to a
> thousand opportunities and a thousand joys.
> Happiness must be beyond or the fire will not
> burn as brightly as it might. . . .(30)

Cowperwood's character seems to have been sketched with this passage as a guideline. His ego has been bolstered from a very early age because he has the kind of aptitudes his society most desires. If he had been born with the temperament of a poet, as Eugene Witla or Dreiser himself, the society would have had nothing but disapproval for him. His role models in _The Financier_ consider him to be "inexpressibly sound and deep-thinking financially" [63] because he expresses the conventional views of his society. This sense of self-satisfaction and its source are clearly pointed out in the novel: "Cowperwood smiled his hearty, genial smile. He was feeling very comfortable under the evidence of approval. He looked bright and cheery in his well-made clothes of English tweed" [53]. "It was fine to be getting on this way in the world and having such a good time" [55].

The bemused ironic tone quite clearly suggests that Cowperwood is under narrative scrutiny. In sketching Cowperwood's childhood and adolescence in such great detail, Dreiser wanted us to see the moral and intellectual bankruptcy of the society whose product Cowperwood is. For Dreiser did not believe in the individual as a separate entity who was personally responsible for the growth of his moral self. He explained his philosophy thus in _Notes on Life_:

> At birth, the individual is entirely an hereditary product. Immediately after birth, this hereditary product is either in harmony or in conflict with his environment. Images and example and after these, moral teachings, social procedure, and tabu, the struggles for possession, and the rejections for want of this or that come to be registered by the mind mechanism, to be compiled, synthesized, and contrasted with what results few if any - not even the creature doing the registering - can predict or, when they occur, understand.(31)

If Cowperwood's imagination has been seized by the likes of Steemberger and Grund, Dreiser wants us to put the blame in the right place. Young Cowperwood by no means lacks intelligence. He is, the novel informs us, a bright, alert, inquisitive child, wanting to find answers to questions about "economics and politics", "pondering, pondering, pondering - one fact astonishing him quite as much

as another, for he could not figure out how this
thing he had come into - this life - was organized"
[10]. The answers that adults provide him are inane
and obviously out of touch with the reality he sees
around him. The story of Adam and Eve that his
mother tells him does not satisfy him, and for good
reason. If he goes to the fish tank to find an
answer, he should not be unduly blamed. Certainly,
what he sees there seems a perfect analogy for the
behaviour of American business in the
mid-nineteenth century. As it is, Dreiser felt
that "the strident voices" on the American scene -
those of the "money barons, the trusts, the
landlords, the stock jugglers, together with their
handmaidens, the Comstockers, boards of moving-
picture censors, busy ministers, vice-crusaders
sly agents (tools and fools) of religious and
financial organizations" were intent on "a program
of mental shoddy and souffle such as no healthy
animal nation bent upon even a semi-respectable
career of constructive thought and constructive
action could possibly accept and mentally live."
(32)
    Cowperwood's imagination has been starved in
all other directions except that of finance. In a
nature unsuited to finance the result might have
been disastrous but Cowperwood, fortunately, has
the right mental aptitude and he flourishes. The
narrator of The Financier, however, has only an
amused smile for his philosophical speculations.
His lesson at the fish tank has no authenticity in
the eyes of the narrator who considers it a
"tragedy" [11]. It is a conclusion arrived at by a
ten year old and the syntax reflects that. The
language throughout the narration of this incident
is apparently condescending. The inexperienced
child has found a simplistic clue to questions of
profound moral and philosophical import. The
amused detachment of the narrator is clear
throughout the rendering of the episode which ends
with the narrator saying, "He went on home quite
pleased with himself 'at his solution" [14].
Dreiser's remark to Dr. Sculley Bradley about this
passage - "It is Frank, not me!"(33) - clears any
doubt as to his intention.
    Critics often quote this passage to prove that
the lobster and the squid sequence is Dreiser's
metaphor for the nature of life. However, his own
remark to Dr. Bradley indicates that he was talking
of the current business practices and not the

nature of reality. The episode of the fish tank brings home to the reader the heroic cast in which the businessman of the time liked to see himself. Life was a fierce battle and he, the successful businessman, was the conqueror. The analogy miraculously transforms the stock market - for Cowperwood later recalls the same image to describe the stock market - into a Darwinian world. Dreiser appropriates these analogies of the battlefield from his contemporaries in order to mock them. In Dreiser's fiction, they become a tool of satire when placed alongside other incongruous analogies and rendered in the ironic language of the narrator.

Judged by the standards of his own society, Cowperwood succeeds miraculously. He makes money in plenty. By the time he is thirty-four years of age, he has "a banking business estimated at nearly two million dollars" and "personal holdings aggregating nearly half a million" [275]. He has become a petal of that "American Beauty rose" in whose service millions must bleed.(34) He has made his place in the select company of millionaires whose biographies were frequently printed by the likes of Success magazine.

There is, however, a twist here. Unlike the success manuals which, as Hofstadter points out,(35) never initiated their readers into the intricacies of finance, insisting all the time on the importance of cultivating certain traits of character, Dreiser painstakingly sketches all the minute factual details. These details, as Dreiser paints them, are not heroic. They are, simply, sleazy. Though "finance is a great art" and Cowperwood is a financier by instinct, the trouble, according to the novel, is that his mind has been fixed on one limited version of the art: "only in the form in which he saw it manifested in Third Street" [39]. And the way it is practised in Third Street requires no subtleties of intelligence to be comprehended. Dreiser wants to make it absolutely clear that "the huge and Aladdin-like adventures" (36) that the great financiers of the day indulged in are not a demonstration of the superiority of their mental equipment - as it was generally claimed and believed - but of the social power they have usurped. The early chapters of The Financier are devoted to deglamorizing the operations of high finance. In Dreiser's fictional world, we are asked to believe that what is required to succeed

is not daring but "connections", a word that
appears many times in many contexts throughout the
Cowperwood trilogy. Characters like Grund have
"connections" in the Senate and make money on the
"tips" they get regarding the passage of certain
bills. A key passage of The Financier describes
how political influence-peddling and amassing of
wealth through the stock market go hand-in-hand:

> A scheme had been on foot to make Texas a
> State of the Union, and a bill was finally
> passed providing a contribution on the part of
> the United States of five million dollars, to
> be applied to the extinguishment of this old
> debt. Grund knew of this, and also of the
> fact that some of this debt, owing to the
> peculiar conditions of issue, was to be paid
> in full, while other portions were to be
> scaled down, and there was to be a false or
> prearranged failure to pass the bill
> appropriating the five million dollars at one
> session, in order to frighten off the
> outsiders who might have heard and begun to
> buy the old certificates for their own profit.
> Grund knew of this. The Third National knew
> of Grund's knowledge through him; and
> Cowperwood, as teller, was also informed in
> some way. He told his wife about it
> afterward; and so his son, in this roundabout
> way, heard it, and his clear, big eyes
> glistened. He wondered why his father did not
> take advantage of it and buy some Texas
> certificates himself, but the latter was too
> honest, too careful. So this was the way
> money was made. Men schemed and planned, and
> then they reaped big profits. Grund, so his
> father said, and possibly three or four
> others, had made over a hundred thousand
> dollars apiece. . . . When he grew up, Frank
> told himself, he was going to be a broker, or
> a financier, or a banker, and do some of these
> things. It was so easy for him to see how
> they were done. You had to get in with people
> - that was how: you had to know what was going
> on. . . . He walked to school each day
> thinking of these things; but he was sick of
> school and books. What did his teachers know
> about money? Nothing. What did these other
> boys know of what was going on in Third
> Street? Not a thing. Why, a man might get

down in there and get rich before anybody knew
anything about anything. He wondered that the
street was not crowded with people like
Steemberger and Grund. It was so easy. He
could see how it was. [21-2]

Dreiser's purpose, clearly, is to show how
little "risk taking" there really is in the way
finance works in Third Street. For the businessman
prided himself on just that. Doing business, the
popular gospel preached, required a heart of steel
and an adventurous spirit. What Andrew Carnegie
wrote in The Empire of Business is typical. "The
business man", he claimed, "plunges into and tosses
upon the waves of human affairs without a life-
preserver in the shape of salary; he risks all."
(37) According to this foamy rhetoric, business is
no humdrum, routine matter of daily life, but a
glorious, perilous existence.

For Dreiser, writing in the early decades of
the twentieth century, when works of Lincoln
Steffens, Ida Tarbell, Charles Edward Russell and
Thorstein Veblen were taking the veneer off the
glorious image of business, this romanticization of
the businessman seemed utterly devoid of truth.
Throughout the trilogy, Dreiser attempts to educate
the reader into the operations of finance, with the
single purpose of showing that what counts in
business is not so much innate ability as
"connections". In themselves, the operations of
finance are ridiculously simple, at least as
portrayed in the trilogy. In a highly ironical
passage in The Financier, Dreiser scuttles the
mystique of this tough world:

It was while Cowperwood was working under
Rivers for Tighe that he learned all those
subtleties of the stock-market system which
afterward stood him in such good stead. By
degrees he picked up all the technicalities of
the situation, and all the terminology, though
the latter was not more than an hour's lesson
the first day, given succinctly by Rivers. A
"bull," he learned, was one who bought in
anticipation of a higher price to come; and if
he was "loaded up" with a "line" of stocks he
was said to be "long." He sold to "realize"
his profit, or if his margins were exhausted
he was "wiped out." A "bear" was one who sold
stocks which most frequently he did not have,

in anticipation of a lower price, at which he could buy and satisfy his previous sales. He was "short" when he had sold what he did not own, and he "covered" when he bought to satisfy his sales and to realize his profits or to protect himself against further loss in case prices advanced instead of declining. He was caught in a "corner" when he found that he could not buy in order to make good the stock he had borrowed for delivery and the return of which had been demanded. He was then obliged to settle practically at a price fixed by those to whom he and other "shorts" had sold. [80]

It is instructive to compare this portrayal with Norris' description of the stock-market. Norris' stock-market is as mysterious as the ways of nature itself, with real bears and bulls ready to tear apart the unwary. Dreiser, on the other hand, wants his reader to shed the romantic notions associated with the stock-market. It is useful to recall the comments made in the novel regarding Cowperwood's scheme to bring the city loan at par, a scheme which gained Yerkes, the Cowperwood prototype in real life, an honourable mention in the D. N. B.:

The plan Mr. Cowperwood developed after a few days' meditation would be plain enough to any one who knew anything of commercial and financial manipulation, but a dark secret to those who do not. [178]

In the first place, Dreiser goes on to say, the city treasury did not need any loans except to profit the city politicians. As to the actual sale of the loan certificates, Dreiser devotes a long paragraph to initiating the reader into the way "manufactured fluctuations" [179] are created so that the watered stock is "unloaded" on the "outsiders" while the "inside ring" makes all the money without taking any risks. The men who come to Cowperwood & Co. to invest in stocks are men with "tips". Dreiser gives a detailed description of the corruption in the city government: how city bonds "work" for some and not for others. The magical pass key, as Cowperwood learnt in his cradle, is "connections" and he cultivates them with assiduous care. The result, expectedly, is a bounteous harvest:

> "This political world is a great world,"
> Cowperwood said to himself. "These fellows
> have access to ready money. I must go slow;
> but I can go slow, and they will make me
> rich." [176]

Dreiser thus ruthlessly undercuts the
businessman's career, while staying within the
conventions of the mythic mode which structured
itself on the eminent peaks of this career, each
achievement more spectacular than the last one. The
financier in Dreiser's novel ventures nothing and
yet gains phenomenal profits. Thus, the handling
of the State loan, Cowperwood's next big venture
after the City loan, and a venture by which great
political capital was made by the money barons,
turns out to be an equally underhand affair. The
financing of the State loan, about which the papers
make such a "palaver", is, in reality, no more than
a trick:

> These great financiers who worked in the
> street, how he envied their reputations! They
> walked so defiantly, so freely. The papers
> spoke of them so respectfully, fawning. He
> was a mere note and stock broker; but he knew
> how these tricks were turned. Money was the
> first thing to have - a lot of it. Then
> reputation of handling it wisely would treble,
> quadruple, aye, increase its significance a
> hundred and a thousand fold. First you
> secured the money. Then you secured the
> reputation. The two things were like two legs
> on which you walked. Then your mere word was
> as good as money, or better. [125]

When this monologue occurs in Chapter XII, the
reader already knows how these two most important
things are secured, having been told by Dreiser
about the devious manipulations and wirepulling
that go on in the commercial and political
quarters. We have been told that "The condition of
the finances of the State and city were most
reprehensible" and "favoritism" was the rule [60].
The popular myth, on the other hand,
propagated that the rich man had amassed his wealth
through hard work and virtuous conduct. Carnegie
was one of the shining examples and in _Triumphant_

89

Democracy and elsewhere he preached the doctrines of hard work, self-reliance and such with great self-exultation. Cowperwood, however, is no country bumpkin or a farm hand starting life as a boot black or an office boy as Carnegie, Alger, Marden and others were telling aspiring youth to do. Nor are there other rags-to-riches stories in the novel.

Indeed, Cowperwood could not have been born in a better place. Money, as his uncle Seneca says, is bred in his bones. He does not start life totally unassisted. He knows the right people and all the right things, and to top it all, even gets a legacy of fifteen thousand dollars. In giving us these facts, Dreiser is doing the same things he did in his interviews with the successful men of his period. Even though the format of Success magazine did not allow for it, Dreiser prodded his subjects to find out how far their success depended on their own merits and how far other factors were responsible. He researched their backgrounds to check if their claims about self-reliance were correct and provided the information when it disclosed facts contrary to their stated claims.(38)

Dreiser is one of the first American novelists to challenge the popular belief in the fluidity of the social and economic system which allowed the son of a poor immigrant to aspire to become a Carnegie, a Vanderbilt, a Rockefeller - those who had risen from poverty. However, it has been pointed out by researchers that "most - perhaps 90 percent - of the industrial leaders in our group [1870-79] were reared in a middle or upper-class milieu." The typical business leader, as Gregory and Neu describe him, was not a "new man", "an escapee from the slums of Europe or from the paternal farm". Statistics, instead, provide a totally different profile: "American by birth, of a New England father, English in national origin, Congregational, Presbyterian or Episcopal in religion, urban in early environment, he was rather born and bred in an atmosphere in which business and a relatively high social standing were intimately associated with his family life."(39)

Cowperwood's antecedents, right down to his Episcopalian denomination, exactly match this profile. Dreiser, obviously, had done his research well. His choice of details shows a remarkable sociological astuteness as compared to that of the other novelists of the age. Henry James' Newman, Fitzgerald's Gatsby and Norris' Jadwin, unlike Dreiser's characters, follow the popular stereotype of the businessman's poor childhood.

Another very important clue regarding Dreiser's narrative intention lies in his choice of the hero. Critics bring in such autobiographical similarities as Yerkes' and Dreiser's "varietistic" tendencies and their devotion to art. Both are said to have gone on to success from a background of poverty. These reasons, however, do not explain the novel's thematic purposes. Moreover, these similarities are only skin deep. Dreiser came from a very poor, Catholic background whereas Yerkes was a Quaker. While he was a fourth generation American, Dreiser was the son of German immigrants.

If Dreiser's own words are to be taken seriously, the choice, rather than being autobiographical, was due to the man's social, sociological and philosophical import. Not only did Dreiser want to explode the rags-to-riches myth with all its heroic paraphernalia, he wanted to point out another falsehood. The businessman in his heroic armour was considered the indispensable provider of essential goods and services without whom civilization would come to a standstill. For his hero, however, Dreiser chose a figure who makes his fortune first by looting the city treasury, and then by manipulating the stock market. The practice of "stock-jobbing" was considered to be unethical both by the entrepreneurs as well as the religious leaders. Edwin Freedley in his popular 1853 handbook on business wrote that "there is a wide and essential difference between speculation and trade, two things which are very apt to be confounded together in theory and practice." In Freedley's opinion, speculation is lottery and a speculator looks to "sudden and eccentric enrichment" whereas the trader makes money out of honest work.(40) Dreiser showed that real money was being made not in supplying or manufacturing but in stocks.

Cowperwood himself does not think very highly of his vocation. A broker. he comes to think in The Financier, is nothing more than "a gambler's agent". The selling of stocks and bonds is "incidental to the actual fact, the mine, the railroad, the wheat crop, the flour mill, and so on" [85]. "A man, a real man, must never be an agent, a tool, or a gambler - acting for himself or for others - he must employ such. A real man - a financier - was never a tool. He used tools. He created. He led" [85]. The lure of quick money, however, is too much for him. With all the treasury money at his disposal, he finds it hard to resist the temptation even though his own sense of manhood is violated by it. When the Chicago fire brings down his holdings in a crash, he blames himself for not listening to his better judgement. "'I wish I were out of this d--d stock-jobbing business,' he said to himself. 'I wish I had never gotten into it'" [335].

Thus, in the eyes of the narrator, Cowperwood is not a pioneer like Jay Cooke, the ideal commercial figure in The Financier. Nor is he an inventor like Edison or Westinghouse. Cowperwood's innate unwillingness to take any kind of risk is emphasized many times throughout the novel. Right from his thirteenth year, what he wants is "A quick, clear, easy profit" [37]. His greatest need is security, not adventure: "He wanted to make himself so secure financially that even lack of quick thinking later on would not subject him to distress and regret" [105].

Critics like Pizer who see Cowperwood's ruin by the Chicago fire as another example of his heroic stature which only "inexorable forces"(41) can subdue fail to notice its actual function in the novel. The fire in The Financier destroys Cowperwood only because he has spread himself "pretty thin" [280]. The other pillars of the Philadelphia business community survive without much discomfiture. In fact, most of them make a windfall out of it. As Cowperwood himself senses, the situation has two aspects. "If only he had the means 'to go short' on this market! If only doing so did not really mean a ruin to his present position. . . . He could not take advantage of it, however. He could not be on both sides of this market. It was either bear or bull, and of necessity he was bull" [343]. The failure of the house of Jay Cooke is a disaster very similar to the Chicago fire and it works in Cowperwood's favour because this time he has no holdings of his own to protect. That there is no mystery to such windfalls becomes clear when we see them repeated three times during the course of the trilogy. Every disaster spells ruin to the small investors while bringing tremendous profits to the insiders. The third time, however, when the American Match fails, the big financiers close the stock market on Cowperwood's advice. They thereby cut off the opportunity for the would-be Cowperwoods.

Thus, it is not adventurousness but "subtlety" that helps make Cowperwood a millionaire. Mencken complained that Cowperwood of The Financier was "hard, commonplace, unimaginative", "little more than an extra-pertinacious money-grubber, and not unrelated to the average stock broker or corner grocer."(42) The question is whether Dreiser wanted him to be any thing else, regardless of Mencken's admiration for the supermen of business.

Dreiser wanted to present the financier in his true colours as a foil to his heroic self-estimates bolstered by the estimations of his society. The novel simultaneously provides these two conflicting viewpoints. In the novel, side by side with the deromanticized version of the narrator, Cowperwood is also presented through his own fantasies as well as the approving eyes of the commercial society. To his wife, Lillian, he looks like "a young warrior" [99] just as he himself comes to see his brokerage activities as "battling" [661]. The heroic mode of perception employed by the commercial class is brought into focus by a very apt image. It is pointed out that Cowperwood's "solid, corrective brain . . . stood like a mailed knight at the draw-bridge of his fortune" [235]. The stock-exchange, presented humorously by the narrator, is transformed into a mighty sea when seen from Cowperwood's eyes. "God, what a struggle! The fights! The cries of the sinking! Strength was the thing" [230]. "They were all Hawks - he and they. They were all tigers facing each other in a financial jungle" [354], runs Cowperwood's chain of thought. In another, equally grim image, Cowperwood sees the world as a huge millstone: "Strength and weakness - there lay the key, the answer. Between upper and lower wheels of strength lay weakness. Were you strong, or were you weak? If you were not strong enough to win, heaven help you! In the center of life were its great prizes, where intolerant men were always battling as he had battled, as he was battling still. The weaklings had to die" [661]. Cowperwood's mental world is a frightening nightmare. In this self-created arena, complete with moats and fortresses, the knight Cowperwood rides steadfastly towards the "fairy-land, full of delight". Contrasted with the ease with which Cowperwood and other businessmen in the novel get their wealth, his private Darwinian world presents the same incongruity as is the basis of Don Quixote's irony.

In a revealing passage, the narrator meditates on the nature of social conditioning: "The spirit of man may, as the idealistic metaphysicians have it, be a reflection of a perfect unity which governs the universe, or it may not. It depends on how one conceives the governing spirit of the universe. But of the mold into which this spirit is born, who shall say? There are time moods, and nation moods, and climate moods, and they bring forth great clouds of individuals curiously minded" [247]. The imagery Cowperwood adopts, then, is influenced by the contemporary national mood. The country, during the latter half of the nineteenth century, was exalting the struggles of the businessman from its pulpits, in its newspapers and in its universities. If Cowperwood thinks of himself as a glorious warrior and of the world as a pitched battlefield, he is in very good company.

In the novel he is described in similar heroic terms by other characters, all emanating from the comfortable, upper stratum of the society. To one of his young mistresses, Florence Cochrane, whom the narrator describes as "mildly intellectual at this time, engaged in reading Marlowe and Jonson", he is a "great personage of the Elizabethan order" [245]. To Berenice, he "seemed a kind of superman" [468]. In fact, heroic epithets are very common with Berenice. In The Stoic, "'Welcome to London!' were her first words. 'So Caesar has crossed the Rubicon!'" [92]. While waiting for his arrival, she sends him poetic telegrams: "The sun shines on the England you step upon. It is a silver door that opens upon your greatest achievement and your greatest fame. The sea has been grey without you. Oro del Oro" [88]. The narrator, rather than approving of this kind of romanticization, wants us to see how inappropriate is this rhetoric. Chapter LX in The Titan discusses the effect of the newspapers on the mind of Berenice:

> This editorial battle-cry, flung aloft during the latter days of the contest at Springfield and taken up by the Chicago papers generally and by those elsewhere, interested Berenice greatly. As she thought of him - waging his terrific contests, hurrying to and fro between

94

New York and Chicago, building his splendid
mansion, collecting his pictures, quarreling
with Aileen - he came by degrees to take on
the outlines of a superman, a half-god or
demi-gorgon. [527]

The narrator not only does not use such heroic
images, but also puts into serious doubt the
estimates of those characters who do. The women of
his time, he says earlier in The Titan, live in
a romantic world of the Middle Ages [63]. They can
love, the narrator tells us, only the inflated
image of a man rather than the reality. Nowhere in
the novel does the narrator describe Cowperwood in
exalted terms. When he does describe him as a
warrior or a general, it is always in mock-heroic
terms and always as a plunderer. Thus, "with
franchises once secured - the reader can quite
imagine how - he could present himself, like a
Hamilcar Barca in the heart of Spain or a Hannibal
at the gates of Rome, with a demand for surrender
and a division of spoils" [40]. Similarly, "And now
the enemy had been heartened by a great victory.
His aldermen, powerful, hungry, fighting men all -
like those picked soldiers of the ancient Roman
Emperors - ruthless, conscienceless, as desperate
as himself, had in their last redoubt of personal
privilege fallen, weakened, yielded" [539]. When
Cowperwood is planning the gas war and sees himself
as a great fighter, the narrator undercuts his
pretensions with deflating irony:

Cowperwood rose suddenly, straight and
determined - a trick with him when he wanted
to really impress any one. He seemed to
radiate force, conquest, victory. "Do you
want to come in?"
"Yes, I do, Mr. Cowperwood!" exclaimed
Sippens, jumping to his feet. . . . He looked
like a chest-swollen bantam rooster. [45]

Cowperwood's "fraudulent" lieutenants in The Titan
are compared to the "decoy sheep at the stock-
yards" [47]. They fight his adversaries with
"Trojan vigor and complacency" [56]. The narrator
calls him "A Marauder upon the Commonwealth" [511].
This view is totally divergent from Cowperwood's
own; in The Stoic he sees himself as a Ulysses
[88].
Cowperwood's view of business as a battle

arena is thus rendered suspect when seen in the
total perspective of the novel. Through the use of
various narrative devices such as irony, parallels,
juxtaposition and the narrative voice, Dreiser lets
the reader know how little basis Cowperwood's
world-view has in actuality. He makes it clear
that Cowperwood has never grown. The philosophy he
has honed out so intelligently at the age of ten
serves him just as well in his sixties. Several
times, Cowperwood is called a boy by the narrator.
After one of those frequently occurring "lobster
and squid" monologues, the narrator comments in
The Financier: "It is not possible to say how a
boy of twenty-one should come by such subtle
thoughts; but he had" [103]. He is still a "boy"
at the age of thirty four [287]. Not only does he
have a "babyish" face [98], but mentally he never
grows out of the infantile fantasies of power.

The irony, unfortunately, has lost its bite
for the critics. Thus it seems to be a universally
acknowledged truth that Cowperwood is Dreiser's
mouthpiece, that Dreiser approves and admires his
"force". The fact is that nowhere in his writings
did Dreiser speak approvingly of the heroic
businessman. The following passage is extremely
relevant to the understanding of the novel:

> What our corporation masters most desire and
> contemplate with great pleasure is the jungle
> - the lion stepping forth to find its easy
> prey. The "king" of beasts or men roars and
> looks abroad at the herds frightened and in
> flight. It is useless to introduce here the
> fact (if it is a fact) that these lords
> temporal are unconscious of what they do and
> of where they are going, that as individuals
> they have good intentions and good will toward
> all. For the perpetuation and progress of
> democracy, it is far more important that they
> be accepted at their appearance value - what
> they appear to be doing as self-willed,
> self-motivated individuals. As such, there is
> not room for them in any scheme or dream of
> democracy. They will and must be stopped by
> those who believe that democracy is possible
> and that it is a humanely agreeable
> relationship to be maintained, or they will
> stop democracy.
> Make your mental choice now. If you wish
> most to live in a world of moderation, having

and holding in limited and harmless ways,
having and holding as men in the happier times
and lands may have held, you cannot possibly
permit or endure any of these incursions and
the unrestricted materialistic displays of
want or individualistic power and parade which
now in America, as elsewhere in the world, are
all too manifest. Men should not return, as
they already are returning, and, in many
places, are already returned, to the awe and
cringing, and the fear, not of equitable
authority, but rather of inequitable authority
and power. Today, on the lips of almost all
Americans are such words as the chief, the big
fellow, the boss, the <u>king</u> of this or that -
from potatoes to oil companies - and, instead
of open statements of belief and confessions
of faith in a simpler and more equitable
world, there are all too many fearful
whisperings as to the danger, as to the
limiting power of such things ⌊social reforms⌋
on strong, creative men and their right to
incentive. . . .(43)

As the passage shows, Dreiser was fully aware of
the power of metaphors to shape reality. The
Cowperwoods, by creating a jungle for themselves,
also determine the nature of the world for others.
The novel is Dreiser's attempt to tell his readers
that the world can be conceived of in other, more
amenable, metaphors and that Cowperwood's claim to
heroism is fictitious. "He was like a canny wolf",
says the narrator in <u>The Financier</u>, "prowling in a
forest of trees of his own creation" [398].
      Apart from pointing out the heroic epithets,
taken out of their context, critics consider other
"proof" of Cowperwood's greatness to be his
creation of the Chicago street railway system. He
is supposed to be one of those who usher in the new
dawn of technology. To quote just one of these
opinions:

      Cowperwood is also cast in a much more heroic
      role in <u>The Titan</u> than in <u>The Financier</u>.
      In the first novel, though we sympathize with
      Cowperwood's desire to succeed, we still sense
      that he is essentially a shark among sharks
      and that his success will benefit only
      himself. In <u>The Titan</u>, however, both
      Cowperwood and Dreiser stress that

> Cowperwood's business activities will also
> benefit mankind because an improved and
> extended city transportation system is a good
> thing even if it has been created by underhand
> means and even if it brings great riches to
> one man.(44)

Pizer, sadly, is putting words in Dreiser's mouth.
The novel does not support his conclusion. First,
Dreiser gives very little space to the actual
"creative" manifestation of Cowperwood's genius.
Secondly, the narrator points out other
alternatives to the problem of building the city
transit system. Dreiser believed in "the public
control of public utilities"(45). Chapter LIX of
The Titan is suggestively titled "Capital and
Public Rights", and it gives the narrator's support
to public ownership of city transit.

The role Dreiser gives Cowperwood is not that
of the builder and the creator but that of the
exploiter. Indeed, Cowperwood conforms to his
habit of attaining "quick and easy" profit in The
Titan as well as The Stoic. The street
railways are simply a means for him to "unload"
unheard of amounts of watered stocks on the market.
As far as innovation is concerned, Cowperwood
blocks new entrepreneurs in the field who have
invented new systems of traction. He is also
opposed to the elevated rails because they will not
yield immediate profits. Dreiser shows in The
Titan that Cowperwood is forced into building them
because his opponents have taken a lead and the
public will turn against him if he does not follow
suit [321-2]. Thus, instead of being a harbinger
of the new dawn of technological progress, he
retards it by his resistance to change. Dreiser
felt that the multi-millionaires had "seized" the
great inventions "in order to set themselves apart
as rich men . . . and by reason of that contrast to
obtain a feeling of individual distinction and
worthwhileness, which otherwise, in so far as they
themselves were concerned, they could not feel."
They "had no more idea of improving the conditions
of the many than they had of giving all that they
had to the poor."(46) The narrator of The Titan
considers Cowperwood's street railways to be
instruments of exploitation only, though they serve
the populace of Chicago: "His street-railway
properties were like a net - the parasite Gold
Thread - linked together as they were, and draining

two of the three important 'sides' of the city"
[472]. Dreiser goes into painstaking descriptions
of Cowperwood's devious ways, "an amazing
hocus-pocus" [473], which was known, according to
the D. N. B., as the "Chicago traction triangle".
So much for the "heroic" role of Cowperwood.

On the other hand, there are many indications
that, contrary to critical opinion, Cowperwood is
not "Dreiser's concept of the great man".(47)
Rather, the blurring, of which value-conscious
critics like Matthiessen have accused Dreiser,
occurs because of the critics' inability to
perceive the inherent irony in the novel. The
heroic role of Cowperwood is a creation of his own
self, as well as that of his fawning admirers. The
narrative consciousness, on the other hand, forces
us to question it. It forces us to examine
ourselves and see if we, too, have not succumbed to
the Cowperwood "condition". The narrator of The
Financier comments that "Your cautious citizen of
average means, looking out through the eye of his
dull world of seeming fact, is often the first to
forgive or condone the grim butcheries of theory by
which the strong rise" [194]. The reason Dreiser
presented these misguided estimates lies in his
desire to paint "the actual mentality and movement
of the country".(48) He dehabilitates the reader
by presenting these critically. The following
passage from the novel is quite representative of
Dreiser's ironic tone:

> It should be said of Cowperwood, Jr., that
> during all these years he was exceedingly
> democratic. He appeared at times a little bit
> removed and superior or distant, but solely
> because he was thinking. He had a cheerful
> hearty way of greeting people which was in the
> main entirely disconnected from what he
> thought of them. Even at this early age he
> was a keen judge of men, and he saw at once
> without much philosophic or sociologic
> knowledge just how the world was arranged.
> There were the weak and the strong, physically
> and mentally. Some men were destined for
> success by their temperament - that he could
> see; others were cut out for failure by the
> same token. You could not expect a weak,
> spindling, half-constructed figure of a man
> with no brain and no force to cut a figure in

the world, and you could not possibly expect a
great dynamic soul like Steemberger not to be
heard of. [40]

The divergence from the narrative viewpoint here
becomes clear when Cowperwood's view of Steemberger
as "a great dynamic soul" is contrasted with an
earlier description of the latter as a fat man with
the face of a pig [20].

Apart from that tell-tale clue, there are
several other indications in the novel that "the
weak and the strong" theory has no approval from
the narrator who wants us to see and evaluate it in
the context of other ideas and men. Hence Dreiser
reminds us in <u>The Financier</u> of the Philadelphia
which is "crowded with historic memories" [1]. It
is full of "notable buildings". These include the
"Independence Hall" and the "Public Ledger
Building", monuments which would remind any
sensitive human being of the hopes and dreams of
the people as vested in the Declaration of
Independence and the American Constitution. But
"things that would have affected some men's lives
radically" [121] do not have much significance for
Cowperwood.

How inept Cowperwood's philosophy really is
when it comes to interpreting the really profound
issues of life becomes clear when he sees Lincoln,
"the great war President". Though he responds to
the "sad, meditative calm" of Lincoln's face, he
cannot account for the "sense of great worth and
dignity" that sweeps over him. Lincoln seems to
him to be "one of the world's really great men" and
yet he is hard put to understand Lincoln's aims in
terms of his own lobster and squid philosophy
[123-4].

Moral considerations are invoked many times in
absolutely unequivocal terms, clearly indicating
that "philosophic and sociologic knowledge" are
accorded the same high respect by the narrator as
by those of us who find the survival of the fittest
a barbaric philosophy. Near the end of Chapter XV
of <u>The Financier</u>, after telling us about the
"inside ring" of such "strong" men as Butler and
Mollenhauer and their ingenious techniques of
"bleeding" the treasury, the narrator comments:

These organizations . . . grow like a rank
growth of weeds in a small community. They
fatten and are added to until, if you attempt

to trace them out, you reach by wider and ever-widening circles the very body and blood of the people themselves. We are all sinners, either directly or indirectly, if no more than by the fact that we do not protest. If we do not protest, it is evident that this idea is not so very shocking to us, certainly not enough to irritate us to the point of protesting.

We plead the difficulty of life, the necessity; life is so hard to regulate; the individual man is so weak, and so on. All of us are too busy grasping at immediate gains to trouble about far-off evils and errors. So - Any how, the city treasurers and assessors did not need to account for more than the principal of the sums intrusted to them; and from this sprang all the hurry and enthusiasm of private speculation, which was so profitable and satisfactory to so many individuals. [164-5]

The novel is an attempt on the part of Dreiser to "shock" his readers to "the point of protesting". After describing Stener who is all blown up with the thought of controlling street car lines - the same thought that keeps Butler, Simpson, Mollenhauer, Cowperwood and numerous small fries preoccupied - the narrator remarks:

He strolled up the street thinking, with no more idea of the importance of the civic duties and the nature of the social ethic against which he was offending than if they had never existed. [273]

Civilization, according to the narrative point of view, is not struggle but co-existence. The narrator speculates that the desire for fair play is part of man's nature, that "ideality" is as much instinctive as "materiality".

Perhaps the two go hand in hand. Before Christianity was man, and after it he will also be. A metaphysical idealism will always tell him that it is better to preserve a cleanly balance, and the storms of circumstance will teach him a noble stoicism. Beyond this there is nothing which can reasonably be imposed upon the conscience of man. [250]

The narrator brings up the same questions in the
epilogue of the novel. "Why were the beatitudes
dreamed and how do they avail?" he asks [779]. In
The Titan he defends Governor Altgeld and the
Haymarket martyrs for their part in the
"dissemination of stirring ideas". After the
Haymarket incident, "Man thought . . . somewhat
more accurately of national and civic things"
[186-7]. These words point out how distant Dreiser
felt from the prevailing social Darwinistic
philosophy. It is extremely difficult for me to
see how critics have ignored all this evidence and
proceeded, instead, to form conclusions such as
this: "Beneath the 'illusion' of democracy -
beneath the idea that all men are created equal in
a just and equitable society - is the truth of
life: the battle is to the cunning and the strong,
and Christian morality and Puritan conventions are
a distortion of man's very nature."(49) On the
contrary, in fact, as the following passage from
The Financier suggests, Dreiser believed in the
possibilities of democracy:

[A] second bailiff . . . recited in an
absolutely unintelligible way that beautiful
and dignified old court-call, which begins,
"Hear ye! hear ye! hear ye!" and ends, "All
those of you having just cause for complaint
draw near and ye shall be heard." You would
have thought it was of no importance in the
world, this beautiful and noble statement
based on the majesty of the law in so far as
it is based on the will of the people; but,
nevertheless, it was. Only custom and
indifference had allowed it to fall so badly
from grace. [548-9]

Obviously, the narrator thinks there is
something about human beings which separates them
from the Black Grouper, the lobsters and the
squids. The trouble with Cowperwood, then, is his
inability to realize this and his tendency to
naively read allegories where they do not exist.
According to the narrative voice in The Financier,
his "moral nature" has "no material or spiritual
existence": "He had never had, so far as he had
reasoned at all, a fixed attitude in regard to
anything except preserving himself intact and

succeeding" [102]. He is essentially a limited man, however clever he may be in the prevailing methods of finance. In a passage at the beginning of Chapter LXVIII occurs this revealing comment:

> It would be too much to say that Cowperwood's mind was of the first order. It was subtle enough in all conscience - and involved, as is common with the executively great, with a strong sense of personal advancement. It was a big mind, turning, like a vast searchlight, a glittering ray into many a dark corner; but it was not sufficiently disinterested to search the ultimate dark. He realized, in a way, what the great astronomers, sociologists, philosophers, chemists, physicists, and physiologists were meditating; but he could not be sure in his own mind that, whatever it was, it was important for him. [700]

"The great business of the individual", Dreiser wrote elsewhere, should be to "question the things he sees - not some things, but everything - stand, as it were, in the center of this whirling storm of contradiction which we know as life, and ask of its source and its import. Else why a brain at all?"(50) Against the "grim butcheries of the theory" which sees life as a grim combat, Dreiser juxtaposes the ideal of a reflective, contemplative life. Opposed to Cowperwood is an ordinary man like Mr. Thomas, "a man with convictions". For those who proclaim Dreiser to be contemptuous of the masses, Mr. Thomas' character in The Financier provides an interesting challenge:

> Mr. Thomas was a rather well-set-up man of fifty-five, with a full but not over-heavy body of perhaps five feet nine inches tall and a nicely proportioned Socrates-like head. . . . His hair and beard were blackish gray, and his whole make-up breathed a certain well-preserved vitality of body and solidarity of thought. He was quite a personage, intellectually, even if he was a flour merchant. [586-7]

Men like Lincoln and Socrates, the astronomers, the sociologists and the philosophers have the capacity to seek out the "ultimate dark". Dreiser's ideal men are imaginatively stirred by high ideals and mysteries of nature. Their knowledge has taught them humility and the futility of personal aggrandizement. They are fully aware of the insignificance of the individual in the scheme of the universe.

Cowperwood, we are told in The Titan, attains "no real understanding" [552]. This is because, in Dreiser's opinion, his moral nature is deficient, in fact non-existent. We see in The Financier that, to the end, he is chasing illusions of fame and power: "master and no master, prince of a world of dreams whose reality was sorrow!" [780]. Power, Dreiser thought,

> where it is anything other than generous and admirable leadership by mind is an illusion of the thinnest and most sordid and most trivial character, and . . . it cannot accomplish anything for any one. It can only retard and should be set aside. Mind, of necessity, apparently, must constantly work toward an extension of opportunity for all, not merely for a chosen few. And in such extension only is delight and peace to be found. There is no other reason for living. And knowledge of this is the essential knowledge.(51)

Cowperwood never achieves this understanding in his mad rush for more and more wealth. In the words of The Financier, he has a "narrow-minded" obsession with one idea, and that is, a rise to fame "via money" [137-8]. This prevents him from attaining his full human stature which comes, according to Dreiser, only when one can look unflinchingly in the face of life, bereft of all feelings of self-grandeur. For Cowperwood, we are informed in The Titan, there "was no ultimate peace, no real understanding, but only hunger and thirst and wonder" [552]. A remark Dreiser made elsewhere helps us to understand Cowperwood's nature:

> It may be . . . questioned how many human brains actually reach full maturity. Many obstacles stand in the way of full development, such as physical, social, educational, or economic handicaps. Religions, castes, tyrannies, tyrants, and inherited taboos and fears have endlessly blocked the way. . . .(52)

In a sense, Cowperwood is a very insecure
individual who compensates for his anxieties
through dreams of power. Dreiser believed that "an
insane, an impossible pursuit of money or vice" was
caused by "a deep-seated neurosis" which, in its
turn, was "due to the repression of every other
normal instinct".(53) Cowperwood comes to regard
the jungle world as the reality and, though he
manages to remain on top of every crisis, the
strain of living in the jungle is quite real for
him, however dubious it may be in real terms. He
cannot relax for a single moment, for he must
either hunt or hide, depending upon how strong the
adversary is. He muses in The Financier that if one
does not keep one's eyes open, "the hungry lot of
fish" [81] will "snap" one up. That his greatest
need is security, not adventure, becomes clear from
the following words in the novel: "He wanted to
make himself so secure financially that even lack
of quick thinking later on would not subject him to
distress and regret" [105]. Earlier, we have been
told: "He must succeed; he must work; he mustn't be
a spindling figure like some of these poor things"
[41].

Cowperwood, seeing failed brokers commit
suicide, comes to believe that "Surely life was
grim" [93]. He concludes that "honor would
ultimately accrue most to him who held his own.
There was no honor for the failure" [102]. He sets
his life goals to be "wealth, prestige, and
dominance" [68]. And he has concluded that those
people who cannot "protect themselves" in "all
circumstances" are indeed "foolish" [68].

Dreiser suggests in The Financier that the
only way Cowperwood can feel "significant" is
through the accumulation of wealth. For, in his
society, "fame went with great wealth greatly
achieved" [594]. Ever since his childhood, he has
been told that one can become a "man" only through
success in the world of business, which becomes
associated in his mind with the jungle and the
battlefield:

> There were just two faces to the shield of
> life from the point of view of his peculiar
> mind - strength and weakness. Right and
> wrong? He did not know about those. . . .
> But strength and weakness - oh yes! If you had
> strength you could protect yourself always and
> be something. If you were weak - pass quickly

to the rear and get out of the range of the guns. [476]

However, the metaphors of battle are not Cowperwood's invention. Other businessmen in the novel use them too. As already mentioned, they are also employed by the wives and mistresses of the businessmen out of their own desire to participate vicariously in the glory of these men. "To Berenice" in The Stoic, Cowperwood's "announcement of this Charing Cross control was an occasion for celebration. For was it not she who had originally suggested this London adventure? And now here she was at last, finding herself a part of a great world of affairs such as in the past she had only dimly envisioned" [114]. In The Financier, Cowperwood seems "all-powerful" [246] to his wife, Aileen. In The Titan, likewise, Antoinette, his secretary and mistress, gives in to the attraction of "this smart, hard office and this strong man. He came out of such a marvelous world, apparently" [134]. The "virus Cowperwood" [124], to use a phrase from this novel, is truly contagious. It permeates all sections of society and wastes human potential by diverting people away from more satisfying pursuits. "[A] more trade-ridden commonwealth", the narrator of The Titan laments, "might not have been found anywhere at this time within the entire length and breadth of the universe" [478].

Cowperwood starts life as a highly intelligent child but his society sees to it that he becomes, like his father and the other business figures, a "capable machine". The Cowperwood of The Titan is "little more than a walking mathematical formula" [521]. Though, as we see in The Financier, he started with the capacity of aesthetic response [115], he soon loses it. The "varied dreams of advancement which germinate and swim" inside his brain [195] crowd out all other feelings. Even the fathering of children is somehow "acquisitive" for him. As Dreiser told Dudley, "the making and holding of great wealth destroys delicacy".(54) He repeated the same charge in an essay entitled "Some Aspects of Our National Character": "If you want to see America illustrated rather clearly as to its cultural, or lack of cultural, results contemplate the American millionaire. He has, if he has not now, the prevailing idea that money is power; he worshipped and slaved for it in the hope that it

would make him wonderful in the eyes of all
men."(55)

It is, then, hard to agree with the popular
critical opinion as to Cowperwood's aesthetic
sensibility. We learn in The Titan that he
collects paintings and other artistic objects
because those he looks up to do so. "Addison had
four or five good pictures - a Rousseau, a Greuze,
a Wouverman, and one Lawrence - picked up Heaven
knows where. A hotel-man by the name of Collard, a
dry-goods and real-estate merchant, was said to
have a very striking collection. Addison had told
him of one Davis Trask, a hardware prince, who was
now collecting. There were many homes, he knew,
where art was beginning to be assembled. He must
begin, too" [56].

Similarly, Cowperwood wants, as a possession,
Berenice, who, true to her name, brings victory to
his search for social supremacy. Instead of being
"idealized", the Berenice-Cowperwood relationship
is very much in keeping with the rest of the
novel.(56) She, like Daisy Buchanan in The Great
Gatsby is a dream girl, symbolic of a "higher"
social realm in the hero's mind. Cowperwood wants
her, not so much due to her personal attraction, as
for her ability to get him accepted in "the charmed
circle" that alone can make him feel significant.
This is made very clear by the narrator of The
Titan: "Quite as in some great racing-stable an
ambitious horseman might imagine that he detected
in some likely filly the signs and lineaments of
the future winner of a Derby, so in Berenice
Fleming, in the quiet precincts of the Brewster
School, Cowperwood previsioned the central figure
of a Newport lawn fete or a London drawing-room"
[358].

Though Cowperwood finds the old money so
desirable that he spends his life seeking a "social
passport" to these "better and higher earthly, if
not spiritual, realms" [471], the narrator presents
them from a satirical perspective:

The functions which these people provided were
stupid to the verge of distraction; really
they were only the week-day receptions and
Sunday-afternoon calls of Squeedunk and
Hohokus raised to the nth power. The
purpose of the whole matter was to see and be
seen. Novelty in either thought or action was

decidedly eschewed. [60]

However, these vacuous people are necessary to
Cowperwood because only they can provide him with
the approval he has sought all along. For money
alone does not satisfy him. It must symbolize
power, heroic deeds, battles won. "[H]e had not by
any means attained the height of his ambition. He
was not yet looked upon as a money prince. He
could not rank as yet with the magnates of the East
- the serried Sequoias of Wall Street. Until he
could stand with these men, until he could have a
magnificent mansion, acknowledged as such by all,
until he could have a world-famous gallery,
Berenice, millions - what did it avail?" [439]. The
"rarefied reaches of social supremacy" [492], where
rests "the gorgeous throne of his own construction"
[485], remain his ultimate destination.

The novel ends with an enigmatic comment from
the narrator: "How strange are realities as opposed
to illusion!" [550]. Cowperwood, however, remains
a "prince of a world of dreams" in his adherence to
illusion. "[F]or him was no ultimate peace, no
real understanding, but only hunger and thirst and
wonder. Wealth, wealth, wealth! A new grasp of a
new great problem and its eventual solution. Anew
the old urgent thirst for life, and only its
partial quenchment" [552]. The portion life
accords him contains nothing but "sorrow, sorrow,
sorrow" because, instead of searching for "peace"
and "understanding", he has attempted "hewing life
to his theory - hammering substance to the form of
his thought" [503]. Just as the narrator had
juxtaposed Cowperwood's narrow life against the
majesty of the night sky, so in The Titan we are
asked to see it in the context of the prolific
world of nature. On a bright June morning, while
Cowperwood sits "reading a fiscal report of one of
his companies and meditating on his affairs",
Berenice reminds him of the vast, infinite,
mysterious processes of life he has no time to
contemplate. "Cowperwood, previously engrossed in
financial speculations, was translated, as by the
wave of a fairy wand, into another realm where
birds and fledglings and grass and the light winds
of heaven were more important than brick and stone
and stocks and bonds. . . . It suddenly came to
Cowperwood, with great force, how comparatively
unimportant in the great drift of life were his own
affairs when about him was operative all this

splendid will to existence, as sensed by her"
[392-3]

Only a contemplation of "the great drift of
life", Dreiser wrote a number of times, can give
one any joy in life. In the vein of the nineteenth
century romantics, Dreiser said that the real
poverty was an inability to perceive the beauty of
nature. The tragedy of America, he thought, was
that instead of pursuing "the really worth while
things in life", "all those things which can only
be pursued in leisure and which without leisure are
barred off; all those things by development of
which man has made himself superior, or at least
potentially superior, to the ape", his country men,
"our monopolists above all", were busy pursuing "in
vain the phantom of happiness", not realizing "how
small a thing is that Money which we have inflated
into a national pneumatic god."(57)

In The Stoic, Dreiser further elaborates on
what, according to him, are the worthwhile things
in life. In his old age Cowperwood becomes dimly
aware of a different, richer kind of existence. He
is made to realize that his "quest for power, fame,
prestige" [2] has really taken him nowhere; that,
in fact, his mind has moved "treadmill fashion"
[230], going nowhere and yet in perpetual motion.
He has been, as Berenice puts it, "like some big
engine or machine that's tearing full speed
somewhere, but doesn't know exactly where" [11].

The realization, however, comes too late for
Cowperwood to change his life in any effective way.
Though he questions the ultimate worth of his
involvement in the London traction deal, he goes on
with it to the end of his days as a matter of
habit, mainly because he is ill-equipped to do
anything else with his life. "There's a lot of
nonsense to all this, you know", he confides to
Sippens. "Here we are, you and I, both of us
getting along in years, and now running around on
this new job, which, whether we do it or not, can't
mean so much to either of us. . . . What
astonishes me is that we can get so excited over
it" [113]. Such statements of self-doubt are
repeated many times throughout this novel.
Cowperwood of The Stoic is a prisoner behind his
desk rather than a master. He has finally got
tired of repeating the "tricks" of the game.

Opposed to the false ideals of luxury and
snobbery, the ones Cowperwood has chased so
assiduously, are the values of the Norwegian sea

folk who live in close harmony with nature, unspoiled as yet by the commodity culture of the industrialized world. By bringing in the contrasting value systems of Norway and India - as he understood them - Dreiser hoped to present to his readers the view that Cowperwood's cultural inheritance was at fault. The geographical difference between Norway and India serves to emphasize the point Dreiser is trying to make: Cowperwood's social Darwinistic philosophy with its heroic implications is not the only basis of social organization, human life can be organized on a more peaceful and harmonious pattern. The Norway episode also ensures that the novel's moral meaning does not depend too heavily on the last four chapters dealing with Berenice's experience in India, one of the least satisfying portions of the trilogy.

The values these cultures promote are unheroic and communal as opposed to the heroic and individualistic ones of Cowperwood's ethos. The life of the Norwegian fishermen is qualitatively superior to Cowperwood's even though they have few material possessions and little cash. They love books and music. The names of Greig, Hamsun, Ibsen and Bjornson "caused Cowperwood to pause and think how small a part literature had played in his life, and to suggest to Berenice that she give him some of the books she had been reading" [222].

The natural splendour of Norwegian sea-side mountains and man's peaceful existence there make Cowperwood realize the emptiness of his mode of life. He comes to admit "that these people had more from life in sheer beauty, simple comfort, and charming social customs than he and thousands of others like him who were so strenuously engaged in accumulating money. As for himself, he was getting old, and the best part of his life was already gone. What, really, lay ahead for him? More subways? More art galleries? More irritations due to public opinion?" [224].

The realization, however, has come too late for any radical change. Cowperwood must go on pretending to be fit and excited. He discovers the pleasures of "the simplicities of a genuine home" in the peace and modest scale of Pryor's Cove for "the first time in years" [245]. The complications of his business deals, however, leave him with no time for them.

As a final irony, Cowperwood's original quest

is rewarded at a time when he has lost the capacity to revel in it. Crippled by Bright's disease and surrounded by the colours and atmosphere of autumn, Cowperwood is suddenly, of no effort of his own, allowed entry to that magical realm he has been seeking all his life. The British aristocracy, in the shape of Lord Stane, fulfills his life-long ambition when a social affair is held in his honour at Tregasal. Dancing to "the rhythmic measures of the waltz" - a dance which takes us back to the previous occasions symbolizing Cowperwood's efforts to invade the upper echelons - he utters, perhaps the most loaded words in the entire trilogy: "Isn't it wonderful, Bevy? You, this place, these people! This is what I've been seeking all my life!" [232-3].

In a metaphorical sense, then, Cowperwood has finally arrived. This, we realize, is the "center of life" Cowperwood has envisioned as his ultimate goal. Only, the victory, the dubious distinction of being part of a moneyed aristocracy, is so utterly hollow, even to the victor. How little this artificial world has to do with the real issues of life becomes clear when Cowperwood is stricken immediately after his statement. What Cowperwood wants at the most fulfilling moment of his life is something "the wonderful lamp called money" [93] cannot buy: "Air, Air; I must get outside!" [233].

The processes of old age and death catch up with him to the "disruption of all his plans". In the last days, his categories are of no avail to him. On his death bed, it is not the distinctions between the strong and the weak that seem to have any relevance but, rather, "goodness of heart and intention" [255], qualities Cowperwood has disdained.

The final comment on Cowperwood's way of life is made in the lines from the Bible the Reverend Hayward Crenshaw reads at his grave side. Their eloquent poetry reminds the reader of the vast gulf between Cowperwood's aspirations and the dictates of Christianity, between the egalitarian ideals of early Christianity and its present approval of the hierarchal society. For even in death, Cowperwood has not been able to resist making a statement about his status: "as her carriage came into full view of the tomb, Aileen was again and finally impressed by her husband's power of self-presentation" [272].

The novel, perhaps, could have been satisfactorily concluded with Cowperwood's death. For, it has been amply demonstrated to the reader by now that Cowperwood's way is not the right way, that "real peace" and "understanding" lie in a different direction. However, Dreiser does not end here, to the dissatisfaction of most of his critics. They find Berenice's conversion totally out of character. It is necessary, I believe, to probe the reasons for Dreiser's need to continue the narration of The Stoic beyond Cowperwood's death.

Perhaps the most important of these was Dreiser's need to make a definitive moral statement, something which is not at all out of character if we look at his other novels. He had introduced Ames at a very late stage in Sister Carrie and saddled him with a large moral burden. In Jennie Gerhardt he had made Lester confess to Jennie about his moral failure. Cowperwood, however, is very much like Clyde in the sense that both of them lack a "spiritual existence". Both of them are so deeply conditioned by the values of their society that Dreiser saw little hope of change. They are characters truly determined by their environment.

Berenice's role, therefore, should be seen in the context of Dreiser's didactic purposes. She is there to point out Dreiser's faith that the vicious cycle could be broken and human beings jolted out of their accepted attitudes and habits. Though we are told in The Titan that she has worshipped "power and success in every form" [447] and has been attracted by "Cowperwood's theory of things" "in spite of her splendid mind" [531], Dreiser has faith in her ability to grow. Youth, he believed, has a "plastic" mind. Dreiser brings about her transformation through a device he uses in several of his novels: by introducing her to books of literature and philosophy. Cowperwood, we are told several times, had never been interested in books. Berenice, we learn in The Stoic, has been led away from "the whole Western materialistic viewpoint" [286] by her reading of the Bhagvad-Gita. Thus, true to Dreiser's dictum that "Life is to be learnt as much from books and art as from life itself - almost more so",(58) Berenice comes to find "truth and understanding" via "a little volume" [286].

The right way of action is presented also

through the mouth of Dr. James, who seems to me to be the closest to Dreiser's philosophy of life as explained elsewhere in his writings. He brings Berenice back to the problem of poverty in the middle of New York: the "neglected children, whose chance for physical and mental survival is practically non-existent" [304]. The chapter ends with a total refutation of "Cowperwood's theory of things":

> Her entire life, as she realized . . . had been spent in the pursuit of pleasure and self-advancement. But now she knew that one must live for something outside of one's self, something that would tend to answer the needs of the many as opposed to the vanities and comforts of the few, of which she herself was one. What could she do to help? [306].

Despite the generally negative critical response, this ending is not a violation of the thematic unity, as the trilogy has been concerned with the problem of individual versus social good right from the beginning. Its opening in Philadelphia, the questions raised about city administration and public transit, the thorough exposure of "how great fortunes are, usually, made"(59) and the favourable presentation of such figures as Abraham Lincoln, Mr. Thomas the flour merchant, the Haymarket anarchists and Governor Altgeld, are all indications of Dreiser's need to explore the true meaning of the "contract social" and the "need of balance" in society. This balance is described very simply in The Titan: "The strong must not be too strong; the weak not too weak" [551].
Seen in the light of these thematic concerns, the Cowperwood trilogy comes across as a troubled examination of what Dreiser considered to be the degradation of America's original democratic ideal, rather than as a romanticized depiction of the "captain of industry".

NOTES

1. Philip L. Gerber, The Titan Theodore Dreiser (Twayne Publishers, Inc., New York, 1964) 88.

2. Theodore Dreiser, A Hoosier Holiday, 171-2.

3. Richard Lehan, Theodore Dreiser: His World and His Novels, 97.

4. Dreiser, "Myth of Individual Possession," Notes on Life, ed. Marguerite Tjader and John J. McAleer (University of Alabama Press, 1974) 122.

5. Reported by Albert Mordell, My Relations with Theodore Dreiser: Haldeman-Julius as a Writer on Freethought; Some Reflections on Freethought: And Haldeman-Julius Publications in Freethought (Haldeman-Julius Publications, Girard, Kansas, 1951) 3.

6. Quoted in F. O. Matthiessen, Theodore Dreiser, 135.

7. Unsigned interview, "Theodore Dreiser Now Turns to High Finance," Theodore Dreiser: A Selection of Uncollected Prose, 196.

8. Dreiser, "True Art Speaks Plainly," Sister Carrie, 473.

9. Unsigned interview, " Author of Sister Carrie," Theodore Dreiser: A Selection of Uncollected Prose, 149.

10. Dreiser, "True Art Speaks Plainly," Sister Carrie, 473.

11. Dreiser, "The Loneliness of the City," Theodore Dreiser: A Selection of Uncollected Prose, 157.

12. Quoted in Matthiessen, 131.

13. Matthiessen, 131.

14. Gustavus Myers, History of the Great American Fortunes (1907; Charles H. Kerr & Company, Chicago, 1911) 1: v.

15. Myers, 1: iii.

16. Myers, 1: iii, iv.

17. Dreiser, The Titan, 552.

18. See Swanberg, Dreiser, 176. Also see Dreiser, The Titan, 189 and America is Worth Saving, 280.

19. Dreiser, The Stoic (Doubleday & Company, Inc., Garden City, N. Y., 1947) 304.

20. See Henry Nash Smith, ed., Popular Culture and Industrialism: 1865-1890 (Doubleday & Company, Inc., Garden City, N. Y., 1967) 81-161. Also, Donald P. De Nevi and Helen M. Friend with John Bookout, ed., Muckrakers and Robber Barons: The Classic Era 1901-1912 (Consensus Publishers, Danville, California, 1973) 31-113.

21. Matthiessen, 132-3.

22. Matthiessen, 157, 158.

23. Matthiessen, 148.

24. Edgar Lee Masters, quoted in Matthiessen, 144.

25. Dreiser, "The American Financier," Hey Rub-A-Dub-Dub: A Book of the Mystery and Wonder and Terror of Life, 74, 77.

26. Dreiser, "'Vanity, Vanity,'" Saith the Preacher," Twelve Men (1919; The Modern Library, New York, 1928) 263-86.

27. Eric Solomon, "A Source for Fitzgerald's The Great Gatsby," Modern Language Notes 73 (March 1958) 186-8.

28. Dreiser, The Financier (Harper & Brothers, New York, 1912) 2.

29. Dreiser, Jennie Gerhardt (1911; The World Publishing Company, Cleveland, 1926) 15.

30. Dreiser, Jennie Gerhardt, 303-4.

31. Dreiser, "Physical and Chemical Character of Man's Actions," Notes on Life, 60.

32. Dreiser, "America and the Artist," Theodore Dreiser: A Selection of Uncollected Prose, 237.

33. Quoted in Mookerjee, Theodore Dreiser: His Thought and Social Criticism, 54, fn.58.

34. John D. Rockefeller, quoted in Hofstadter, Social Darwinism in American Thought 45.

35. Hofstadter, Anti-Intellectualism in American Life (Alfred A. Knopf, New York, 1963) 255.

36. Dreiser, Twelve Men, 268.

37. Andrew Carnegie, The Empire of Business (William Briggs, Toronto, 1902) 190.

38. See Dreiser, "A Talk with America's Leading Lawyer: Or What Success Means," Theodore Dreiser: A Selection of Uncollected Prose, 119-23.

39. Frances W. Gregory and Irene D. Neu, "The American Industrial Elite in the 1870's: Their Social Origins," William Miller, ed., Men in Business: Essays in the History of Entrepreneurship (Harvard University Press, Cambridge, Mass., 1952) 202, 204.

40. Edwin T. Freedley, A Practical Treatise on Business: or How to Get, Save, Spend, Give, Lend, and Bequeath Money: With an Inquiry into the Chances of Success and Causes of Failure in Business (1853; Arno Press, New York, 1973) 166.

41. Pizer, The Novels of Theodore Dreiser, 164.

42. H. L. Mencken, A Book of Prefaces (Garden City Publishing Company, Inc., Garden City, N. Y., 1917) 114.

43. Dreiser, "The Myth of a Perfect Social Order," Notes on Life, 299.

44. Pizer, The Novels of Theodore Dreiser, 189.

45. Dreiser, Letters, 1: 378.

46. Dreiser, America is Worth Saving, 10-1.

47. Lehan, 100.

48. Dreiser, Letters, 2: 478.

49. Lehan, 113.

50. Dreiser, "Life, Art and America," Hey Rub-A-Dub-Dub: A Book of the Mystery and Wonder and Terror of Life, 257.

51. Dreiser, Letters, 1: 383.

52. Dreiser, "The Necessity for Youth and Age, Old and New," Notes on Life, 225.

53. Dreiser, "Neurotic America and the Sex Impulse," Hey Rub-A-Dub-Dub: A Book of the Mystery and Wonder and Terror of Life, 132, 126.

54. Quoted in Dudley, 306.

55. Dreiser, "Some Aspects of Our National Character," Hey Rub-A-Dub-Dub: A Book of the Mystery and Wonder and Terror of Life, 54.

56. See, for example, Matthiessen, 146, and Pizer, The Novels of Theodore Dreiser, 193.

57. Dreiser, America is Worth Saving, 281.

58. Dreiser, "Life, Art and America," Hey Rub-A-Dub-Dub: A Book of the Mystery and Wonder and Terror of Life, 276.

59. Dreiser, Letters, 1: 209.

Chapter Five

DREISER'S "HALF-EQUIPPED KNIGHTS" IN SISTER CARRIE
THE "GENIUS" AND AN AMERICAN TRAGEDY

In the Cowperwood trilogy, Dreiser had attempted to
dissolve the aura around the heroic figure of the
"captain of industry" and show how fortunes are
really made. The trilogy painted a world of high
finance, which relied on inside connections and
underhand deals rather than brave battles fought on
the much-touted battlefields. This was Dreiser's
answer to the propounders of "the You Can idea"
who professed that "any boy, working like Carnegie,
perhaps reading Success . . . could, from that
point, if he would, leap into the arena of life and
succeed."(1) The trilogy, in this sense, dealt
with the public and the social aspects of the myth
rather than confining itself to the strictly
personal. Though the inflated public and self
images of Cowperwood are constantly compared with
his inner spiritual vacuity, the focus remained on
the body politic and the ripple effect of
Cowperwood's private corruption.
        Thus, in Sister Carrie, The "Genius",(2)
and An American Tragedy,(3) Dreiser went on to
study the impact of the heroic myth on the lives of
individuals. The protagonists of these three
novels are the victims of the same "condition" that
afflicted Cowperwood. Unlike the protagonists of
Jennie Gerhardt and The Bulwark, the novels where
Dreiser dealt with characters who refused to live
by the myths of their society despite a great
personal cost, having seen through them, Carrie
Meeber, Eugene Witla and Clyde Griffiths are
entirely immersed in the values of their society.
They think and act within the framework of the
popular myth. The limitations of the characters
and their guiding world-view are brought out by the
ironic structures of these novels. The novelist's
wider vision evaluates the restricted vision of his

characters.

I shall examine the three novels as ironic structures, concerned with evaluating the prevalent social myths of the period. I see them as Dreiser's attempts at an analysis of the popular linguistic moulds that determine the way his characters perceive and respond to the world around them. Instead of being the merely naive "self-projections" that they are taken to be, these novels are a serious comment on the modes of socialization promoted in American society and the human product that they create.

According to Dreiser's perception of the problem, Americans were being manipulated into losing their individuality. "Movies, radios and newspapers contribute their share of setting millions of plastic minds in a mold which produces the same sort of figurative marbles running down a trough - until they fall off".(4) He repeatedly tackled this process of the plastic mind taking the impress of its environment. His novels begin at the very beginning, with the adolescence of his protagonists. He catches them, to use some words from Sister Carrie, "[w]arm with the fancies of youth" [2], at the "formative period" [2], and points out the meagre heritage that has been passed on to them.

The desires of Carrie, Eugene and Clyde have a remarkable similarity in that they all presuppose that "happiness" is to be found in a particular physical space described in Sister Carrie as the "walled city" [328]. However, as the image suggests, there is a wide gulf between the desire and the destination and the way is beset with dangers which paralyze the soul of the aspirant. It is a quest which, in the novelist's terms, is ultimately destructive. The novels, on the one hand, recreate the world of romance that these protagonists have created for themselves, and, on the other, juxtapose it with the bemused irony of the narrative voice. They thereby expose the ideological imperatives embedded in the language of public discourse.

The "walled city" has a special connotation for Dreiser. It does not mean simply "the city" as opposed to the country but, rather, a special part of the city itself, the part created by and sequestering wealth. Hurstwood, for example, perceives Carrie to have entered the "walled city" when he sees her name on the billboards and the fire signs. Dreiser, living across the river, in close proximity to it, describes himself as an outsider who feels judged and mocked by the symbolic messages emanating from the "walled city":

> But over the river from all this is another picture which disturbs me even more than my present surroundings, because, as seen from here, it is seemingly beautiful and inviting. Its tall walls are those of a fabled city. I can almost hear the tinkle of endless wealth in banks, the honks of automobiles, the fanfare of a great constructive trade life. At night all its myriad lights seem to wink at me and exclaim, "Why so incompetent? Why so idle, so poor? Why live in such a wretched neighborhood? Why not cross over and join the great gay throng, make a successful way for yourself? Why sit aside from this great game of materiality and pretend to ignore it or to feel superior?"(5)

The passage indicates how acutely Dreiser identified the keywords that defined the nature of public life in turn of the century America. Thus, even when one has refused to join the fray, one cannot escape without being branded as "idle" or "incompetent". That is to say, the "walled city" defines others' identity by its very existence. The outsider cannot remain neutral to it. One only "pretends" to be superior unless one has tested oneself by applying to its portals. And as "America's leading lawyer", one of the eminently successful people Dreiser interviewed for Success magazine, told him, a man "owes it to himself to endeavor to prove that his estimate of himself is correct. We all need to. If he fails, he will be learning his limitations, which is better than never finding them out. No man can justify inaction."(6) Thus, the journey to the "walled city" is overladen with moral meaning. It becomes a test of an individual's "worth".

This social imperative, propagated by the gospel of success, supplies the pattern of Dreiser's novels. He adopts the popular theme - virtuous young men's victorious "battle" in the city against formidable adversaries - and submits it to critical scrutiny. The three novels chosen for discussion here display common structural and linguistic features that can only be accounted for by their relationship to the popular narratives of the period, that is, adolescent fiction, businessmen's autobiographies, Sunday school sermons and newspaper accounts. When read against this backdrop, these novels come across as bitter diatribes against those who control the reins of power in Dreiser's society.

Carrie's journey to the city is described in two prominent patterns of imagery, common in the public discourse of the time. These patterns, one derived from the world of chivalric romance and the other from that of pilgrimage literature, are used interchangeably throughout the novel. Carrie is alternately described as a knight-errant and a Christian pilgrim.

Most critical assessments consider Dreiser's use of martial and religious imagery unartistic and yet another example of his lack of style. However, as I hope to establish, Dreiser, in his decision to use the two patterns, made a very acute artistic choice. To his contemporary readers the combination should have come as no surprise. They were very used to seeing it everywhere in the media. The perceptive ones would have seen it as a very effective satirical device. If today's readers have trouble making sense of the pattern, it is because the context has been forgotten and not due to a problem with Dreiser's style.

The novel introduces a heroic pattern in the opening paragraphs. The narrator describes Carrie as a "half-equipped little knight . . . venturing to reconnoitre the mysterious city and dreaming wild dreams of supremacy" [2]. A little later on, she is referred to as a "little soldier of fortune" [45, 57]. Chapter VI is entitled "The Machine and the Maiden: A Knight of Today". The pattern is reinforced when the affluent part of Chicago is described as "the walled city" [328]: "Men were posted at the gates. You could not get in. Those inside did not care to come out to see who you were" [241]. The image of the "walled city" is reiterated in several chapter titles such as "A Witless Aladdin: The Gate to the World" (Ch. XVI), "A Glimpse Through the Gateway: Hope Lightens the Eye" (Ch. XVII), "The Ambassador Fallen: A Search for the Gate" (Ch. XXVI), "Without the Walled City: The Slope of the Years" (Ch. XXXIII) and "The Spirit Awakens: New Search for the Gate" (Ch. XXXVII).

Further augmenting the image pattern are

120

references to Fortune as a military figure and to its army. Carrie, as already mentioned, is a "little soldier of fortune". The metaphor recurs in several chapter headings: "Intimations by Winter: An Ambassador Summoned" (Ch. VIII), "The Counsel of Winter: Fortune's Ambassador Calls" (Ch. X), "Of the Lamps of the Mansions: The Ambassador's Plea" (Ch. XII), "His Credentials Accepted: A Babel of Tongues" (Ch. XIII), "The Ambassador Fallen: A Search for the Gate" (Ch. XXVI), and "The Way of the Beaten: A Harp in the Wind" (Ch. XLVII). All these references paint the city as a battlefield with a mediaeval touch, mock-heroic in the beginning, and getting more sinister with the decline of Hurstwood.

The pilgrimage imagery is also introduced quite early in the book. Carrie's journey to the city is likened to an "adventurous pilgrimage" [11]. The traditional imagery of the religious quest appears in several chapter headings: "The Lure of the Material: Beauty Speaks for Itself" (Ch. VII), "The Lure of the Spirit: The Flesh in Pursuit" (Chs. XX and XXI), "The Blaze of the Tinder: Flesh Wars with the Flesh" (Ch. XXII), "A Spirit in Travail: One Rung Put Behind" (Ch. XXIII), "A Pilgrim, An Outlaw: The Spirit Detained" (Ch. XXVIII), "The Kingdom of Greatness: The Pilgrim Adream" (Ch. XXX), and "The Spirit Awakens: New Search for the Gate" (Ch. XXXVII). That the pilgrimage and the heroic patterns intermingle in several chapter headings quoted above is self-evident.

It is interesting to recall here that Sister Carrie almost got titled "The Flesh and the Spirit".(7) The chapter headings quoted above are vestiges of this earlier title and indicate the thematic importance of the controlling metaphor of pilgrimage.

It should be apparent that both the patterns are equally important to the structure of the novel and, at times, coalesce. Both patterns have one element in common, however discordant they may seem on the surface: they both refer to questing figures who move in a landscape fraught with deadly impediments.

Despite the fact that these patterns recur so persistently in the text, only one critic has considered them important enough to attempt an extended explanation. In a paper entitled "Sister Carrie: A Modern Pilgrim's Progress",(8) James

Mulqueen considers the metaphor of pilgrimage to be a deliberate inversion of Bunyan's allegory on Dreiser's part with the intent of criticizing the materialism of Industrial America. However, as far as the heroic quest pattern is concerned, Mulqueen expresses his inability to decipher its import.

Although Mulqueen's half-explanation is not very satisfactory, it is better than those provided by such eminent critics as F. O. Matthiessen, Kenneth Lynn and Donald Pizer who find the phrase "half-equipped little knight" "hackneyed" and "sentimental" and dismiss it as another example of Dreiser's lack of discrimination.(9) If these critics had consulted contemporary sources before condemning Dreiser so categorically, they would not only have felt a greater respect for his acuity but would also have discovered some startling insights into the nature and function of symbols in general.

It is the contemporary discourses and their tonalities that allow us to decode Dreiser's symbolic patterns. They present the possibility that Dreiser may not simply be inverting Bunyan's allegory as Mulqueen considers the case to be. In reality, Dreiser is responding to the appropriation of the allegory by the apologists of the businessman-hero. The same thing would apply to his use of the imagery of knight-errantry in the novel. We should consider the possibility that instead of going directly to the heroic romances, Dreiser is referring to its use in the eulogies of the businessman's glorious deeds. It seems to me that Dreiser is making fun of those who had taken over these symbols for the sake of personal glorification by reappropriating them himself.

I propose that this is exactly what Dreiser does in <u>Sister Carrie</u>. He is parodying the heroic imagery used by the contemporary American businessman. When Dreiser calls Carrie "a half-equipped little knight", he is deliberately echoing the rags-to-riches discourses which transformed the poor rural youth travelling to the city into martial heroes. By calling her "half-equipped", however, he underlines the fact that the odds for succeeding in the "battle" were against people like Carrie. The irony is deepened even further by Dreiser's choice of a female protagonist as the success literature reserved the martial role for men. It conceived of the woman's role in the image of the lady of romance whose only function was to welcome the knight home when he came back laden with spoils. Dreiser's mock-heroic purpose becomes apparent when we juxtapose the two images. He tears down the pretense maintained by a male-dominated capitalist society that the American woman was somehow outside the pale of "the survival of the fittest" ethic.

For the contemporary reader who was familiar with the business discourse, Dreiser's wry irony would have been immediately apparent. As Bertrand Bronson points out, ironic composition gains its effect "by virtue of the fact that all the while a tacit comparison with another image is proceeding. This silent process is the very core of irony."(10) The businessman dressed in the guises of the heroic knight and the Christian pilgrim must be retrieved by us if we are to appreciate Dreiser's ironic thrusts.

The military metaphors of a "walled city" and of soldiers doing battle are not Dreiser's own fabrications, then. They have been appropriated by him in order to mimic the world-view generated by the businessman-hero who had so enthusiastically adopted the Carlylean epithet to describe himself. Dreiser explores the analogy in all its ramifications: if the businessman was a captain, the rest had to become soldiers perforce. In the same way, if he chose to don the mantle of the pilgrim, the American city automatically became the wilderness. By drawing the two metaphors together in Sister Carrie, Dreiser exposed the strange symbolic alliances in the minds of the creators of these symbols.

Dreiser's satiric thrust becomes even clearer in his portrayal of Drouet as "A Knight of Today". Unlike Carrie, who must work in a sweat shop for four and a half dollars a week because she is only "a half-equipped little knight", Drouet is a full-blown knight. However, unlike Frank Norris' businessmen who are described in overblown heroic imagery, Dreiser's businessman-knight is described in these mock-heroic terms:

> He appeared to great advantage behind the white napery and silver platters of the table and displaying his arms with a knife and fork. As he cut the meat his rings almost spoke. His new suit creaked as he stretched to reach the plates, break the bread, and pour the coffee. [45]

The "Half-Equipped Knights"

This knight has few heroic or human qualities to recommend him:

> He bobbed about among men, a veritable bundle of enthusiasm - no power worthy the name of intellect, no thought worthy the adjective noble, no feelings long continued in one strain. A Madame Sappho would have called him a pig; a Shakespeare would have said "my merry child"; old, drinking Caryoe thought him a clever, successful businessman. [49]

The last clause is savagely ironic. The businessman-knight falls miserably short when he is judged by standards such as those of the narrator, Sappho and Shakespeare. Only another businessman considers him worthy of esteem. Elsewhere in the novel, the businessmen gathered at the club are described as "rotund, rosy figures, silk-hatted, starchy-bosomed, beringed and bescarfpinned to the queen's taste" [121]. Juxtaposed against the image of the knight-errant, these descriptions appear singularly funny. Similarly, while the businessman prided himself as the steadfast pilgrim, Dreiser symbolically links him to Belshazzar in Chapter XXXII, entitled "The Feast of Belshazzar: A Seer to Translate".

What we see in these instances is a systematic attack on the adversary through a mimicry of his favourite symbols. When we see the sacred symbols of the elite in the distorted mirror of the literary work, we get what Burke calls a "perspective by incongruity", a perspective the writer creates by "violating the 'proprieties' of the word in its previous linkages".(11) However, we are bound to miss the irony if we do not take the literary work as "the answer or rejoinder to assertions current in the situation in which it arose".(12) For example, the irony implicit in Dreiser's description of the rotund, overfed and overdressed businessman, similar to Veblen's ironic descriptions in The Theory of the Leisure Class, can only be appreciated when we realize that the businessman prided himself on his thrift and industry.

Instead of taking the "assertions current in the situation" in which the literary work arose, our critical terminology accounts for everything with words such as materialism, industrialization and urbanization. However, this vocabulary is unable to capture the dramatic cross-firing that goes on in the literary works. Their vital energy, which is often supplied by the writer's wrath against the adversary, goes entirely unnoticed when we limit our discussion by using such broad terms.

For example, apart from the highly ironic controlling metaphors of the religious and military quests, the novel is also replete with subtle jabs at the adversary's language that can only be grasped if we are familiar with it. "Industry", for example, was a sacred word for the business and religious leaders of the time. Honest industry was considered the sure formula for attaining riches as well as Godliness. Dreiser makes fun of the formula by, on the one hand, allowing Carrie to make her fortune through prohibited channels, and on the other, by commenting on the discrepancy between the pieties of the success literature and the actuality:

> Here was Carrie, in the beginning poor, unsophisticated, emotional, responding with desire to everything most lovely in life, yet finding herself turned as by a wall. Laws to say: "Be allured, if you will, by everything lovely, but draw not nigh unless by righteousness." Convention to say: "You shall not better your situation save by honest labour." If honest labour be unremunerative and difficult to endure; if it be the long, long road which never reaches beauty, but wearies the feet and the heart; if the drag to follow beauty be such that one abandons the admired way, taking rather the despised path leading to her dreams quickly, who shall cast the first stone? [368]

In this strategically important passage, only four paragraphs away from the conclusion, Dreiser's references to "honest labour", "righteousness" and "the admired way" are openly provocative as they undermine the symbolism frequently resorted to in the Sunday school preachings of such "stewards of the Lord" as Carnegie, Vanderbilt, Rockefeller, Sr. and Gould. The narrator maintains that the much touted "straight and narrow path" does not exist.

Passages like these indicate that the novel can be read as a strategic response to the "gospel of wealth". Contrary to the "glorious drama of poverty"(13) staged in the annals of rags-to-riches

125

literature, the novel maintains that honest labour does not pay; that it is nothing more than "a steady round of toil" [10]. It maintains that people do not fail because of "sinfulness", as the captains of industry insisted, but because of such inexorable factors as the aging process, the loss of will power, the loss of status, malnourishment, discouragement and labour laws. The novel illustrates the impact of these factors as a counterpoint to the philosophy which blamed the poor's lot on their "sinfulness". In stressing the importance of environment, while also blaming and satirizing those who were responsible for its creation, Dreiser aligned himself with the radical forces of his society who were struggling to overthrow the plutocratic rulers of the United States of America.

Thus, like most literary works, Sister Carrie also displays the desire of its author to seek "vengeance" against the adversary through ridicule. It systematically tears down the "eulogistic coverings" of the opponent, coverings that the opponent had so carefully contrived for himself by stealing away the traditional honorific symbols and role models.

"Vengeance", however, is not the only authorial motive, according to Burke. An equally important motive is a desire to provide "consolation" to one's allies.(14) The symbols of authority are desanctified with a view to demystify the world for us.

The writer thus provides us with a perspective through upsetting the customary linkages of dominant discourse. The novel contains several such addresses to the reader: on the true nature of money, on the nature of morals, and on the nature of society. They gain in irony when we realize that they are in an adversarial relationship with the symbols and the ideology of the American businessman. They are formulated as rejoinders to the authorities and propagate an alternative world-view.

I believe that when Dreiser stressed the role of environment over so-called "free will", he was responding to the prevailing philosophy which considered poverty to be the result of sin and idleness. By claiming that environment, and not individual decisions, determined the outcome of a life, Dreiser exonerated the poor from the charges of moral failure, while challenging the claims of

the rich who explained their wealth in terms of
mental superiority as well as Christian virtue. For
if environment was the sole arbiter, no one need be
considered superior or inferior. Both wealth and
poverty could then be understood in scientific
terms and something might be done to achieve a more
equitable social order. The narrative asides like
the following in Sister Carrie are rhetorical in
their nature since they deliberately engage the
official world-view:

> A man's fortune or material progress is very
> much the same as his bodily growth. Either he
> is growing stronger, healthier, wiser, as the
> youth approaching manhood, or he is growing
> weaker, older, less incisive mentally, as the
> man approaching old age. . . . Rich men are,
> frequently, in these days, saved from this
> dissolution of their fortune by their ability
> to hire younger brains. These younger brains
> look upon the interests of the fortune as
> their own, and so steady and direct its
> progress. If each individual were left
> absolutely to the care of his own interests,
> and were given time enough in which to grow
> exceedingly old, his fortune would pass as his
> strength and will. He and his would be
> utterly dissolved and scattered unto the four
> winds of the heavens. [239-40]

Dreiser here shreds to pieces the myth of the
Nietzschean Superman who owed nothing to any one in
his march to the top. Similarly, when Carrie
smugly congratulates herself for having found a job
in the theatre by unremitting effort and criticizes
Hurstwood for not doing the same, the narrator's
comment exposes the hypocrisy of a social system
that blames the victim for his misfortune:

> "Why don't he get something?" she openly said
> to herself. "If I can he surely ought to. It
> wasn't very hard for me."
> She forgot her youth and her beauty. The
> handicap of age she did not, in her
> enthusiasm, perceive.
> Thus, ever, the voice of success. [279]

With total disregard for the narrative texture
and referentiality, American critics have read
Sister Carrie as a semi-autobiographical,

sentimental portrait of an artist. However, I see it as the portrait of a potential artist who will never attain her stature because of the deficiencies caused in her by her environment. The "illusions of ignorance and youth" [1] with which she began at the age of eighteen are never overcome by her.

In Chapter VI, the narrator comments on the limitations of Carrie's mind: "Her imagination trod a very narrow round, always winding up at points which concerned money, looks, clothes or enjoyment" [39]. It is not that Carrie is born with a mind incapable of experiencing the finer pleasures of life. Contrary to popular critical opinion, there is no such inexorability of destiny in Dreiser's conception of character. Her intellectual and creative powers are limited because she has not had the benefit of good schooling: "She was a fair example of the middle American class - two generations removed from the emigrant. Books were beyond her interest - knowledge a sealed book" [2]. Near the end of the novel, she does enjoy reading Balzac when Ames recommends Le Père Goriot to her, and the book is shown to accomplish a widening of her sympathies.

In several places Dreiser complained bitterly that American youth was being deprived of humanity's rich cultural heritage. "Life", he believed, "is to be learned as much from books and art as from life itself - almost more so, in my judgement. Art is the stored honey of the human soul, gathered on the wings of misery and travail. Shall the dull and the self-seeking and the self-advertising close this store on the groping human mind?"(15) Throughout Sister Carrie, Dreiser continues to contrast uninformed reaction to social environment with that of the poet and the philosopher, as he had done in The Financier too. In Sister Carrie Sappho, Shakespeare and Epictetus represent an alternate world-view.

Carrie, however, has tutors like Mrs. Hale and Mrs. Vance who are totally immersed in the values of their society: "the gossip of the manager's wife formed the medium through which she saw the world. Such trivialities, such praises of wealth, such conventional expression of morals as sifted through this passive creature's mind, fell upon Carrie and for the while confused her" [77]. As a result, "She did not grow in knowledge so much as she awakened in the matter of desire" [86].

Dreiser's criticism of the American society is of the same grain as was that of Matthew Arnold's regarding Victorian society. Both societies neglected to cultivate the civilizing forces of culture, preferring philistinism instead. As Dreiser told Dudley, his hope as a writer was "to see mind and body united again", for "Nothing counts without mind and taste".(16) Similarly, the essays in Hey Rub-A-Dub-Dub were written in the hope of promoting "a sounder approach to life than is now voiced".(17) According to Dudley, "he prized above everything . . . the hope of a social fabric, backed by learning and imagination - what he called 'artistic vision.'"(18)

Dreiser's concern is not so much with the "human condition", as his critics suggest, as with a social condition. He is concerned with a society that deprives its members of a sound emotional and intellectual development. Carrie's shortcomings are not simply personal; she represents, for Dreiser, "the average American debarred from every avenue of intelligence or effort save that which relates to money."(19) This "little soldier of fortune" should be seen as representative of a whole regiment of "little knights" who are going to lay siege at the "walled city". Dudley paints the martial mood of business America at this time very succinctly: "It is formidable - this period of our development. Out of their high schools and fresh-water colleges what of the past were schoolboys remembering? Almost nothing it would seem, but the myth [sic] of Xerxes, Hannibal, Alexander, Caesar, Attila, Napoleon, who in their days and countries came singly and were paragons. But now in this land of machinery every boy was a potential conqueror, or he was a nobody."(20)

Instead of the military values of heroism and prowess, Dreiser advocated brotherhood. He urged that we should try to "unravel the tangled affairs of men first, and make them smooth. . . . We will be concerned with making things good, and with living so that things shall be better. . . . [T]here will be naught but hope, unfaltering trust and peace."(21) And until that time comes, he advised the individual to become "non-striving", "resisting actively and successfully the illusions of mental and spiritual growth or achievement via the amassing of material wealth or earthly distinctions, honors, or powers. These are the things that are to be actively resisted in the sense of one's refusing to succumb to their allure and, instead, in their place, to cultivate moderation, simplicity, self-restraint, and repose."(22) These qualities, so reminiscent of the Eastern philosophy of renunciation - Dreiser was deeply influenced by Buddhism - are presented in Sister Carrie through the character of Ames who does not want to be rich: "What good would it do? A man doesn't need this sort of thing to be happy" [237]. Elsewhere in the novel Dreiser presents the same belief through the narrative commentary:

> [I]t is the higher mental development that does away with such thoughts. It is the higher mental development which induces philosophy and that fortitude which refuses to dwell upon such things - refuses to be made to suffer by their consideration. . . . It is the Epictetus who smiles when the last vestige of physical welfare is removed. [241]

Against this narrative stance is pitted the attitude of Carrie and other characters who continue to chase "idle phantoms" [214] all through their life. Carrie never breaks the hold of her social conditioning even though she comes palpably close to it. She continues to be swayed by the spectacle of wealth and its reports in the media. She reads about the doings of the rich and gets very discontented. "She lived as much in these things as in the realities which made up her daily life" [228].

I, therefore, find it very hard to see the novel as the quest of an aesthetic sensibility towards artistic fulfillment as some critics have done. Dreiser shows that Carrie will never become an artist; she continues to work in the popular theatre that he so thoroughly condemned. Carrie of the last chapter, sitting in her rocking chair, unable to give up the lucrative popular stage for serious theatre, represents the fate of the artist in a capitalistic society. This co-opting of the artist was a major concern for Dreiser as evidenced by the fact that in The "Genius" he went on to portray another co-opted artist.

Ames warns Carrie that, if she did not leave the commercial theatre, her "power to act will disappear" [356]. However, the narrator does not lead us to hope that she will change. She "troubled over it in her rocking chair for days".

"Still, she did nothing - grieving. It was a long way to this better thing - or seemed so - and comfort was about her; hence the inactivity and longing" [357].

There is no disjunction in the two roles of Carrie, that of the "little soldier of fortune" and that of an actress in commercial theatre. Many critics have complained of such a disjunction because they find her transformation from a parvenu to an artist hard to believe.(23) However, the point of the novel is precisely that Carrie has not been transformed. Social environment has seen to it that "knowledge" remain a "sealed book" to her while she chases "phantoms" in a frightening social Darwinian jungle.

That is the way the novel ends. Instead of reading the last chapter as a sentimental outburst, a paean to the emergence of a young artistic sensibility, as many critics have done, I read it as a bleak prophecy about the fate of an individual gifted with artistic talent in the turn of the century America. There is little hope that Carrie will leave commercial theatre - as well as her suite at the Waldorf - and devote herself to serious art.

A true artist, Dreiser believed, must serve the "truth" and work for "the well-being of the future". He must portray "the wretched results of modern social conditions".(25) Sister Carrie must be read in the context of this belief: as an assessment of individual lives surrounded by a culture manufactured by plutocrats. However, when this novel and other literary works are read in complete detachment from the dominant discourse of the period of which they are the products, their cultural role is denied. There is, as I have tried to point out, a world of difference between discovering allusions to mediaeval romances and Pilgrim's Progress in Sister Carrie and discovering that Dreiser was only reappropriating what had been wrongfully usurped.

Dreiser returned to the theme in The "Genius". Like Sister Carrie, this novel is also concerned with an examination of the nature of art and the artist's situation in the American society. The nurture and treatment of an artist becomes the test of the level of civilization a particular society has reached. Dreiser did not believe that the individual had an entity apart from his social milieu. He held that the intellectual level of individuals in a society was determined according to the general level of civilization of the social order. This interconnection between the artist and his society is presented in "The Problem of Genius":

> A man of genius, like every other human being is limited by his environment, hence by the ideas and knowledge of the times; he cannot perform miracles. He can only excel, and usually in a unique and creative manner, in a function which others master to a lesser degree. . . . And the environment of its day may as readily frustrate as further it.(25)

It would be appropriate, then, to say that Eugene Witla is a case study upon whose success or failure as an artist depends a favourable or unfavourable judgement of the American society. The crux of the problem, therefore, is to determine whether Dreiser considers Eugene to be a good artist. And if he does not, then, what, according to him, are the reasons for Eugene's failure?

As to Dreiser's own estimate of Eugene's stature, his letter to Mencken provides a clue: "Please note that the title "The Genius" [sic] is quoted." One of the reasons for this choice was "to convey the exact question which I mean to imply".(26) If we take this suggestion seriously, the strategy for analysing the novel would be to see the character as a limited one and look for the novelist's reasons for making it so.

However, as with his other novels, very few of Dreiser's critics seem to have grasped this aspect of the novel. Once again, their analysis gets bogged down in tracing similarities between the novel and Dreiser's own life. There is no doubt that the novel takes off from autobiography and that a knowledge of Dreiser's life is a prerequisite to understanding it. However, when the critics fail to see the implied irony, claiming that the raison d'être of the novel is simply "to explain and to justify Dreiser as an artist", (27) they underestimate Dreiser's art. The impression of the novel that one gets from these analyses is that of a petulant writer who wanted nothing more than to even his score with his enemies. Since all these critics happen to be among the foremost voices of American criticism, Dreiser's questions about the conditions of art and the artist in America have remained undebated.

This approach of the critics is troubling. A good analysis of the novel, one would think, would be the one which began with the premise that the critic's task is to determine the level of distance between the hero and the novelist, since Dreiser did intend to imply irony. Only when the critic has accomplished this task can he be in a position to state whether the novel stands or fails. However, one sees no such questions being raised and answered. As a result, The "Genius" is perhaps the most neglected and the least understood novel in the Dreiser canon. It has suffered the fate of being dismissed as unassimilated, naive autobiography by practically all his modern critics despite the fact that early readers like John Cowper Powys, E. L. Masters, Randolph Bourne and F. Scott Fitzgerald, to name just a few, praised it most enthusiastically. Literary fashions, needless to say, do change. Yet I find it curious that these modern critics have not questioned the reasons for the swing in opinion. If the novel could appeal to so many distinguished contemporary readers, there must be more to it than simple adulation.

E. L. Masters' review in the Chicago Evening Post is a good indicator of the reasons the novel struck home. To Masters, The "Genius" was "an American story", "a chronicle of as well as against America". He thought that Dreiser had been able to lay his hand on some basic truths about American society: "He understands what a man almost a genius must contend with in this disorderly land of rhetorical freedom and societal tyranny and banality. He knows that the American soil is not productive of genius; and hence Witla, the hero, a name which connotes witless, goes thru the experience that would come to a genius, but fails in the main thing as a genius would not fail." Pinpointing one of the most vital aspects of the novel, Masters continued: "For one thing the American atmosphere stunts his unfolding; for another his nature is unstable, his ideals shift and fade from vision; for another the love of money-making diverts his attention from art."(28)

Masters' pronouncement deserves close attention, not only because he was a close friend of Dreiser's, but also because Dreiser himself uttered similar sentiments many times, both in his

novels as well as in his non-fictional writings and
speeches. In an essay entitled "Some Aspects of
Our National Character", he complained that America
had lost sight of its originally stated goal. "We
were to do tremendous things, not for the human
pocketbook but the human mind and soul. Our
children and our children's children were to be
free, progressive, fearless, mentally and
spiritually alert, entirely loosened from the
trammels and chains of superstition and the
degradation of poverty and want." On the contrary,
"The truth is that America has not as yet had an
intelligence or a culture worthy the name. It has
no visible intellectual purpose, unless it be that
of getting money."(29) In another essay, entitled
"Life, Art and America", he reiterated the charges:
"To me the average or somewhat standardized
American is . . . absolutely devoid of true
spiritual insight, correct knowledge of the history
of literature or art, and confused by and mentally
lost in or overcome by the multiplicity of the
purely material and inarticulate details by which
he finds himself surrounded."(30) He raised the
matter again in another important essay called
"America and the Artist". His words here
illuminate the contexts of The "Genius" as well as
Sister Carrie:

> I will say that for one not incorruptibly
> fevered with artistic convictions, standards,
> desires, and ideals, the material and sensual
> gauds of America this day - the enormous
> prices offered for shoddy as opposed to silk
> and fine wool and linen - certainly tend to
> wean him from more serious efforts. One must
> desire, and desire much, to do that which is
> beautiful and honest - today, here - as
> opposed to that which is tintinnabulary and
> meretricious; for the fumes of those twin, and
> to so many irresistible, fleshpots - notoriety
> and cash - will assuredly call him from his
> lean and soul-searching labor. But when ever
> has the true artist failed to adhere
> desperately and without shadow of turning to
> that which is true and beautiful? For these
> shall he not put aside kin and country, and
> with these only as his guides - his pillar of
> cloud by day, his beacon of fire by night - go
> forth?(31)

Sister Carrie makes it clear that Carrie does not
have the needed asceticism. She makes a choice, or
rather passively accepts "the material and sensual
gauds" instead of making art her "pillar of cloud"
and "beacon of fire". This holds true for Witla as
well. Unlike Dreiser, who chose not to accept the
challenge thrown at him by the enticing voice of
the "fabled city", beckoning him to leave his
"wretched neighborhood" and "cross over and join
the great gay throng", Eugene abandons his art to
seek the goals of material success.

The novel explores the reasons for this
deviation, tracing its roots to Eugene's early
childhood and adolescence. And once again, Dreiser
reaches the verdict he had given in Sister Carrie
as well as The Financier. Eugene, like their
protagonists, has been won over by the gospel ot
success. At sixteen, Eugene "was overawed by the
fact that the world demanded practical service -
buying and selling like his father, clerking in
stores, running big business" [12].

Eugene has a low opinion of himself from the
very beginning and this feeling is reinforced by
the opinions of others. His family do not care for
his interest in literature and art and disapprove
of Eugene devoting time to reading and sketching.
His sister thinks that he "dreamed too much" and
his father considers him to be "naturally lazy".
The local editor views him as "lackadaisical and
rather moody" [13, 22]. When Eugene tells Stella
Appleton, a town beauty, that he would like to be
an artist, she pretends not to hear him. The
Alexandria society has no need or appreciation for
a budding artist. True to its name, it cares only
for deeds of adventure and warfare. (Interestingly,
Herrick used the name with a similar symbolic
weight.)

Though Eugene is enchanted by "A soaring
buzzard poised in speculative flight", "a rose in
bloom, a tree swaying in the wind" [11-2], and
quotes Yeats' poetry, he is uncomfortably conscious
of the differentiations of wealth. "He thought it
must be nice to be rich. So he dreamed" [26]. Like
Carrie, he too wants to go to the city. "He did
not think so much of Alexandria. Some time he was
going to get out of it" [23]. Chicago evokes the
complex of feelings in him with which the reader of
Dreiser is already familiar. To the small town
dweller, the big city is the "much larger world
outside" [30], offering promises of wealth as well

as sexual fulfillment. Eugene comes to believe that the love of a girl is somehow dependent on his monetary status. When he finds that the girl he would like to befriend prefers a more prosperous boy-friend, he becomes conscious of his "position in the world" [31]. The town dandies who wear nice suits and have money to make week-end trips to Chicago or Springfield seem to him to get all the girls. The dreams of love and the dreams of wealth are intertwined in Dreiser. The woman and wealth both need to be conquered as proof of a man's virility.

The dreams around the city are built on the evidence of magazines and newspapers. In Eugene's case, as in Dreiser's own, the newspaper acts as the precipitator. In a scene reminiscent of Dreiser's own departure for Chicago, Eugene's journey begins. Like Dreiser's and Carrie's, his, too, is steeped in romance. However, it is not just a spectacle but, as usual, a testing ground. "He must succeed. That's what the world was made for. That was what he was made for" [36]. Chapter IV describes Eugene's approach to the city and his euphoria over it. Once again, Dreiser resorts to his favourite strategy of generalizing Eugene's experience and making out of him a mythic archetype. The landlady, on seeing Eugene, thinks: "This was what Chicago did to the country. It took the boys" [39]. To get into Chicago's "great banks, great office buildings, great retail stores, great hotels" [39] - the four invincible fortresses in Dreiser's fable land which overawe and abash his characters - is, however, fraught with danger. "Underneath, of course, was struggle. . . . This city demanded of you your very best, or it would have little to do with you. Youth in its search for something - and age - were quickly to feel this. It was no fool's paradise" [39].

This attitude to the towering commercial buildings in the downtown core is not unique to Dreiser. Louis Sullivan, the well-known Chicago architect, believed that these buildings, commissioned by powerful businessmen, promoted feudal relationships by cowing people down and making them feel subservient.(32) The Cliff Dwellers by Henry Fuller, a novel favoured by Dreiser, suggested through martial imagery and spatial metaphors that the bankers and the stock-brokers behaved like feudal warriors and were ripping apart the democratic fabric inherited from an earlier, more egalitarian America.

Eugene reacts to the heart of the business
district and the luxurious homes of the rich just
as Carrie and the young Dreiser did. They make him
feel that "he was destined to be a failure" [40].
As in Sister Carrie and the autobiographies, there
are extended descriptions of Eugene's visits to
these areas of the city. The disparities between
the rich and the poor are graphically presented.
Eugene meets "shabby men, sunken eyed, gloomy,
haggard", and the sight teaches him that "the City
could be cruel" and that "you could fail so easily"
[43].

Though he has read the works of Carlyle,
Emerson, Thoreau and Whitman, they fail to impress
on him that one need not see life in the stark
contrasts of success and failure. Instead of going
their way, that of asceticism and social
responsibility, he opts for the world represented
by Michigan and Prairie Avenues. Two events boost
his sagging confidence and make him feel that he
might one day get to them. One is his success with
a woman, a relationship which he conducts with "an
air of superiority". "This was, in its way, his
first victory of the sort, and it pleased him
mightily. . . . What, he thought, did the silly
boys back in Alexandria know of life compared to
this? Nothing. He was in Chicago now. The world
was different. He was finding himself to be a man,
free, individual, of interest to other
personalities" [46]. The other is a raise in his
salary. "Eugene thrilled. That would be really a
rise in the world. . . . His visions began to
multiply. One could get up in the world by trying.
The energetic delivery he had done for this laundry
had brought him this. Further effort in the other
field might bring him more. And he was young yet"
[47].

When he visits his home town, he finds "that
his old world was no world at all". "Of these
fellows none knew the visions that were now surging
in his brain. Paris - no less - and New York - by
what far route he could scarcely tell." He does
not realize that "the difference was in him only.
He was the one who had undergone cataclysmic
changes" [59]. Bristling with "vanity and deep
egotism" [61], he lives in his dream world
unmindful of the hurt he causes other people by
using them as his tools. Thus, while he uses Ruby

to alleviate his sexual needs as well as to find companionship in a city he otherwise finds "artificial and cold" [75, 108], she is not good enough to take along to the city. He gets betrothed to Angela who "was purer than Ruby" and "he knew that she would make any man an ideal wife" [81]. While he sleeps with Ruby, he offers tributes of sacred love to Angela, calling her "the fair Elaine of Arthur's court" [91].

Eugene's association of Angela with "the fair Elaine" echoes a common trend of the period. The woman was the prize awarded to the man successful in battle. In a passage reminiscent of Carnegie, Eugene thinks of the city as the great battlefield. However, unlike Carnegie, he alternates between moods of buoyant hopefulness and total impotence:

> Here were Jay Gould and Russell Sage and the Vanderbilts and Morgan - all alive and all here. Wall Street, Fifth Avenue, Madison Square, Broadway - he knew of these by reputation. How would he do here - how fare? Would the city ever acclaim him as it did some? He looked wide eyed, with an open heart, with intense and immense appreciation. Well, he was going to enter, going to try. He could do that - perhaps, perhaps. But he felt lonely. He wished he were back with Angela where her soft arms could shut him safe. He wished he might feel her hands on his cheek, his hair. He would not need to fight alone then. But now he was alone, and the city was roaring about him, a great noise like the sea. He must enter and do battle. [101]

The critics who see the novel as simple autobiography fail to realize that Eugene of the above paragraph is not at all like Dreiser. For Dreiser, by the time he reached New York, had already come under the influence of Balzac, Tolstoy, Spencer, Huxley, Tyndall and Wallace. And these thinkers and artists, he wrote, had taken away his desire for material success. According to Helen Dreiser, The "Genius" was "a composite of the lives of three men",(33) partly Dreiser's but also drawing on the lives of two other men. One of them was Dreiser's predecessor as the editor of the Delineator who committed suicide at an early age, probably because the "battle" of life overwhelmed him. The other was a contemporary artist, Everett

Shinn, who made a promising beginning as a member of the avant-garde Ash Can School and went over to more lucrative things like painting murals for banks and art directing in Hollywood.

These two did not become great artists, and nor will Eugene, because of the division in their lives compelling them to prove their selfhood through amassing wealth, an activity which destroyed Shinn mentally and the other man physically. An interview Dreiser gave in 1914 is relevant to the novel: "It never occurred to anybody that greatness could be achieved as a writer, a musician, an artist. Therefore all the potentially great men poured into business."(34) Those who started as good artists initially degenerated into the best-selling variety because they preferred prosperity to artistic integrity:

> In almost every case they succeeded in writing but one book, before the iron hand of convention took them in hand. Will Payne wrote The Story of Eva, a fine piece of American realism, and then quit, - started to make a decent living by writing for the Saturday Evening Post. Stephen French Whitman wrote Predestined and then quit. Not a thing since. Norris wrote McTeague and The Octopus. Then he fell into the hands of the noble Doubleday who converted him completely to The Pit, a bastard bit of romance of the best seller variety. Hamlin Garland wrote Main-Travelled Roads, his one book by the way, then diluted a clear realistic vision with as much sweetness and light as he thought would keep him respectable, - on the calling lists of American manufacturers of plows and elevators and saws, possibly, and sell a few more books, after which, - well, you know the rest. Even Chambers wrote one good book, The King in Yellow, proving that he could have written more of the same. Then he deliberately chose the best seller grade I fancy. Unquestionably, Jack London did so. I have read several short stories which proved what he could do. But he did not feel that he wanted want and public indifference. Hence his many excellent romances.(35)

The craving for success, that is commercial success, was endemic, Dreiser thought. No wonder that Eugene chooses the same road. However, here it is necessary to point out the misconceptions that have arisen due to a misapplication of autobiographical material. Since the critics start with the premise that Dreiser craved for the trappings of wealth and admired the successful businessman, they are unable to see the implied criticism in Eugene's response. The fact is that Dreiser refused to compromise his art for the sake of monetary gain. As Masters points out: "America should awake to the significance of the fact that Dreiser is not striving for popularity or to make money. He is not writing to propitiate American standards."(36) The meaning of the novel becomes clearer once we get the correct data on Dreiser's life.

Eugene, then, is not Dreiser, that is, the committed artist, but a potential artist whose talent goes to seed because he adopts the standards of his society as to what constitutes achievement. Instead of being able to say no to the temptations and the pseudo-challenge of the "walled city", he gets "over-whelmed" by its magnitude. The result is that inanimate things take over the role of adversary and make him visualize life in metaphors of bitter struggle:

> He had marvelled at wealth and luxury in Chicago, but here it took his breath away. It was obviously so much more fixed, so definite and comprehensible. Here one felt intuitively the far reaches which separate the ordinary man from the scion of wealth. It curled him up like a frozen leaf, dulled his very soul, and gave him a clear sense of his position in the social scale. He had come here with a pretty high estimate of himself, but daily, as he looked, he felt himself crumbling. What was he? What was art? What did the city care? [103]

Chapter XXII elaborates on this aspect of Eugene's life to the point of prolixity, reminding the reader of Ripley Hitchcock's advice to Dreiser: "Pray, let the reader infer something for himself. It is not necessary to go into all the details." (37) It is surprising how many readers have missed Dreiser's emphasis despite the overwhelming presence of such passages as the one just quoted. The chapter depicts in great detail Eugene's "chief

trouble with his present situation". He is shown
as being made dissatisfied with his lot by the
display of material splendour around him, just as
Carrie was, "and he came to the conclusion that he
was not living at all, but existing. Art as he had
first dreamed of it, art had seemed not only a road
to distinction but also to affluence. Now, as he
studied those about him, he found that it was not
so." As the narrator makes clear, the affluence
Eugene is dreaming of is the kind enjoyed "in that
world of real luxury which was made up of the
so-called four hundred - the people of immense
wealth and social position." Eugene loses esteem
for his art because it would not get him anywhere
near them. "Why, art, outside the fame, was
nothing. It did not make for real living." "How
would it be if he never came into this luxury, was
never allowed to enter society, was never permitted
to live as wealth was now living! The thought hurt
him. He felt an eager desire to tear wealth and
fame from the bosom of the world" [148-50]. Thus,
"shabby materialism" [200] comes to represent for
Eugene the be-all and end-all of life, when it
becomes associated with the fame and glory which
his society accords only to the warriors of the
marketplace. The question, as Dreiser saw it, was
not just that of man's attraction for material
goods. Rather, wealth is coveted by Cowperwood and
Eugene for its prestige value, for the supposed
"greatness" it confers on them. Because American
society invests social climbing with radiant
symbols borrowed from religion and literature, its
members come to feel that true self-affirmation can
only be had in that direction. As a result, Eugene
spends less time perfecting his art and more in
dreaming about what to the narrator is
"vainglorious life" [299].

As has already been noted, the dreams are not
always about conquering but have a darker side as
well. The fear of failure, of slipping down the
ladder, is a part of the experience in the journey
to the "walled city". Apart from "overindulgence"
[250] in sex it is this morbid fear which causes
Eugene's nervous breakdown. Though both reasons
are presented in the novel, the latter has not been
noticed. Chapter X in Book II makes the connection
quite clear. In his confused state Eugene thinks,
"If one failed of strength in any way, if life were
not kind in its bestowal of gifts, if one were not
born to fortune's pampering care - the rest was

misery" [251]. When he comes back to New York in this defeated state, the city "depressed him greatly, for he had always hoped to be an integral part of this magnificence and display and now he was not - might never be again" [299]. At the nadir of his mental and physical decline, he sees the world in the same grim images Cowperwood employs: "It was a horrible picture to him in his present condition. It was like the grinding of the millstones, upper and nether. These were the chaff. He was a part of the chaff. He was a part of the chaff at present, or in danger of becoming so. Life was winnowing him out. He might go down, down, and there might never be an opportunity for him to rise any more" [307-8].

As a day labourer, he behaves entirely differently from Dreiser who had undergone a similar experience. Dreiser wrote in an essay, "The Toil of the Laborer": "And as I thought of the meagerness of their wages, the manner in which I had driven them, and the profitless luxury, in so far as they were concerned, to which their labor tended, I resolved that I, for one, would have nothing more to do with it."(38) Eugene, on the contrary, "used to look at the wounded ground, the piles of yellow mud, the dirty Italians, clean enough in their spirit, but soiled and gnarled by their labor, and wonder how much longer he could stand it. To think that he, of all men, should be here working with Deegan and the guineas! . . . He longed for Carlotta, longed for a beautiful studio, longed for a luxurious, artistic life. It seemed that life had wronged him terribly, and yet he could do nothing about it. He had no money-making capacity" [390].

Eugene comes to believe that "One had to be strong, eager, determined, and abstemious if wealth was to come" [394], the qualities the self-help writers emphasized so much. He makes up his mind that "[h]e was going to climb again in the world and be happy with Angela. He was going to be an artist or a business man or something. Look at Hudson Dula. Owning a lithographic business and living in Gramercy Place. . . . Maybe he could be an art director or a lithographer or something" [399]. Angela wonders whether he will really "set himself to the task of climbing slowly and surely".

The symbolic act which marks the beginning of this new journey towards the upper reaches of the social pyramid is the change of costume. Eugene gives up his "ultra artistic appearance, abandoning his flowing tie and the rather indiscriminate manner he had of combing his hair", in favour of "severe simplicity" [394]. "Certain artists whom he met in times past and recently, were quite commercial in their appearance - the very successful ones" [394]. He still wears "a soft hat", which the owner of the advertising agency finds very "unbusinesslike" [414]. Eugene soon gives it up for "a stiff derby" [428].

Eugene's meeting with Summerfield brings out the conflict at the heart of the novel. Eugene, who has little faith in the value of art, is daunted by the demeanour of the businessman, the man who is believed to deal with "the real world". The imagery is familiar:

> This man was getting on his nerves already, . . . making him think that the quiet realms of art were merely the backwaters of oblivion. Those who did anything, who were out in the front row of effort, were fighters such as this man was, raw products of the soil, ruthless, superior, indifferent. . . . If he could be strong, defiant, commanding, what a thing it would be. Not to wince, not to quail, but to stand firm, square to the world and make people obey. Oh, what a splendid vision of empire was here before him. [418]

From Summerfield, he acquires "some of that eager personage's ruthlessness and began to manifest it in his own attitude" [420]. Soon enough, he begins to look "more like a young merchant than an artist" [428]. "From a lean, pale, artistic soul, wearing a soft hat, he had straightened up and filled out until now he looked more like a business man than an artist, with a derby hat, clothes of the latest cut, a ring of oriental design on his middle finger, and pins and ties which reflected the prevailing modes" [433]. This description is very reminiscent of Drouet and Hurstwood. The symbolic significance of these sartorial changes is clear from the fact that Dreiser repeats them three times within a space of thirty pages.

Eugene's reaction to the offer made by his next employers, Kalvin Publishing Company - Dreiser's hint to the reader that Eugene has surrendered to the Puritanical work ethic - indicates why he would never be a good artist:

Eight thousand a year! Was he eventually
going to become a great business man instead
of an artist? . . . Eight thousand this year!
Ten the next if he made good; twelve, fifteen,
eighteen - He had heard of such salaries in
the advertising field alone, and how much more
would his investments bring him. He foresaw
an apartment on Riverside Drive in New York, a
house in the country perhaps, for he fancied
he would not always want to live in the city.
An automobile of his own, perhaps; a grand
piano for Angela; Sheraton or Chippendale
furniture; friends, fame - what artist's
career could compare to this? Did any artist
he knew enjoy what he was enjoying now, even?
Why should he worry about being an artist?
Did they ever get anywhere? Would the
approval of posterity let him ride in an
automobile now? He smiled as he recalled
Dula's talk about class superiority - the
distinction of being an artist, even though
poor. Poverty be hanged! Posterity could go
to the devil! He wanted to live now - not in
the approval of posterity. [440]

Critics have seen nothing of import in
Eugene's rise in the business world. To them it
has meant a tedious retelling of Dreiser's own rise
in the field of popular magazines. In fact, here,
too, the link between autobiography and fiction is
slight. First, Eugene forgets all about painting
as soon as he enters the business world. Dreiser,
on the other hand, did not stop writing. As the
accounts of Dudley and Swanberg show, he came back
to writing as soon as he had recovered from his
nervous breakdown and, though he was penurious,
refused to give in to the prevailing standards:
"[H]is trouble was that he was asserting his own
artistic individuality. He was not doing factual
pot-boilers cut to order, but sketches he wanted to
write, which had only a slight story line and were
therefore hard to place." Nor did he lose sight of
his vocation when with the Butterick's: "Apparently
he had no time to work on Jennie Gerhardt, but
the dream of writing novels persisted. To one of
his editorial colleagues, Charles De Camp, he
talked with such certainty of his future that years
later De Camp wrote him, 'I remember the days we
used to walk up town from 7th av & 15th st and how

confidently you predicted what you have done.'"(39)
As an editor, he "found space for informative
articles". The June 1906 issue of Broadway Magazine
carried a manifesto which declared that it was
starting with "new and refreshing ideals", getting
rid of "the cheap, the vulgar, and the commonplace
policy which once guided it".(40) As editor of
Delineator, he published articles about Jane
Addams and Emma Goldman, using innuendo and irony
to make them acceptable to the bosses. As William
Lengel, his assistant editor and, later, editor of
Cosmopolitan, said, "He made a strong virile
magazine for women".(41) And he never buckled
under the pressure of the management, letting a
story stand despite the fact that the management
found its heroine totally unacceptable on account
of the fact that she smoked. Thus, Dreiser's
acceptance of the editor's role was not a
transformation comparable to Eugene's progress from
a painter to an advertising executive. There was
no contradiction between Dreiser's two roles of
editor and writer and, apart from working on short
stories and prose pieces, he resumed work on Jennie
Gerhardt, finishing twenty more chapters while
still on the job.
    If one came to the novel with this knowledge
about Dreiser's personal life, or without the
knowledge of what his critics have written about
him, it would be hard to miss the implied irony of
these lines in The "Genius": "He tried to think
just what it was each magazine should represent,
and who and where was the man who would give to
each its proper life and vigor. At once, for the
adventure magazine, he thought of a man whom he had
met years before who had since been making a good
deal of success editing a Sunday newspaper magazine
supplement, Jack Bezenah. He had started out to be
a radical writer, but had tamed down and become a
most efficient newspaper man" [477-8].
    The other very vital difference between
Dreiser and Eugene Witla concerns their life styles
at this stage in their careers. While Eugene's
dreams are made of material possessions and status
only, Dreiser led a comparatively modest life. He
paid off the debts accumulated during the years of
his mental breakdown and started a publishing firm
with B. W. Lodge which republished Sister Carrie.
The novel had remained out of print for seven
years. The rest of the money was "saved so that he

could be free to write about life as he saw it. He
and his wife lived now in a comfortable apartment
on Morningside Drive, but even so, he says: 'I was
a very simple person with no money to spend on
luxuries.' They worked hard and saved."(42) This
self-estimate is confirmed by the testimony of
Mencken.(43)

The similarities between the creator and his
hero are, thus, rather minimal. There is even
disagreement about the reasons for Dreiser's
falling out with his employers, Dudley reporting
that he left the job himself because he was getting
tired of it and Swanberg giving the popular story
about the Thelma Cudlipp affair. Even if Thelma
Cudlipp could be considered equivalent to Suzanne
Dale of the novel, the dissimilarities are too
pronounced to allow us to consider Eugene a copy of
his creator.

The fact of the matter is that Dreiser in this
novel is concerned with an issue rather than a
personality. As the biographical information
shows, the implied criticism of Eugene does not
apply to Dreiser himself, who never lost sight of
his vocation. To see Eugene Witla as Dreiser in
disguise, attempting to glorify himself, is to
underestimate Dreiser's personal integrity as well
as to fail to appreciate his concerns in the novel.
If the novel is read on its own premises, without
being clouded with misleading biographical
information, the implied criticism of Eugene's ways
becomes quite clear.

Eugene is a creature of dreams. Dreiser, as a
purveyor of "reality", presents these dreams in the
light of the day to show us how paltry they really
are, and how destructive of Eugene's talents. In
addition to this question of wasted potential,
there is also the concern that Eugene's commercial
success is not for good. Just when the dream seems
to have been realized, the "heartache" returns. As
Eugene finds out, the apartment on Riverside Drive
cannot provide complete happiness. Unfortunately,
"the road downward" described in Sister Carrie
[244] is dangerously close to it and a constant
threat. As Colfax tells Eugene in The "Genius":
"I want to tell you something! You're going in
there now with full authority, but don't you fall
or stub your toe or get sick or make any mistakes.
If you do, God help you! if you do, I'll eat you
alive!" [478]. Eugene "felt as though the red cap
of a cardinal had been put upon his head, and at

the same time an axe suspended over him" [479]. He feels that the assistants under him "could turn on him as lions on a tamer and tear him to pieces!" [509]. Eugene is unable to see the real nature of the publishing concern, so overwhelmed is he by the metaphors of battle. However, while he considers himself to have given "the best fight", the cause, according to the narrator, does not deserve it. For the publishing concern deals in nothing but "mental pabulum" [476-7].

Another interesting aspect of the theme is brought out through Eugene's relationship with Suzanne. Though Eugene is so insecure within himself and his position with Colfax so tenuous, Suzanne sees him as a demi-god. The Suzanne-Eugene relationship is, in many ways, comparable to Cowperwood-Antoinette and Cowperwood-Berenice relationships. All three women see their men with a halo of glory around them and love the man's image more than anything else. The moment Eugene loses his job, he also loses his charisma. Suzanne's first thought on hearing that Eugene has lost his job is, "He was not quite so powerful" [671]. A year later, she thinks, "Was he the able person she had really fancied him to be? . . . Would she not be more interested in one who was sharp, defiant, indifferent - one whom she could be compelled to adore and fight for rather than one who was constantly adoring her and needing her sympathy? A strong, solid, courageous man - was not such a one her ideal, after all?" [730].

The relations between the sexes are thus dominated by stereotypes: those of the strong, aggressive, heroic male and the soft, dependent, beautiful woman who worships, as well as is dominated by, this image of glorious perfection. The women, therefore, by believing in the myth of the virile man of wealth, are agents as well as victims of mystification. As the narrator in The Titan suggests, the women of his society perceived the world through a "rose-tinted mist of romance", living in a "high world of fancy. . . . Their husbands must be models, worthy of their high ideals." The narrator attributes the origin of this "illusion" to the poetry of the Middle Ages. The result is a social order which converts women into parasites and "objects of art" and men into heroic conquerors [63]. It is interesting to recall that Marguerite Tjader was chided by Dreiser for being "Nothing but a parasite", "wasting [her]

life" for a "few pieces of furniture". She was
asked by Dreiser to read Veblen's Theory of the
Leisure Class.(44)
    While Eugene looks "so powerful" to Suzanne,
deep inside, he is a bundle of insecurities created
by his tenuous hold on the ladder of success. When
the ladder is taken away from underneath, he
collapses entirely. At this stage on the "road
downward", he is similar to Hurstwood: "If Eugene
had been ten or fifteen years older, the result
might have been suicide. A shade of difference in
temperament might have resulted in death, murder,
any thing" [680]. Eugene, however, does not follow
Hurstwood's course because of "his natural desire
to work" [680], which, along with the therapeutic
effect of the preachings of Christian Science,
eventually lifts him out of his depression.
Moreover, unlike Hurstwood, he is lucky to have the
support of his sister and her husband. "There were
long talks with Myrtle and Bangs - arguments upon
all phases of mortal thought. . . . There was the
taking up and reading or re-reading of odd
philosophic and religious volumes, for he had
nothing else to do" [695]. Books, as in the case
of Berenice, are the road to mental health.
    Eugene goes back to painting after a turbulent
period lasting three years. Yet, the novel is
ambivalent as to the quality of his work. He sells
very well, getting commissions from bankers to
supply ornaments to the structures of commerce. But
the question whether he has really achieved the
status of a genuine artist remains unresolved.
However, that is only because the modern reader
does not have the clues Dreiser's contemporary
audience had. Burton Rascoe, for example, states
that the quotation marks in the title indicate
Dreiser's conviction of "Witla's second-ratedness.
It is as if he had said, 'Here is a man of talent
who, if it were not for his essential weakness of
character, would be a genius.'"(45) Dudley,
similarly, saw it as an indictment of American
society which destroyed artistic talent by luring
it towards commercial success: "In a store, and
doing well". She thinks that Fitzgerald was so
taken with The "Genius" perhaps because "he found
himself there".(46)
    The early readers, then, did not see the
conclusion as a triumphant self-affirmation. It is
hard to understand what makes the modern critics
think otherwise. For it is difficult to ignore the

clues Dreiser has provided throughout the book. The character of Witla, even if we ignore Masters who thinks the name means "witless", emerges in the novel as that of an illusion-ridden being who hankers after fame, power and money. He has been drawn as a character seeking affirmation through the conventional social ideal of monetary success rather than through devotion to his art. In the end, he is persuaded to return to art only by the insistence of the friendly art-dealer and not because he has an uncontrollable urge to create. It is hard to accept the prevalent attitude, given the total context of the novel, that what we see in the last pages is a nascent genius who has just been through his <u>Sturm</u> <u>und</u> <u>Drang</u> period.

There is a very important clue which further detracts from this view. It is the biography of Everett Shinn, the painter who, according to Dreiser, was one of the three characters who served as the prototype of Witla. Everett Shinn was a member of the group of painters who called themselves "The Eight" and were made notorious by their detractors under the name of "The Ash Can School". The school, according to art histories, brought a wave of fresh air to the hothouse-bred art of genteel tradition and, because of the similarity in their aims, their work was often compared to that of writers like Frank Norris and Jack London.(47) The reasons Dreiser chose Shinn as a prototype instead of Robert Henri or John Sloan, the more illustrious members of the group, can only be explained in terms of Dreiser's sense of thwarted promise, not because of uncontrollable circumstances but because of a personal weakness for wealth. Mahonri Sharp Young's study of the group brings out some facts which illuminate the novel. According to Young, Shinn was "the cleverest" of "The Eight". However, he was also "the only one of the group who felt the attraction of pretty actresses, great ladies, and rich men. He was dazzled by the rich just as he was dazzled by women and the theatre: they made his heart leap for joy." "Shinn had more talent and facility than any of The Eight. He could do anything easily. The trouble was that he didn't do his best work all the time. His career has an unexpected shape. The worst sin for an artist is not to advance, and Shinn could not say, with Beethoven, that his work was better than it used to be." "Shinn was the only one of The Eight whose career as an artist was interrupted. The others all did the best work they could and devoted their lives to painting. Shinn was the only one who continued to turn out illustrations, which did not improve. This highly talented man turned out a great deal of incredibly bad work." "For him, art was not all that serious. He could do it, but with no high sense of mission. He was a hard worker who got the job out, but it was just a job to him. . . . He was the only one who never became a full-time artist." "Shinn learned the art of getting on only too well." Very interesting from our point of view is the sidelight thrown by Young on the direct relationship between Shinn and Witla: "Too much has been made of Shinn's being the model for Dreiser's The Genius [sic], particularly by Shinn himself. . . . Usually people, hurt and angry, deny that they are models for fiction, but Shinn gloried in it."(48)

Similar opinions of Shinn are expressed by Daniel Catton Rich and Homer Saint-Gaudens. The picture that emerges is that of an artist with promise who squandered his talent for the sake of making easy money by decorating rich people's houses, and working as a scenic designer and a motion picture art-director.(49)

It is easy to see that Witla is a "composite" of all those artists who, according to Dreiser, compromised themselves because they did not have a strong belief in the value of art and prostituted it for paltry aims. Consequently, far from being a romantic exaltation of the artistic self at the cost of society, as critics consider it to be, the novel is a troubled questioning of the values of a society which puts so high a premium on material success. And this was the reason Dreiser had no trouble in shifting back and forth between The "Genius" and the Trilogy of Desire; not because, as Lehan thinks, they are "merely less personal accounts of the same kind of story",(50) but because there too Dreiser was dealing with the nature of man's response to material wealth. Those who see these novels as mere phantasies of the "dream-self", biographies of the potent superman in different guises, have somehow overlooked the emphasis Dreiser wanted to put on economic relationships in society.

Once this common bond among the novels is perceived, there remains no need to see Dreiser's career in distinct stages in which each succeeding

The "Half-Equipped Knights"

stage seems to negate the preceding one. In fact, this simplistic point of view fails to take into account the fact that Dreiser worked on all these novels simultaneously. It is, of course, true that The Titan, An American Tragedy, The Stoic and The Bulwark were published far apart from one another. However, Dreiser had actually started working on them along with Jennie Gerhardt and The Financier. This proximity of their genesis is indicated in the commonality of their themes and inspiration. They all deal with man's relationship and response to money. Those who have been unable to see this unifying thread have also found it hard to understand how the so-called superman worshipper went to the other extreme of writing about a non-entity. However, to a reader who comes to his work without these preconceptions, there hardly appears a drastic shift of focus among the themes of The "Genius", the Cowperwood trilogy and An American Tragedy. The subject remains the same: the acculturation of a young hero in the values of his society.

For those looking for variety and novelty, Dreiser's insistence on the economic aspect of life may seem repetitious. Dreiser, however, thought that the pursuit of wealth had become a national obsession and he considered this preoccupation utterly degrading and pathetically wasteful of human potential. In 1918, disillusioned with the road the post-World War America seemed to be taking, he said to Dudley: "A few more years and an idea outside of business won't get a show anywhere."(51) To William C. Lengel, who had sent Dreiser a telegram asking him to suggest possible contributors to Hearst's International, he wrote after listing a long array of names: "I would like to write a genial study of Americans, giving them full credit, to be called, - Get There, Eli. And I might add two words to the title, thus: But Where?" The reason he did not write it is made clear by the editorial note of Elias: "The last paragraph was circled in pencil by the editor, Ray Long, who noted: 'I'd like to see him do it, but we couldn't order it.'"(52) What Dreiser did, instead, was to go on with An American Tragedy. For this is the time he was starting work on the novel. The title for the article proposed to Lengel powerfully conveys the novel's theme as well its relationship to the preceding novels.

An American Tragedy is, perhaps, the most

acclaimed of Dreiser's novels, drawing praise even
from such an arch-enemy as Stuart Sherman. And
there is surprisingly little disagreement as to
Dreiser's purpose here. It would indeed be hard to
see Clyde as a superman or an artistic genius!

What has not been discussed, however, is, once
again, the relationship of the novel to the popular
discourse of the time. Clyde, like Dreiser's other
characters, is deeply influenced by the
pronouncements of the gospel of wealth. He, too,
lives in the hope of attaining an ideal state of
being which will be realized by undertaking a
perilous journey through the wilderness of the
American city.

What makes An American Tragedy different from
the other novels is its scope and breadth. Dreiser
felt that this time he had been able to encompass
the totality of American experience. In a letter
to a reader, he explained the novel's genesis:

> I had long brooded upon the story, for it
> seemed to me not only to include every phase
> of our national life - politics, society,
> religion, business, sex - but it was a story
> so common to every boy reared in the smaller
> towns of America. . . . My purpose was not to
> moralize - God forbid - but to give, if
> possible, a background and a psychology of
> reality which would somehow explain, if not
> condone, how such murders happen - and they
> have happened with surprising frequency in
> America as long as I can rémember.(53)

Dreiser thought that by providing "a background"
and "a psychology of reality", he could compel
American society to examine itself and realize that
the murderer was the product of its institutions.
He hoped to make it see that the attitudes it
fostered as desirable were actually destructive.

Dreiser's attacks on the social institutions
mentioned in his letter are bitter. He holds them
directly responsible for creating a mythology which
portrays success in money-making as the apex of
human achievement. Clyde's failure of insight is
firmly related to his milieu. Clyde is very much
like his predecessors, possessing an "exotic sense
of romance" [22]. Like Cowperwood he gets out of
school "because he already felt himself very much
belated in the race" [36]. He gets work as an
assistant to a soda-fountain clerk and thinks: "He

would work and save money and be somebody." To this very sound sense of business practice, the narrator adds an ironic rejoinder: "Decidedly this simple and yet idyllic compound of the commonplace had all the luster and wonder of a spiritual transfiguration, the true mirage of the lost and thirsting and seeking victim of the desert" [38].

This key passage clarifies many aspects of the theme in a most economic way. It manages to convey how this crude commercialism was blessed by the Church so that a bestseller of 1924 described Jesus as a shrewd businessman, making true Emerson's prophecy that "the gods of the cannibals will be a cannibal, of the crusaders a crusader; and of the merchants a merchant."(54) The word "mirage", which was the novel's original title, describes the narrator's attitude to Clyde's quest. Also, it underlines the ironic tone which mocks, throughout the novel, Clyde's as well as his society's mythos which "links business with religion, explains religion by business, and then uses business terms as religious terms."(55)

The Green-Davidson hotel, with its gaudy and over-ornate decorations, is described from this dual viewpoint. For Clyde, it symbolizes the ultimate in perfection: "Could it be possible that he would be admitted to such a grand world as this - and that so speedily?" [44]. The overweening voice of the narrator, however, criticizes not only Clyde's own illusions but the taste and the wisdom of the entire society: "In short it was compact, of all that gauche luxury of appointment which, as some one once sarcastically remarked, was intended to supply 'exclusiveness to the masses.' Indeed, for an essential hotel in a great and successful American commercial city, it was almost too luxurious. Its rooms and hall and lobbies and restaurants were entirely too richly furnished, without the saving grace of either simplicity or necessity" [42].

The gaudy and expensive American hotel and restaurant became a powerful symbol for Dreiser. With its luxurious appointments and its ability to screen people on the basis of money, such a place conferred status on the ones inside while evoking dreams in those barred out. Their impact on Carrie, Drouet and Hurstwood was repeatedly brought out in Sister Carrie. Cowperwood takes care to stay in the most expensive hotel on his exploratory visit to Chicago, a fact which impresses Addison.

The hotel has this magical effect on Angela as well. For her, "The luxuries of the modern hotel . . . were a foretaste of what was to be an enduring higher life. These carpets, hangings, elevators, waiters, seemed in their shabby materialism to speak of superior things" [200].

The world of the hotel seems to Clyde "a realization of paradise", "a marvelous-marvelous realm" [49-50]. "And there was music always - from somewhere" [45]. It symbolizes for him not just aesthetic perfection, but also "social superiority" [54]. "Such grandeur. This, then, most certainly was what it meant to be rich, to be a person of consequence in the world - to have money" [58]. In Clyde's imagination, from now on, beauty and wealth become linked. The world of the hotel is fantastic and, "Aladdinish", an adjective that is used many times throughout the novel. The people in it are "so very different from most of the people in the streets or anywhere, as he saw it" [55].

The car accident forces Clyde to leave his job at the hotel, but not before it has had a formative influence. "And so, of all the influences which might have come to Clyde at this time, either as an aid or an injury to his development, perhaps the most dangerous for him, considering his temperament, was this same Green-Davidson, than which no more materially affected or gaudy a realm could have been found anywhere between the two great American mountain ranges" [58]. Clyde and the other bell-boys are convinced from what they see here that "the chief business of life for any one with a little money or social position was to attend a theatre, a ball-game in season, or to dance, motor, entertain friends at dinner, or to travel to New York, Europe, Chicago, California" [59]. Clyde also learns that to attain this world, one has "to get into something where there was more chance to do something and be somebody" [176]. The vagueness of "something" brings out the airy nature of the advices of the self-help manuals which were high on the virtues of character building and absolutely vague as far as concrete suggestions were concerned. As Clyde writes to his mother after his accident, "I want to do something in this world. I want to be successful. . . . I got to get on in this world" [182]. He plans to get into a line "where I can work up".

Clyde's metaphors of ascent are juxtaposed to the ones used by his mother, a device which pinpoints the intermingling of the commercial and the religious spheres. His mother's letter predictably draws on the Puritan's metaphors of pilgrimage: "I had hoped and prayed that you would return to the straight and narrow path - the only path that will ever lead you to success and happiness of any kind." "Oh, my son, if you only knew how you must be on your guard to avoid these pitfalls. And you have such a long road ahead of you. . . . Will you stop and listen to the voice of our Lord that is ever with us, guiding our footsteps safely up the rocky path that leads to a heaven more beautiful than we can ever imagine here?" From her advice to Clyde that he ask his "rich and successful" uncle for a job in his "great collar business" [183-4], it appears that adherence to "the straight and narrow path" is synonymous with diligence in business.

As becomes clearer later on, there is virtually no difference between the road to heaven and that leading to material success. The great "pitfalls" on both roads are those of drink and sex. Clyde realizes that if he really wants to "get on", he must learn to control his sexuality. Watching the "company of seemingly mentally and socially worldly elect", he comes to feel that "[p]robably one could not attain to or retain one's place in so remarkable a world as this unless one were indifferent to sex, a disgraceful passion of course." "These various distinguished individuals . . . for the most part seemed to be unaware of, or at least unaffected by, that element of passion, which, to his immature mind up to this time, had seemed to propel and disarrange so many things in those lesser worlds with which up to now he had been identified" [188-9].

In an essay entitled "Neurotic America and the Sex Impulse", Dreiser had speculated that there was a connection between excessive desire for material wealth and status and the restrictions imposed upon the sexual impulse. He felt that life would be easier and happier if human beings could be made to accept their sexuality. But as things stood, sexuality, instead of being successfully suppressed, had become perverted and, instead of being dictated by emotions, had itself become a commodity.(56) Dreiser's attribution of asexuality to the "socially elect" can be understood only in this light. They have attained their place by successfully resisting the perils of the flesh. The sign of their virtue, as the Puritan clergymen would say, is their accumulated wealth.

Clyde resolves to be a good boy and thinks that "if he worked very steadily and made only the right sort of contacts and conducted himself with the greatest care here, one of these very remarkable men . . . might take a fancy to him and offer him a connection with something important somewhere, such as he had never had before, and that might lift him into a world such as he had never known" [189]. Clyde's plan is one which has animated every rags-to-riches novel.

As to the "socially elect" themselves, Samuel Griffiths and his family consider themselves as role models for the less fortunate. When Clyde talks to him of "ever since I heard of you and your big company", it pleases him no end. "Plainly he and his achievements had stood in the nature of an ideal to this youth" [195]. Shortly after follows a narrative discourse which is very pertinent to the discussion here, that is, the linking of success in money making to moral growth:

> For while Samuel Griffiths, as well as his son Gilbert, realized that this was small pay (not for an ordinary apprentice but for Clyde, since he was a relative) yet so inclined were both toward the practical rather than the charitable in connection with all those who worked for them, that the nearer the beginner in this factory was to the clear mark of necessity and compulsion, the better. Neither could tolerate the socialistic theory relative to capitalistic exploitation. As both saw it, there had to be higher and higher social orders to which the lower social classes could aspire. One had to have castes. . . . It was necessary when dealing with the classes and intelligences below one, commercially or financially, to handle them according to the standards to which they were accustomed. And the best of these standards were those which held these lower individuals to a clear realization of how difficult it was to come by money - to an understanding of how very necessary it was for all who were engaged in what both considered the only really important constructive work of the world - that of material manufacture - to understand how very essential it was to be drilled, and that

sharply and systematically, in all the details
and processes which comprise that constructive
work. And so to become inured to a narrow and
abstemious life in so doing. It was good for
their characters. It informed and
strengthened the minds and spirits of those
who were destined to rise. And those who were
not should be kept right where they were.
[196]

The passage brings out all the important
aspects of Dreiser's theme. Also, it contains the
quintessence of the popular social philosophy of
the times. Success in money making becomes
symbolic of one's higher intelligence and one's
"election". It follows, then, that the test be as
hard as possible. Those born with natural ability
will manage to "rise" from the "very bottom" while
the lazy and the unintelligent will be weeded out.
The irony of it, as Dreiser sees it, is that those
who preach the doctrine do not practise it
themselves. Gilbert, for example, is born to
wealth. And so is his father who inherited money
from his father while Clyde's father was left out
of the will.
    It is this social philosophy which is
reflected in the set-up of the factory as well as
that of Lycurgus, a name quite ironical in its
phonetic similarity with "lucre". Clyde must work
his way up from the shrinking room in the basement.
In his social life, the same distance is symbolized
by the presence of Wykeagy Avenue with its fabulous
mansions side by side with the wretched slums which
are joined to it by a bridge on the river Mohawk
which traverses the town. Though they are
described realistically, their symbolic import
becomes clear in the light of the overall water and
bridge imagery in Dreiser. Clyde finds a room on
Thorpe Street, "a thoroughfare enormously removed
in quality if not in distance from that in which
his uncle resided". Here, in the "commonplace
brown or gray or tan colored houses, rather smoked
or decayed" live "many drab and commonplace figures
of men and girls", employed in the many factories
of the town [210]. Working in "the basement world"
of the factory, Clyde dreams of the "beautiful
Wykeagy Avenue" which "evoked a mood which was as
of roses, perfumes, lights and music. The beauty!
The ease!" [209-11]. The world of poverty is
described by Dreiser as the "under-world of toil"

157

[108].

The social import of Wykeagy Avenue becomes clear from the opinion of Mrs. Griffiths, "who took no end of satisfaction in the grace and rank of her own home in this street. She and her husband had been so long climbing up to it" [237-8]. One's residence determines whether one is "anybody" or a "nobody" [230]. Clyde, on his visit to his uncle's house, becomes very sad. "If he could enter upon this world, find some way" [246]. Yet, this "marvelous" "high world" is beyond his reach as "the lines of demarcation and stratification between the rich and the poor in Lycurgus was [sic] as sharp as though cut by a knife or divided by a high wall" [274-5].

Though a high wall separates the two worlds, "[n]otices in the local papers almost every day as to their coming and going here and there" [282] impinge themselves upon the consciousness of the less-privileged. "At times, after reading these accounts he had pictured to himself, even when he was off somewhere with Roberta at some unheralded resort, Gilbert Griffiths racing in his big car, Bella, Bertine and Sondra dancing, canoeing in the moonlight, playing tennis, riding at some of the smart resorts where they were reported to be" [330]. Clyde is unable to enjoy the present for itself, so agitated is he by the "vision" of this grandiose future. Even though he is deeply attracted by Roberta, his material ambitions prevent him from treating her with dignity and honesty. "For after all, who was she? A factory girl! The daughter of parents who lived and worked on a farm and one who was compelled to work for her own living. Whereas he - he - if fortune would but favor him a little - !" [330]. The investiture of power on the rich had resulted in a similar sense of insignificance in Carrie: "What, after all, was Drouet? What was she?"(57) Ironically, Roberta's love for Clyde is tempered by the same thoughts: "Roberta, after encountering Clyde and sensing the superior world in which she imagined he moved, and being so taken with the charm of his personality, was seized with the very virus of ambition and unrest that afflicted him" [275]. Minor characters such as Dillon and his group have similar expectations from life. They are overawed by the rich and wish to be like them at some point. All of them have a tremendous reverence for the houses and inhabitants of Wykeagy Avenue. Like them, and like Carrie and Eugene, Clyde often travels to the rich part of the city to admire the houses:

> Their great house closed and silent, except for gardeners and an occasional chauffeur or servant visible as he walked from time to time past the place, was the same as a shrine to him, nearly - the symbol of that height to which by some turn of fate he might still hope to attain. [330]

This is what Samuel Griffiths had wanted: that his "achievements" become an "ideal" for the nation's youth. Many times throughout the novel Dreiser refers to these houses as "shrines" and situates them at a "height". That this is how the rich thought of their homes becomes apparent from the booklets of Elbert Hubbard, that great favourite of business, entitled Little Journeys to the Homes of Great Businessmen. The homes, quite obviously, were not just for living but also for impressing and inspiring.

These homes possess Clyde's mind to the exclusion of everything else. They symbolize the "height" he wants to attain and everything else is seen in the light of this metaphor. Roberta, he thinks, was "not of his station, really" [331]. Sondra, on the other hand, is a "goddess in her shrine of gilt and tinsel" who gives him hope that "somehow, in some way, he was to be lifted from the lowly state in which he now dwelt. He was, as he now saw it, really too good for the commonplace world by which he was environed" [338].

Clyde does not love Sondra. It is "all that she represented" [338] which he is after. "And what harm, he now asked himself, was there in a poor youth like himself aspiring to such heights? Other youths as poor as himself had married girls as rich as Sondra" [344]. Eugene, too, had aspired for the hand of a rich girl who would allow him to enter the charmed circle. Dreiser felt that such a dream was typically American and grew out of reading the popular sentimental novels: "For years I have been arrested in stories and plays by the poor young man who marries the rich man's daughter. I have had many letters from people who wrote: 'Clyde Griffiths might have been me.'"(58)

Ironically, while Clyde is trying to take a short cut to wealth, others see him as one "who has to make his own way in the world" [245], beginning where "[t]he best people start", that is, at the "bottom" [239], and climbing up by "hard work - saving one's money - looking neat and gentlemanly" [220]. The Starks admire him for his "energetic and ambitious commercialism" [409], which is supposed to prompt him to take his work home. This is the official version of the myth: one begins as a shoe-shine boy and climbs to the top rung of the ladder.

This, according to Dreiser, is the paradox at the heart of the myth. The rich justify their privileges as having been earned through Herculean labour and present themselves as worthy examples to be emulated. The poor are so daunted by this picture that they see the rich as somehow superior in strength and intelligence and themselves as inferior. They begin to see the world around them as over-powering and intimidating and their natural initiative is thwarted:

> Modern business has made American citizens into nothing but trudging asses. There is no great contemporary literature. If there is to be any in the future it will have to take the form of satire or expressions of despair. . . . Big business movements are making it impossible for men to express themselves as individuals. Because they cannot hope to succeed in small enterprises they have lost their initiative and their power to think.(59)

Those who succeed, like Cowperwood, see themselves as Napoleons and Hannibals and Nietzschean Supermen, not realizing that their success depends on many other things apart from their own personality. They, then, take a contemptuous view of the rest of the society, the classic example being Vanderbilt's statement: "The public be damned!" The rest, on the other hand, daunted by the difficulties of "the admired way", lose all interest in ordinary life. This is the way Dreiser explained Clyde's actions. The type of murder he commits, Dreiser thought, was typical of American society. He collected data on at least twenty such murders before settling on the Gillette case.

American society, as viewed from the perspective of Dreiser's novels, is a landscape containing towering mountains with shrines on top and swarms of human beings at various heights. Or, it is a long perilous road, with the "walled city" at the end, brightly lit and noisy within while crowds mill outside, barred from entering. The sea and the jungle provide the accessory imagery.

Clyde's desire to free himself from Roberta, then, is an attempt to escape from "the stark, bald headlands of fact" [388]. Roberta's farmhouse reminds him of "how far he had travelled away from just such a beginning as this!" [427]. Roberta is this "other world from which he sprang" [428], and he is afraid that it might "extend its gloomy, poverty-stricken arms to him and envelop him once more." The path to Sondra, however, is almost impossible to traverse. A dream of Clyde's, almost Bunyanesque, underlines its paralyzing grimness:

> And then falling into a nervous, feverish doze soon thereafter, he found himself dreaming of a savage black dog that was trying to bite him. . . . [N]ow he was in some very strange and gloomy place, a wood or a cave or narrow canyon between deep hills, from which a path, fairly promising at first, seemed to lead. But soon the path, as he progressed along it, became narrower and narrower and darker, and finally disappeared entirely. And then, turning to see if he could not get back as he had come, there directly behind him were arrayed an entangled mass of snakes that at first looked more like a pile of brush. But above it waved the menacing heads of at least a score of reptiles, forked tongues and agate eyes. And in front now, as he turned swiftly, a horned and savage animal - huge, it was - its heavy tread crushing the brush - blocked the path in that direction. And then, horrified and crying out in hopeless desperation, once more he awoke - not to sleep again that night. [479]

The dream is interesting from many angles. On the one hand it describes the enormity of the effort required to reach the holy shrine or the walled city at the top. On the other, it points out in Freudian terms that Clyde's problem is sexual as well. In his own mind, he feels that he cannot climb to the top because of his sexual transgression, a detail which ties in with Dreiser's early statements regarding sexuality and commercial success.

161

An American Tragedy is patterned on the same design as Dreiser's other novels discussed in this study. Like them, it, too, is concerned with the choice between the right and the wrong way and the difficulty involved in that choice. Dreiser's walled city with all its enticements proves much too distracting for most of his characters who, unlike Ames, never learn that one's happiness does not depend on one's admittance to its portals. In the earlier novels, except in the case of Hurstwood's suicide, Dreiser had mainly concerned himself with personal unhappiness due to the feverish scramble for purely material ends. Here, he dealt with the ultimate taboo, namely murder. Clyde's crime is terrible because in murdering Roberta he also destroys his own means of finding contentment and meaning in life. For their love for each other, born of a "chemical" attraction neither can resist, has the capacity to transform the world. It creates, so long as it lasts, "an ecstatic paradise of sorts in the very center of a humdrum conventional and petty and underpaid work-a-day world" [330]. When they are together, even "as commonplace and noisy and gaudy" a place as Starlight amusement park transports them to a level of "ecstasy which was all out of proportion to the fragile, gimcrack scene" [306].

However, this relationship is sacrificed for the sake of "luxury and social supremacy", for the "height" represented by "the Finchley residence in Wykeagy Avenue" [338, 396]. The "social custom and taboos", Dreiser thought, are extremely powerful and few escape their influence. "In short, according to what the individual is environmentally subjected to, those social patterns about him and the impact of which he cannot sensorially escape - so is he."(60) Therefore, he would not resort to sudden conversions in his novels and objected to them in the works of others. In an interesting letter discussing the play of a friend of his, he wrote: "I was a little surprised that the various and moving and troubling actions of the characters, expressing as they did, and beautifully, temperamental afflictions, could have brought about the sudden illumination of your leading character, Leo Gordon, with which you closed the play."(61)

This lack of self-consciousness in Dreiser's characters has upset many of his critics. They are, however, unable to see that while Dreiser denied most of his characters the power to

162

transcend their environment, he did not deny the possibility. The artists and philosophers transcend it and help others see their bondage as well. Ames in _Sister Carrie_ as well as Berenice in _The Stoic_ have seen through the social myths. For both of them, books provide the key to an understanding of life.

Dreiser hoped that his books will do the same for his readers. As Charles Child Walcutt observes, a naturalistic novel is not to be considered deterministic _per se_. "Reading a naturalistic tragedy in which the hero appears to have no freedom, one can know that one is performing an act of freedom in reading the book, and can sense that the author is by no means contained by the determinism which controls his novel, for he appeals to the reader's freedom and idealism as he shows that his hero is trapped."(62) That Dreiser was aware of this process is clear from his symbolic use of books in the novels as liberators of the consciousness of his characters. The reason he wrote novels, he told Dudley, was because people "need to know things".(63)

To call this writer a nihilist, a social Darwinist and a superman worshipper seems untenable in view of his writings. As the evidence shows, Dreiser rejected the prevalent myths built upon a combination of the Puritan ethic, social Darwinism and the heroic quest; all of which presented the world as an adversary, to be fought and conquered through virtue and courage. Like Howells and Herrick, Dreiser opted for the opposing values: "kindness, generosity, love and mercy".(64) Human beings, Dreiser reiterated, can thrive only in an atmosphere of love and security and not in the Darwinian jungle or the Puritan's wilderness. His fiction challenges these symbols as well as their manufacturers.

NOTES

1. Dreiser, unpublished manuscript, _Theodore Dreiser: A Selection of Uncollected Prose_, 277.
2. Dreiser, _The "Genius"_ (1915; The World Publishing Company, Cleveland, 1946).
3. Dreiser, _An American Tragedy_ (1925; The World Publishing Company, Cleveland, 1948).
4. Quoted in Dudley, _Dreiser and the Land of the Free_, 472.
5. Dreiser, _Hey Rub-A-Dub-Dub_, 5.

6.   Dreiser, "A Talk with America's Leading Lawyer," 121.
7.   Pizer, editor's note, Sister Carrie, 436.
8.   James E. Mulqueen, "Sister Carrie: A Modern Pilgrim's Progress," CEA Critic 31 (March 1969) 8.
9.   Matthiessen, Theodore Dreiser, 68; Pizer, The Novels of Theodore Dreiser, 68.
10. Bertrand Bronson, In Search of Chaucer (University of Toronto Press, Toronto, 1960) 30.
11. Burke, Permanence and Change: An Anatomy of Purpose, introduction by Hugh Dalziel Duncan (1935; Bobbs-Merrill, New York, 1965) 90.
12. Burke, The Philosophy of Literary Form, 109.
13. Dreiser, unpublished manuscript, Theodore Dreiser: A Selection of Uncollected Prose, 277.
14. Burke, The Philosophy of Literary Form, 304.
15. Dreiser, Hey Rub-A-Dub-Dub, 276.
16. Quoted in Dudley, 403.
17. Dudley, 405.
18. Dudley, 433.
19. Dreiser, Hey Rub-A-Dub-Dub, 133.
20. Dudley, 207.
21. Dreiser, Ev'ry Month, quoted in Yoshinobu Hakutani, "Theodore Dreiser's Editorial and Free-Lance Writing," The Library Chronicle 37 (Winter 1971) 80.
22. Dreiser, "The Salve Called Religion," Notes on Life, 278.
23. See, for example, Matthiessen, 73; Pizer, The Novels of Theodore Dreiser, 63.
24. Dreiser, "True Art Speaks Plainly," Sister Carrie, 473.
25. Dreiser, "The Problem of Genius," Notes on Life, 177-8.
26. Dreiser, Letters, 1: 183.
27. Pizer, The Novels of Theodore Dreiser, 137. Pizer, however, is only expressing a widely held view.
28. Edgar Lee Masters, "An American 'Genius,'" Chicago Evening Post (October 22 1915); rptd. in Jack Salzman, ed., Theodore Dreiser: The Critical Reception (David Lewis, New York, 1972) 221-2.
29. Dreiser, "Some Aspects of Our National Character," Hey Rub-A-Dub-Dub, 25, 54.

30. Dreiser, Hey Rub-A-Dub-Dub, 252.
31. Dreiser, "America and the Artist,"
Theodore Dreiser: A Selection of Uncollected
Prose, 236.
32. Duncan, Culture and Democracy: The
Struggle for Form in Society and Architecture in
Chicago and the Middle West during the Life and
Times of Louis H. Sullivan (The Bedminster Press,
New York, 1965) 580.
33. Helen Dreiser, My Life With Dreiser
(The World Publishing Company, Cleveland, 1951) 81.
34. Quoted in Swanberg, Dreiser, 176.
35. Dreiser, Letters, 1: 329.
36. Masters, "An American 'Genius,'" 222.
37. Quoted in Swanberg, 167.
38. Dreiser, Hey Rub-A-Dub-Dub, 105.
39. Quoted in Swanberg, 110.
40. Swanberg, 111, 114.
41. Quoted in Swanberg, 129.
42. Quoted in Dudley, 224.
43. H. L. Mencken, Letters, ed. Guy J.
Forgue (Alfred A. Knopf, New York, 1961) 339.
44. Marguerite Tjader, Theodore Dreiser: A
New Dimension (Silvermine Publishers, Inc.,
Norwalk, Conn., 1965) 2, 47.
45. Burton Rascoe, Theodore Dreiser (Robert
M. McBride & Company, New York, 1925) 57.
46. Dudley, 332, 391.
47. John I. H. Baur, Revolution and
Tradition in Modern American Art (Harvard
University Press, Cambridge, Mass., 1951) 15.
48. Mahonri Sharp Young, The Eight: The
Realist Revolt in American Painting (Watson-
Guptill Publications, New York, 1973) 143, 144,
154, 152. Dreiser's relationship with Shinn is
dealt with by Joseph J. Kwiat in "Dreiser's The
'Genius' and Everett Shinn, the 'Ash Can
Painter'," PMLA 67 (March 1952) 15-31. However,
Kwiat does not go into the implications of Shinn's
personal history, finding The "Genius" to be a
positive portrait.
49. Daniel Catton Rich, introduction, Charles
H. Morgan, George Bellows: "Painter of America"
(Reynal & Company, New York, 1965) 12; Homer
Saint-Gaudens, The American Artist and His Times
(Dodd, Mead & Company, New York, 1941) 203.
50. Lehan, 118.
51. Quoted in Dudley, 268.
52. Dreiser, Letters, 1: 347.
53. Dreiser, Letters, 2: 458.

54.   Quoted in Duncan, Communication and
Social Order, 368. The bestseller was Bruce
Barton's The Man Nobody Knows: A Discovery of
the Real Jesus (The Bobbs-Merrill Company,
Indianapolis, 1924).
55.   Duncan, Communication and Social Order,
363.
56.   Dreiser, Hey Rub-A-Dub-Dub, 132-3.
57.   Dreiser, Sister Carrie, 87.
58.   Quoted in Dudley, 451.
59.   Quoted in Dudley, 471-2.
60.   Dreiser, "The Mechanism Called Man,"
Notes on Life, 53, 57.
61.   Dreiser, Letters, 2: 756.
62.   Charles Child Walcutt, American Literary
Naturalism, A Divided Stream (University of
Minnesota Press, Minneapolis, 1956) 27.
63.   Quoted in Dudley, 292.
64.   Dreiser, Ev'ry Month, quoted in
Hakutani, 77.

Chapter Six

DREISER'S CONTEMPORARIES: SOME OTHER VOICES

The predominant social symbols of industrial America which were used to glorify the achievements of the wealthy by representing the pursuit of riches in the frame of a religious or heroic quest attracted many other novelists besides Dreiser. In this chapter, a few of their works are analysed in order to establish how widespread the reach of these symbols was in the national psyche. So far, the focus of this study has been on Dreiser's response to these manufactured symbols of glory. An attempt is made here to identify these symbols in the works of several other major writers of the period.

Their recurrence in these works calls into question the supposed loneliness of the American writer. It helps us place Dreiser in a tradition: as one who was acquainted with the works of his contemporaries, contrary to the popular view which presents him as one of the untutored, uncouth giants of American literature. The commonality of these symbols also casts doubt on the wisdom of the usual critical approach which too often deals with the texts as self-contained entities, without an historical context. The symbolic realm of the novel, according to this approach, is totally privatized, without any regard for the shared social experience of the writer. As I have already pointed out in the earlier chapters, this lack of interest in the historical experience leads to gross misrepresentations. That happens because we fail to take into account the prospective audience of the writer's discourse. And yet we all know what happens when a third party tries to make sense of a dialogue without having access to all the facts. If we want to understand these texts better than we do now, we must find out who is the adversary the author is ridiculing or, conversely, the hero he is glamorizing. And does this hero or adversary have a justificatory vocabulary which the author appropriates in order to reject or accept it?

The present chapter, it is expected, will clarify these issues. Since the purpose is illustrative rather than historical, I have been selective in my choice of texts. My selection has been influenced by the reputation of the novelists and the present availability of the texts. The order of discussion is chronological.

William Dean Howells is perhaps the first American novelist of stature to deal with the new cultural hero in The Rise of Silas Lapham. That was how William Morton Payne, a fellow novelist who later wrote The Money Captain, felt: "It is almost a new species of work - one which might be styled the business man's novel."(1) However, one can see that Howells' originality consists not so much in the subject as in its treatment. As Edwin Cady points out, the novel is "Horatio Alger upside down".(2) Curious are the ways in which popular literature generates the highbrow variety!

The novel touches upon the popular rags to riches myth in all its attendant associations in the American mind. As early as 1869 Howells had been aware of the myth's powerful hold on the American mind. In his review of the autobiography of Horace Greeley, who is referred to in The Rise of Silas Lapham as one of Lapham's favourite writers, Howells wrote that "the history of a man's rise from poverty and obscurity to distinction" was a "perpetual romance", which "delights and touches all, for in this nation it is in some degree the story of every man's life or the vision of his desires."(3)

Romance, of course, was Howells' arch enemy. He felt that it filled people with harmful desires and led them away from a meaningful confrontation with reality. It was false, immoral, egotistical, and detrimental to the spirit of a democratic society. The Rise of Silas Lapham reflects these concerns. The novel examines the dominant ideology and its manifestation in the individual. Proclaiming that the novelists "must examine anew the springs of action, the grounds of conviction",(4) Howells goes beyond the individual actions of characters to relate them to the deeply ingrained cultural beliefs. The self-made man is scrutinized in terms of his psychological motivation, his high self-esteem, his complex links with religion, and his relationship with the society as role model, judge and mentor.

The opening chapter of the novel is a master-stroke of genius. With great economy and tremendous pointedness, Howells succeeds in making us see the process of image-building itself. Even before we are introduced to Silas Lapham, the private citizen, we are presented with his public image, as one in a series of portraits which appears in The Events, the major evening newspaper of Boston, under the title "Solid Men of Boston" [1]. The express purpose of the series is to "encourage the youthful reader to go and do likewise" [5].

As becomes apparent from Bartley Hubbard's irreverent conversation with Lapham, the column always follows a fixed format in which the life of the successful businessman is cast in the shape of a Pilgrim's Progress. Lapham, obviously, has already read a good many of them. For when he is approached by Hubbard, he asks, without any opening remarks, "so you want my life, death, and Christian sufferings, do you, young man?" [3]. Like the protagonist of a typical rags to riches story, Lapham was born on a country farm, the ideal place according to the myth. However, just when he is warming up to the theme, the impatient Hubbard who has obviously read and written piles of these interviews, cuts in: "Worked in the fields summers and went to school winters: regulation thing?" He continues to fill in the details to the consternation of Lapham, "Parents poor, of course. . . . Any barefoot business? Early deprivations of any kind, that would encourage the youthful reader to go and do likewise? Orphan myself, you know" [5]. When Lapham gets angry at this point, refusing to cooperate further if Hubbard makes a "joke" of his life, Hubbard assures him that "it'll come out all right". And so it does:

> "Mr. Lapham," he wrote, "passed rapidly over the story of his early life, its poverty and its hardships, sweetened, however, by the recollections of a devoted mother, and a father who, if somewhat her inferior in education, was no less ambitious for the advancement of his children. They were quiet, unpretentious people, religious, after the

> fashion of that time, and of sterling
> morality, and they taught their children the
> simple virtues of the Old Testament and Poor
> Richard's Almanac." [5]

It is interesting to note that the "simple virtues
of the Old Testament and Poor Richard's Almanac"
are not upheld by either Howells or Hubbard. In
fact, the remark is a "gibe" on Hubbard's part. It
is the intellectual's revenge against having been
forced to kowtow to the powerful: "he trusted to
Lapham's unliterary habit of mind for his security
in making it, and most other people would consider
it sincere reporter's rhetoric" [5]. The portrait
of Lapham is his way of getting even with his
masters who control his pen and yet who do not have
the ability to penetrate his sarcasm. He works on
the article with a great deal of "inward derision"
[21], being forced to write about Lapham's "boyish
trials and struggles" [5], while he must not say
anything about Lapham's garish advertisements which
deface the local landscape and cause a great deal
of unpleasantness to the cultural elite of Boston.
Nor must he write anything about Lapham's ousted
partner, for this is Lapham's sore point: "Lapham
dropped the bold blue eyes with which he had been
till now staring into Bartley's face, and the
reporter knew that here was a place for asterisks
in his interview, if interviews were faithful"
[16-7]. The finished portrait conforms admirably
to the stereotype. Lapham has been reduced to a
figure in a morality play. The interview, instead
of giving the reader a personal glimpse of Lapham,
comes out as a sermon, or rather, a parable for the
young reader:

> Simple, clear, bold, and straightforward, in
> mind and action, Colonel Silas Lapham, with a
> prompt comprehensiveness and a never-failing
> business sagacity, is, in the best sense of
> that much-abused term, one of nature's
> noblemen, to the last inch of his five eleven
> and a half. His life affords an example of
> single-minded application and unwavering
> perseverance which our young businessmen would
> do well to emulate. There is nothing showy or
> meretricious about the man. He believes in
> mineral paint, and he puts his heart and soul
> into it. He makes it a religion; though we
> would not imply that it _is_ his religion.

[20]

The business activity has become "spiritualized". It has become, as the nineteenth century churchmen of America preached, "My Father's business".(5) The work of the world has fused the transcendent realm of the spirit and the material realm of daily life. Lapham's words are charged with emotional intensity whenever he speaks of his business: "I believe in my paint. I believe it's a blessing to the world. When folks come in, and kind of smell round, and ask me what I mix it with, I always say, 'Well, in the first place, I mix it with _Faith_, and after that I grind it up with the best quality of boiled linseed oil that money will buy'" [17]. The selling of paint, according to this philosophy, is a religious act; a sure way to reach God. This investiture of business in a spiritual garb is even more apparent in Lapham's conversation with Tom Corey. Lapham is "deeply moved" when Tom praises his paint, "'It's the best paint in God's universe,' he said, with the solemnity of prayer." Tom Corey, of course, strips it of its transcendental pretensions: "'It's the best in the market,' said Corey; and he repeated, 'I believe in it'" [76]. For Lapham, business is the expression of his godliness; for Corey, just a way of making a living.

As a way of conveying his double-edged view of Silas Lapham, Howells could not have hit upon a more convenient device than Bartley Hubbard's interview. It allows him to go beyond the individual and pass judgement on a whole social class which is so proud of its achievements. It also enables Howells to convey this society's vision of ideal life in its own terms. The irony is subtle. Despite all its power, the business community is made the butt of ridicule by the literary man in precisely the language it usually reserves for eulogizing itself.

Silas Lapham and his compatriots consider themselves "risen Americans" [5] and have given proof of their virtue. The defence of riches in the interview is consistently religious. The social Darwinistic arguments used by the later advocates, with their concomitant imagery of the battlefield and the jungle are conspicuously absent. The world of 1875 Boston is predominantly religious. Lapham's wealth, the "Solid Men of

Boston" series implies, is due to his "Christian sufferings" [3], his Franklinian virtues of "single-minded application and unwavering perseverance" [20].

The reader here is confronted with a paradox. If Silas Lapham is already "risen" by page 6, what does the title mean? For it implies that he will "rise" through the course of the novel. The reader is led to conclude that there is a discrepancy between society's view of what constitutes rising and the novelist's. This view is reinforced by Howells' own comments. In his synopsis of the novel, he wrote: "His after . . . life of adversity from which he does not recover, is sketched. The reader is made to feel that this adversity, consciously and deliberately chosen, is The Rise of Silas Needham."(6) Elsewhere, Howells again stressed this metaphorical juxtaposition of the upward and downward ways:

> I was always fond of Lapham and fonder still of his wife, though I did not realize her so directly from life; he seemed to me of the lasting boyishness which keeps the hearts of Americans sweet. Then, he was finding out, against his selfish ambition and temptations, what a true rise was, and I was following him with pride and joy.(7)

The novel, in Howells' terms, is a discourse against the official view of worth. The article in The Events cleverly polarizes the conflicting viewpoints and generates the narrative tension. It encapsulates a vein of American thought, that troublesome equation in Puritan theology which resulted, ultimately, in establishing the pursuit of wealth as the only way of reaching God. As Lapham himself knows, his life has no meaning apart from his money: "I guess you wouldn't want my life without the money" [3], he says to Hubbard. Also significant is the fact that "the money" is important as a religious symbol in only one sense; and that is determined by how it was earned. If it does not epitomize the virtuous journey from rags to riches, the "regulation thing" [5], it is worthless. In other words, it is symbolic of man's Christian virtues, a proof that he has travelled through the perilous path unscathed.

The novel begins with the presentation of this view, examines it through the course of the

narrative and ends by discarding it. There is a
beautiful symmetry in the structure of the novel.
The first and the last chapters mirror themselves.
The first chapter gives us an uncritical view of
how words like "rise", "trials", "blessing", and
"faith" are used. In the last chapter, the same
words are used, but in a totally different context.
The first chapter presents Lapham as an example
worthy of emulation. For Sewell, however, Lapham's
character becomes a "moral spectacle" [363] only
after he loses his fortune. The first chapter
shows that the world respects only the "trials"
which one has supposedly faced in the accumulation
of wealth. In the last paragraph of the novel, we
are told that not the accumulation but "the loss of
his fortune had been a terrible trial" [365]. The
first chapter portrays Lapham's "rise" as parallel
to the discovery of his paint at "the bottom of a
hole" [20]. The same imagery is used in the last
paragraph of the novel to denote Lapham's true
"rise". "Well," he says, "it don't always seem as
if I done it. . . . Seems sometimes as if it was a
hole opened for me, and I crept out of it" [365].

This scrutiny of accepted meanings begins very
early in the novel. Chapter III provides a glimpse
of the actual operations of Lapham's business, the
unethical way in which he had unloaded his partner.
In Chapter IV, the narrator provides his view of
the matter:

> As he said, Lapham had dealt fairly by his
> partner in money; he had let Rogers take more
> money out of the business than he had put into
> it; he had, as he said, simply forced out of
> it a timid and inefficient participant in
> advantages which he had created. But Lapham
> had not created them all. He had been
> dependent at one time on his partner's
> capital. It was a moment of terrible trial.
> Happy is the man forever after who can choose
> the ideal, the unselfish part in such an
> exigency! Lapham could not rise to it. [50]

Howells assiduously breaks the assumed connection
of wealth with moral rectitude. Nineteenth century
America believed that wealth was the blessing of
God. Howells believed that "there is no system of
favoritism by which a moral man can commend himself
above a sinner to God's love."(8) He blasted the
philosophy which attributes "to the father of all a

design in the injustice we have ourselves created."
(9) The novel posits an inverse ratio between
wealth and religiosity. The decrease of material
possessions is followed by a heightened moral
awareness on Lapham's part. With the progress of
the novel, Lapham realizes that God does not
necessarily shower His blessings in the shape of
riches. When the English party makes an offer for
his land through his ex-partner Rogers, Mrs. Lapham
thinks that the chance has come through
"Providence". Lapham, however, knows better: "I
guess it wasn't _Providence_ raised it up" [279].
Later, he attributes it to the devil.

In the first trial, Lapham had failed to "rise
to it". The subsequent trials find him ready. Left
to his own resources, he passes the test
brilliantly. His wife realizes that "the simple,
rude soul to which her heart clove in her youth,
but which she had put to such cruel proof with her
unsparing conscience and her unsparing tongue, had
been equal to its ordeals, and had come out
unscathed and unstained" [350-1]. It seems as
though Howells was trying to restore the abused
words to their proper sphere. The novel reestablishes the traditional hierarchy of values
where salvation is the topmost concern and
acquisitiveness the most venal sin.

Howells felt that true religion had
disappeared from America. In _A Modern Instance_,
the narrator blasts the "worldly tendencies of the
church" in modern America.(10) Squire Gaylord, who
represents the original brand of Puritanism, calls
the modern church "the Mammon of Righteousness"
[33]. It has diluted its religion to suit the weak
stomachs of the new generation:

> Religion there had largely ceased to be a fact
> of spiritual experience and the visible church
> flourished on condition of providing for the
> social needs of the community. It was
> practically held that the salvation of one's
> soul must not be made too depressing, or the
> young people would have nothing to do with it.
> Professors of the sternest creeds temporized
> with sinners, and did what might be done to
> win them to heaven by helping them to have a
> good time here. [24]

It is this church that has sanctified the wealthy
as the stewards of the Lord.

Lapham's sin is self-pride and a contempt for other approaches to life. This Howells felt to be the reigning attitude of Puritanism. Himself a Swedenborgian, he found Puritanism cold and self-righteous:

[T]he wish to be sincere, the wish to be just, the wish to be righteous are before the wish to be kind, merciful, humble. A People are not a chosen people for half a dozen generations without acquiring a spiritual pride that remains with them long after they cease to believe themselves chosen. They are often stiffened in the neck and they are often hardened in the heart by it, to the point of making them angular and cold; but they are of an inveterate responsibility to a power higher than themselves, and they are strengthened for any fate.(11)

In Howells' eyes, Lapham sins through self-pride and a lack of sensitivity towards the sufferings of others. Though he gratefully provides for the indigent family of the man who had saved his life in the Civil War, it does not make him think of the widespread poverty around him. The dinner scene brings out this limitation of Lapham's mind which hardens him towards the deprivations of the poor. As Daniel Aaron points out, Howells, though unwilling to include the blunt and the shocking, "dearly loved the edged remark casually dropped in the parlor".(12) When Corey Senior remarks about the injustice of the empty mansions while the poor rot in the crowded slums and expresses surprise as to why the poor do not occupy (Howells had used "dynamite" in the manuscript version) these houses, Lapham "wanted to speak up and say that he had been there himself, and knew how such a man felt. He wanted to tell them that generally a poor man was satisfied if he could make both ends meet; that he didn't envy any one his good luck, if he had earned it, so long as he wasn't running under himself" [194-5].

Talking about the lack of compassion in the self-made men, Howells once wrote: "The self-made man, when he has made himself of money, seems to have been deformed by his original destitution, and I think that if I were in need I would rather take my chance of pity from the man who had never been poor." True to this dictum, Bromfield Corey shows

175

more concern for the poor. As to Lapham's
statement that the poor did not get upset by the
display of wealth, Howells believed the opposite to
be true: "the superiority around him . . . puts the
poor man to shame at every turn in life, though
some people, with an impudence that is pitiable,
will tell you that it does not put him to shame;
that he feels himself as good as any one."(13)

Lapham is so preoccupied with his own
achievements, he is always talking about his
journey from poverty to wealth. As Tom Corey says,
"he hasn't got over being surprised at the effect
of rubbing his lamp" [67]. He is always judging
others by his standards. He is extremely critical
of the Coreys for not hustling in the market.
Lapham's sense of his own superiority as well as
the values which uphold it are conveyed to us in a
conversation between him and Corey Senior.

> And you can't ever tell what's in you till you
> try. Why, when I started this thing, I didn't
> more than half understand my own strength. I
> wouldn't have said, looking back, that I could
> have stood the wear and tear of what I've been
> through. But I developed as I went along.
> It's just like exercising your muscles in a
> gymnasium. You can lift twice or three times
> as much after you've been in training a month
> as you could before. And I can see that it's
> going to be just so with your son. His going
> through college won't hurt him, - he'll soon
> slough all that off, - and his bringing up
> won't; don't be anxious about it. [142]

Apparently, Lapham knew his Franklin, who believed
that one's moral muscles grew through exercise, and
the proper exercise, of course, was the
accumulation of wealth. This is, as it were, the
metaphysics of business. Business is said to
"develop" character, inculcate "strength". From
"the pride which comes of self-making" [108],
Lapham judges the Coreys and finds them somewhat
immoral: "My note of hand would be worth ten times
what Bromfield Corey's is on the street to-day. And
I made _my_ money. I haven't loafed my life away"
[120].

Every time Lapham speaks, he casts his life in
terms of metaphors of becoming, of process. He
speaks from the vantage point of a man who has
arrived somewhere. The drama of Lapham's life is

more than one of simple upward mobility, which was
the only way in which the Europeans understood the
efforts of the _parvenu_. To the American man of
wealth, making money represents a process of
character formation, a process of _achieving_
manhood. Only business, Lapham thinks, can build
character: "I could make a man of that fellow, if I
had him in the business with me. There's stuff in
him" [58-9]. According to the businessman,
business is the only way one can reach one's
potential. Manhood is an earned state, acquired
only in one specific way. Every man "should want to
strike out and do something for [him]self" [58].
Money must be earned even though one does not need
it or has inherited it. "I don't like the
principle. I like to see a man _act_ like a man",
Lapham tells his daughter who tries to defend
Corey's "idleness" on the ground of inherited
wealth [58]. Thus, the earning of money is not
simply an essential activity but an absolute. The
novel undercuts this premise by suggesting that
only through his return to poverty does Lapham
regain "the manhood which his prosperity had so
nearly stolen from him" [359].

Incessant work, according to this faith, was
the surest armour against the devil. Activity in a
worldly "calling", said Cotton Mather, was the
second oar of the boat in which a man rowed towards
heaven. In other words, Americans associated
ceaseless activity with heavenward movement. The
implications are most clearly pointed out by Henry
Blake Fuller in a novel admired by Howells. In
With the Procession this total occupation with
work is symbolized as a blindfolded journey on a
road with high walls on both sides with a heavy
burden on one's back.(14) It is only in this light
that we can understand Lapham's smug self-pride. He
scorns leisure: "Well, say I'm fifty-five years
old; and I've _lived_ 'em, too: not an hour of waste
time about _me_, anywheres!" [4]. Tom Corey's life
seems to Lapham to be one of immobility and
indirection: "Now, I suppose that fellow belongs to
two or three clubs, and hangs around 'em all day,
lookin' out the window, - I've seen 'em, - instead
of tryin' to hunt up something to do for an honest
livin'" [58]. The phrase "hangs around" is
repeated three times on this page.

Tom Corey says, "I suppose his range of ideas
is limited" [67]. Lapham has no use for "a more
searching intellectual activity", "a grander social

life", or "art and literature" [66], things the
Coreys appreciate. Lapham has invested his emotions
in his mineral paint. As Corey Senior puts it
rather ironically, the mineral paint business
requires the sense of a "deep inward vocation"
[68]. The Coreys also hint towards the other, more
recent metaphor of success in business. This is
the metaphor of adventure: "But there's no doubt
but money is to the fore now. It is the romance,
the poetry of our age. It's the thing that chiefly
strikes the imagination" [64]. Tom Corey feels
that the vulgarity of business is camouflaged by
decking it in metaphors: "And I don't know that it
was vulgar. Perhaps his successful strokes of
business were the romance of his life -" [66].
Though the Coreys speak of it in their usual
ironical style, the metaphor of romance was a
serious matter to the business community. The
dialogue also points out Howells' attitude to the
businessman. Romance was anathema to Howells. He
disliked its "muscular ideals", its tendency to
picture "duels and battles" as "the great and
prevalent human events". And he felt there was some
truth to the argument that the popularity of the
"tarradiddles of the historical romancers" had
something to do with "the accumulation of riches"
in the country.(15)

The Rise of Silas Lapham is Howells'
protest against the tendency to romanticize
business. He gives the favourite vocabulary of the
businessman an ironic treatment. And he shows that
Lapham's true "rise" can occur only when he has
fallen in the eyes of the world. However, this
"rise" is valuable only to the novelist. The false
self, the self of pride and worldly achievement, is
good copy for The Events and masquerades as an
example of true Christianity. Howells has given a
detailed picture of the operations of The Events
in A Modern Instance. Setting its policies
according to the dictates of the counting-room,
this novel tells us, it not only gives corrupt
businessmen "the benefit of the doubt" [194], it
glorifies them by casting their lives in the mould
of the Christian drama of the soul's journey
towards God.

There is evidence to suggest that the process
of writing The Rise of Silas Lapham left Howells
deeply disturbed. Even though he managed to arrive
at an acceptable resolution, he was perhaps
bothered by the tensions that the novel leaves

unresolved. Though Lapham is purged, The Events, that epitome of what A Modern Instance calls "counting-room" journalism [159], remains. The novelist cannot drive it out of existence. That feeling of impotence was, perhaps, the reason for his mysterious nervous breakdown in 1884. Twelve years later, he told an intimate friend about it:

> Howells' socialism is an answer to grave questions which have arisen in the author's own mind; it is offered as a partial solution of problems which he found confronting himself, compelling attention, refusing to be curtly dismissed. They made their demands - these questions - when Mr. Howells was writing Silas Lapham in the late summer and fall of 1884. His affairs prospering, his work marching as well as his heart could wish, suddenly, and without apparent cause, the status seemed wholly wrong. His expression, in speaking about that time, was, "The bottom dropped out!"(16)

The novel was supposed to prophesy a new, saner type of life through the marriage of Penelope and Tom. Penelope, we feel sure, will never hanker after status and Tom will never exalt business to the realm of romance. However, it seems that this optimism was eclipsed by the presence of The Events in the novel. It seems especially menacing if one comes to the novel via A Modern Instance. The Events is a great source of corruption in the social life of its time. In its power to manufacture myths and convey them to "the young reader", it casts a pall on the innocent world of the novel. Perhaps Howells was not sure that the "force . . . 'which works for righteousness'"(17) to which he attributed Lapham's regeneration, was really operative in contemporary America. His optimism about the efficiency of personal reform must have gone hollow at some point for he failed to incorporate into the novel the image he had transcribed in his notebook: "the young trees growing out of the falling logs in the forest - the new life out of the old. Apply to Lapham's fall." (18) He may have realized that the mild irony of the Austenian comedy of manners that he had chosen as his vehicle in this novel was not a strong enough anodyne for the moral blight he wanted to cleanse.

Yet, for all its shortcomings, <u>The Rise of Silas Lapham</u> remains an impressive achievement. In its honest scrutiny of the canonized millionaires, it brought to the fore the processes of glorification through which the dominant class of a society anoints itself. By choosing a theme which had been so grossly inflated in the popular literature, and treating it anti-romantically, Howells provided a much-needed corrective. The novel is invaluable for the insights it provides into the mind of nineteenth century America.

Howells' radical departure from the conventional opinion of the time becomes even more notable when contrasted with the arch conservatism of George Horace Lorimer. The editor of the once prestigious <u>Saturday Evening Post</u> is scarcely recognized today for his literary achievement. However, two out of the three novels he wrote made the best sellers list at the time. Of course, best sellers need not always be good literature and Lorimer might remain happily obscure if that were the only consideration. However, Lorimer in his role as editor of the <u>Post</u> can scarcely be ignored by a student of American culture. He made the magazine "an American institution",(19) a forum which American presidents, robber barons and other practitioners of words shared together, some lured by the opportunity for big money and others by their desire to reach its three million-strong readership. His critics, usually the intellectuals, charged that the <u>Post</u> literature was produced on the principles of the assembly line, calling Lorimer the "Henry Ford of American literature".(20) And yet, the lure of the gold was so strong that many of them condescended to submit their wares to the autocratic editor. The sales figures show that the editor's taste became synonymous with the taste of middle America. As his biographer remarks:

Lorimer left an indelible mark on his times. He was the articulate voice of millions, the purveyor of entertainment, advice, and political sentiment to a considerable body of Americans. . . . He was a man whom nine Presidents of the United States recognized as the potent spokesman for a sizable block of voters, and whom thousands of writers, both famous and unknown, looked upon as a god. Lorimer was the <u>Post</u> and the <u>Post</u> was

Lorimer.(21)

The wares this "American institution" offered
to its readers - the professed aim was to reach the
"ambitious young men of the great middle-class
American public" - were composed of three elements:
"business, public affairs, and romance". These,
according to Frank Luther Mott, "dominated the
subject matter and ideology of the magazine".

> These overlapped and mingled. Thus business
> articles tended to emphasize the romance of
> large fortunes and the rise of a young man
> from the bottom of the ladder to the topmost
> rung of millionaireship. . . . Even the
> romantic fiction was often based on financial
> deals and the pursuit of wealth.(22)

Beginning with the very first issue of the Post
under his editorship, Lorimer made business the
main focus of his magazine. The Post regularly
published series like these: "American Kings and
Their Kingdoms", "How I Made My First Thousand
Dollars", and "Why Young Men Should Begin at the
Bottom".

What Lorimer considered the "romance of
business"(23) was denounced by his detractors as
crass materialism. Upton Sinclair accused him of
believing that "the one virtue of man is to produce
larger and larger quantities of material things",
that "the masters of world capitalism are
benevolent supermen engaged in conferring the
blessings of civilization upon the inferior races,
but having their efforts imperiled by evil-minded
intriguers called 'reds.'"(24)

Though the truth of Sinclair's allegations
cannot be denied, Lorimer has to be credited for
writing the first novel which concentrated entirely
on the businessman. Howells had seen him in his
relation to the family, as a parvenu in the comedy
of manners. The businessman-protagonist of
Lorimer's Letters From a Self-Made Merchant to His
Son is the apotheosis of perfection. He is the
standard bearer of values, a beacon of inspiration
for the young people who write to him for advice.
He is the Solid Man of the Events series, seen
without the Howellsian framework of irony.

In his homely wisdom, his love of proverbial
phrases, and his role as moral educator, Lorimer's
hero resembles Franklin to a great extent. Lorimer

can be said to be indebted to Franklin even in the
choice of his format. Franklin had written the
Autobiography with the purpose of pointing out to
his son the possibility of self-making. Lorimer's
novel consists of a collection of letters from a
father to his son on the same theme. It contains a
great deal of autobiographical information which is
supposed to set an example for the son. In terms
of their appeal to their audience too, Lorimer and
Franklin are similar. The Letters From a Self-Made
Merchant to His Son and Old Gorgon Graham were both
best sellers.(25) Tebbel relates that the first
novel "became a simultaneous bestseller in the
United States, England, and Germany; it was later
translated into a dozen languages, and survived for
more than forty years, more generally circulated in
all parts of the world than any book of American
authorship since Uncle Tom's Cabin."(26)

The novel's success has to be attributed to
its perfect fit with the dominant ideology. It put
together the prevailing ethos of America in an
extremely readable form. Indeed, grateful fathers
wrote to Lorimer about the miraculous reformation
the novel had caused in the character of their
sons. The novel is remarkable not only for its
originality but for its deep allegiance to the
gospel of wealth. This trait, which can be called
its Americanness, becomes even clearer when we
recall some famous letter-writers of the past.
Walter Raleigh, Francis Osborne and Lord
Chesterfield did not suppose that success in the
worldly realm had anything to do with the spirit.
However, in the case of Lorimer's businessman, they
are harmonized so perfectly that the pursuit of
wealth becomes the only way of reaching God. There
is no grubby materialism about John Graham. Money
is not earned for its own sake. It is justified in
terms of the good life, "the right path" [3].

The word "calling" acts as the bridge between
the material and the spiritual. Wealth for Graham
comes by being diligent in one's "calling". The
material and the celestial are part of the same
continuum for him, just as they are for his
favourite preacher, Henry Ward Beecher. Here there
is no duality between the godly and the worldly,
the monastery and the marketplace. Avarice need
not be condemned since God himself ordained it.
According to Beecher, "The constitution of man, and
of society, alike evinces the design of God. Both
are made to be happier by the possession of

riches."(27)   The   pursuit   of   wealth   is   mandatory
according   to   this   philosophy,   both   as   a   shield
against   the   temptation   of   the   Devil   and   as   a
positive means of achieving grace.

John   Graham's   world   is   permeated   with   God's
presence.   How   close   the   identification   is   in   his
mind   between   his   way   and   God's   will   is   clear   from
his   language,   which   bridges   the   two   spheres   by
interchanging   their   vocabulary.   God   is   described
in   mercantilist   terms   whereas   business   absorbs   the
aura of scripture. To give some examples:

> The   Lord   let   us   in   on   the   ground   floor,   gave
> us   corner   lots,   and   then   started   in   to   improve
> the adjacent property. [30-1]

> Sausage   is   the   one   subject   of   all   others   that
> a   fellow   in   the   packing   business   ought   to
> treat solemnly. [127]

> You've   got   to   believe   that   the   Lord   made   the
> first   hog   with   the   Graham   brand   burned   in   the
> skin. . . . [142]

> You've   got   to   feel   the   same   personal
> solicitude   over   a   bill   of   goods   that   strays
> off   to   a   competitor   as   a   parson   over   a
> backslider,   and   hold   special   services   to   bring
> it back into the fold. [143]

He   visualizes   the   soul   in   the   image   of   a   department
store,   the   sins   and   virtues   being   the   damaged   or
fresh   goods   on   the   shelves.   And   he   measures   his
spiritual health by a regular stock-taking.

Unlike   the   merchants   of   the   Middle   Ages   who,
according   to   Tawney,   made   special   efforts   to
placate   God   on   their   deathbed,   Graham   believes
himself   to   be   a   pious   man.   He   thinks   he   runs   his
business   according   to   the   Ten   Commandments.   He
says   in   Old Gorgon Graham   that   his   "immortal
soul" [20]   is   uppermost   in   his   concerns.   He   is
very   generous   to   charities   and   very   active   in
church.

Letters   makes   clear   the   logic   he   uses   to
harmonize   the   two   spheres.   It   tries   to   justify
John   Graham's   ways   to   his   son.   The   son,
Pierrepont,   is   the   intractable   material   whose
objectionable   behaviour   furnishes   Graham   with   a
"text"   from   time   to   time. The purpose behind the
letters   is   to   point   out   "the   straight   and   narrow

path" [205] to the son. Though the letters seem to
the reader to concern themselves with driving
Pierrepont to a desk in his father's business,
Graham believes that he is discoursing about his
son's "immortal soul".

The "straight and narrow path", we are told,
passes through the Stock Yards John Graham owns.
The journey for the novice must begin at the
bottom:

> The only sure way that a man can get rich
> quick is to have it given to him or to inherit
> it. You are not going to get rich that way -
> at least, not until after you have proved your
> ability to hold a pretty important position
> with the firm; and, of course, there is just
> one place from which a man can start for that
> position with Graham & Co. . . . That place is
> the bottom. [16]

Pierrepont must "work up" to the top and the novel
relates many instances of the dangers of inherited
wealth. When one takes an "elevator" [17] or
"balloon" to the top, the result is destruction.
"Hot air can take up a balloon a long ways, but it
can't keep it there. . . . But in the end there
always comes a time when the parachute fails to
work. I don't know anything that's quite so dead
as a man who's fallen three or four thousand feet
off the edge of a cloud" [245].

The best way to reach the "top" is to "climb".
"The path isn't the shortest way to the top, but
it's usually the safest way." "Life isn't a spurt,
but a long, steady climb" [245-6]. Some people,
Graham says in Old Gorgon Graham, like to "ride
through life on the bumpers of a freight" [255],
rather than strenuously climb up the desired path.
He considers them "hoboes". As the imagery shows,
Graham is very suspicious of any mechanical means
of ascent. Those who get bogged down in bookish
knowledge, learning seven foreign languages instead
of doing some "useful" work, are chastized thus:
"These fellows forget that while life's a journey,
it isn't a palace-car trip for most of us, and that
if they hit the trail packing a lot of weight for
which they haven't any special use, they're not
going to get very far" [157-8]. He hopes that his
son is not one of these reprobates.

That the climbing which Graham is talking

about is not arrivism - a climbing on the social pyramid - but a spiritual ascent becomes clear from the way it is equated in Letters with moral growth:

> Once a fellow's got the primary business virtues cemented into his character, he's safe to build on. [72]

> It isn't the little extra money that you may make for the house by learning the fundamental business virtues which counts so much as it is the effect that it has on your character and that of those about you. [77]

The thought is pursued in Old Gorgon Graham as well:

> Young men are told that the first thousand dollars comes hard and that after that it comes easier. So it does - just a thousand dollars plus interest easier; and easier through all the increased efficiency that self-denial and self-control have given you, and the larger salary they've made you worth. [271-2]

Throughout Letters and its sequel, moral categories are used to differentiate between the rich and the poor, the "captain of industry", and the "private". Thus, we note in Old Gorgon Graham that in Graham's rational world, a man's place in the corporate hierarchy is the index of his virtue.

> If anything unusually good happens, there's an unusually good man behind it, and he ought to be earmarked for promotion; and if anything unusually bad happens, there's apt to be an unusually bad man behind that, and he's a candidate for a job with another house. [204]

Letters reveals how the age reconciled the tenets of Christianity with those of social Darwinism:

> It's been my experience that pride is usually a spur to the strong and a drag on the weak. It drives the strong man along and holds the weak one back. It makes the fellow with the stiff upper lip and the square jaw smile at a laugh and laugh at a sneer; it keeps his conscience straight and his back humped over

185

his work; it makes him appreciate the little
things and fight for the big ones. But it
makes the fellow with the retreating forehead
do the thing that looks right, instead of the
thing that is right; . . . it makes him live
today on tomorrow's salary; it makes him a
cheap imitation of some Willie who has a
little more money than he has, without giving
him zip enough to go out and force luck for
himself. [251-2]

The "strong" are the ones who can resist the
temptations of the flesh. However, they are also
the fighters in the vocabulary of the "romance of
business" Lorimer was so enamoured of. The novel
is replete with the imagery of warfare. The world
of business is a tough, predatory world:
"Naturally, a young man who expects to hold his own
when he is thrown in with a lot of men like these
must be as clean and sharp as a hound's tooth, or
some other fellow's simply going to eat him up"
[32]. "I can give you a start, but after that you
will have to dynamite your way to the front by
yourself" [17].
    The dominating framework of reference,
however, is religious. The "strong" are also the
"good". And the goodness is measured periodically
in the shape of the increased pay cheque. "[A] boy
that's no good has learned just how little work he
can do and keep his job" [60]. Such people never
climb:

[T]hey will never climb over the railing that
separates the clerks from the executives. Yet
if they would put in half the time thinking
for the house that they give up to hatching
out reasons why they ought to be allowed to
overdraw their salary accounts, I couldn't
keep them out of our private offices with a
pole-ax, and I wouldn't want to; for they
could double their salaries and my profits in
a year. But I always lay it down as a safe
proposition that the fellow who has to break
open the baby's bank toward the last of the
week for car-fare isn't going to be any
Russell Sage when it comes to trading with the
old man's money. [22-3]

Earlier, Graham had made clear that the people who
have to break open the baby's bank are the ones who

come late and leave early and who buy drinks for
their friends. Conviviality is a dangerous vice
for Graham because it "takes up a heap of time"
[41].

The workers at the bottom are either the
beginners, who will eventually go up, or those who
have been proven to be no good. They are never
judged in such secular terms as inefficiency or
lack of training. Their faults are in the moral
realm. Under Graham's stewardship, many are
persuaded to lead, according to the sequel, "a
better life" [203]. If men stray off the right
path, the fault, Graham says in the sequel, lies
with their employers:

> The chances are that, to start with, Tom and
> Dick were honest and good at the office and
> sincere at the Sunday-school, and that, given
> the right circumstances, they would have
> stayed so. It was their employers' business
> to see that they were surrounded by the right
> circumstances at the office and to find out
> whether they surrounded themselves with them
> at home. [258]

"Right circumstances" at the office are provided by
seeing to it that the employees are giving their
best to the job. They are not to steal any time
for personal use and not to do any job half-
heartedly, however mean it may be. Graham says in
Letters that "right circumstances" at home have a
contributory effect on a man's life at his job.

> A married man is worth more salary than a
> single one, because his wife makes him worth
> more. He's apt to go to bed a little sooner
> and to get up a little earlier; to go a little
> steadier and to work a little harder than the
> fellow who's got to amuse a different girl
> every night, and can't stay at home to do it.
> That's why I'm going to quit writing these
> letters - I'm simply going to turn you over to
> her and let her keep you in order. [311-2]

Performance on the job, then, should be the
ultimate concern of a man's life. Incessant
activity is the only path to virtue. The earning
of money has become an absolute.

If a man's earning capacity denotes the state
of his moral health, it goes without saying that

John Graham will have to be regarded as one of the
healthiest. His fortune proves that he has adhered
strictly to the process of character building he is
recommending to his son. As a self-made man, he
started his business in a shanty and has expanded
it to the extent of half a mile of factories and
ten thousand employees. We are to believe that all
this has been achieved by practising the Ten
Commandments. We are also to believe that the
material prosperity is the index of moral growth.
"A fellow is a boss simply because he's a better
man than those under him, and there's a heap of
responsibility in being better than the next
fellow", he says in Letters [212]. And in the
sequel he remarks that being a millionaire entails
stewardship:

> Being a millionaire is a trade like a doctor's
> - you must work up through every grade of
> earning, saving, spending and giving, or
> you're no more fit to be trusted with a
> fortune than a quack with human life. For
> there's no trade in the world, except the
> doctor's, on which the lives and happiness of
> so many people depend as the millionaire's;
> and I might add that there's no other in which
> there's so much malpractice. [196]

He is sure that business founded on dishonesty
ultimately smashes up. On the whole it is a pretty
rational world where, he says elsewhere in the
sequel, virtue and vice meet their just rewards.

> Whenever you hear of a man's jumping suddenly
> into prominence and fortune, look behind the
> popular explanation of a lucky chance. You'll
> usually find that these men manufactured their
> own luck right on the premises by years of
> slow preparation, and are simply realizing on
> hard work. [275]

In other words, all millionaires whose businesses
show no signs of smashing up have made it by
practising Christian virtues. To follow his theory
further, the pursuit of this fortune has had a
remarkable impact on their character. Graham tells
his son in Letters that "I have no fears for you
after you've been at work for a few years" [54].
His own character has been built that way. At his
present position on the moral pyramid, he has to be

188

even more watchful of his actions. "The farther you go, the straighter you've got to walk" [180]. "[A] man can't do what he pleases in this world, because the higher he climbs the plainer people can see him" [182].

The best indication of one's spiritual progress is the ability to own one's business:

> [T]he boy who is a good fellow at someone else's expense would not work up into first class fertilizer. That same ambition to be known as a good fellow has crowded my office with second-rate clerks, and they always will be second-rate clerks. If you have it, hold it down until you have worked for a year. Then, if your ambition runs to hunching up all week over a desk, to earn eight dollars to blow on a few rounds of drinks for the boys on Saturday night, there is no objection to your gratifying it; for I will know that the Lord didn't intend you to be your own boss. [20]

The connection between business and godliness is not just presumed in the novel. Lorimer is careful to provide its ideational base. Like a good Puritan, Graham believes that the only way one can reach God is by being diligent in his "calling". One must contribute to increasing the glory of the Lord's creation. For, as Graham says in the sequel, "faith without works" [81] is meaningless. Elsewhere in Old Gorgon Graham he tells his son:

> Never ask a man what he knows, but what he can do. A fellow may know everything that's happened since the Lord started the ball to rolling, and not be able to do anything to help keep it from stopping. [159]

The only proof of one's diligence is the tangible product:

> The fact of the matter is, that we're all in trade when we've got anything, from poetry to pork, to sell. . . . But if we haven't anything to sell, we ain't doing anything to shove the world along; and we ought to make room on it for some coarse, commercial cuss with a sample case. [296]

The only poetry he cares about is the one which

sells things, that is, advertising. Otherwise, he is very contemptuous of aesthetic or intellectual pursuits:

> It would be a mighty good thing if we could put a lot of the professors at work in the offices and shops, and give these canned-culture boys jobs in the glue and fertilizer factories until a little of their floss and foolishness had worn off. [297]

The ideal of workmanship he has in mind is that of ceaseless activity in the interest of providing needed goods. He keeps "very busy trying to see that 70,000,000 people were supplied with their daily pork" [217]. Work keeps the devil away:

> It's been my experience that you've got to have leisure to be unhappy. Half the troubles in this world are imaginary, and it takes time to think them up. . . . Everybody's got to raise something in this world, and unless people raise a job, or crops, or children, they'll raise Cain. You can ride three miles on the trolley car to the Stock Yards every morning and find happiness at the end of the trip, but you may chase it all over the world in a steam yacht without catching up with it. [190-1]

The happiness Graham is talking about is not entirely earthly but spiritual:

> Happiness is like salvation - a state of grace that makes you enjoy the good things you've got and keep reaching out for better ones in the hereafter. [191-2]

Of course, there is nothing unique about equating work with happiness. Many thinkers have done it. It is the neat equation Graham posits among work, wealth and salvation which makes his philosophy unique. The people to be distrusted are of two kinds: those who have inherited wealth and those who earn low salaries. Both shirk work in order to drink and have a good time. Such people are inevitably immoral, "a lovely warning for a Sunday-school superintendent" [116]:

I've met a heap of men who were idling through life because they'd made money or inherited it, and so far as I could see, about all that they could do was to read till they got the dry rot, or to booze till they got the wet rot. [296]

There are many parables in the novel showing how the inherited wealth usually evaporates. "When a fortune comes without calling, it's apt to leave without asking" [7]. That is why Graham is so particular that his son start at the bottom. The people who start poor are luckier according to this philosophy. "I didn't have your advantages when I was a boy", he says early in Letters and you can't have mine" [1].

The wealthy have no excuse for not working. In Graham's world, work and wealth have only a symbolic connection. Wealth is the sign that the person has been industrious. However, one must not think that the ultimate aim of work should be wealth. He says in Old Gorgon Graham that one must go on working regardless of its utility:

[T]he fellow who doesn't enjoy his work and who quits just because he's made money that's the money-grubber; . . . the man who keeps right on is fighting for something more than a little sugar on his bread and butter. [293-4]

He intends to work right until "the Great Call" [27] comes. "[W]hen I retire it will be to the cemetery" [5-6].

In an enigmatic passage in Letters Graham says: "I've put a good deal more than work into my business, and I've drawn a good deal more than money out of it" [263-4]. Money, we are repeatedly told, is pointless. The transcendental nature of his meaning is clearly underscored by his programme for his grandson. "I hope to live long enough", he remarks in the sequel, "to see the kid with us at the Stock Yards, and all three of us with our coats off hustling to make the business hum. If I shouldn't, you must keep the boy strong in the faith" [293].

It almost appears as though Lorimer had set out with the intention of exemplifying Weber's thesis. Graham's life is that of complete devotion to work, done not for the sake of money but for salvation. All sensual and intellectual pleasures are suspect, and the only way he likes to spend his surplus is through charities. He is perfectly sure about his election and sees a direct connection between character and wealth. Like John D. Rockefeller, Sr., Graham can say, "The good Lord gave me the money".(28)

Lorimer has done us a distinct service by providing such a clear explication of the gospel of wealth. His novels are quite unique, for no other novelist, not even Horatio Alger, had explored the intrinsic connection between wealth and virtue in such detail. For though Alger treats vice and virtue as synonymous with poverty and wealth respectively, he does not go so far as to justify the pursuit of wealth as the means of salvation. In Lorimer, it is the earning of wealth, with its necessities of self-control and denial, which results in virtue.

Perhaps only the son of a Baptist preacher - that, too, the preacher whose congregation included P. D. Armour whose portrait the novel is considered to be - could have written these novels. We may question their literary merit, but as sociological documents they provide a rich quarry for the student of American culture.

Though Lorimer's own reputation as a novelist has been eclipsed so thoroughly that few literary histories even mention his name, his importance to American literature can be gauged from the fact that The Pit by Frank Norris was serialized in the Saturday Evening Post right after Lorimer's own novel. The Post was also the outlet for the business romances of Harold Frederic as well as the Merwin and Webster team. In this respect, Lorimer can be said to have inaugurated the romance of business. It is pure speculation on my part but perhaps, in his position as a pillar of the establishment, he provided some fuel for the anti-business sentiments of novelists like Abraham Cahan, Robert Herrick, Theodore Dreiser and Upton Sinclair. Many of these writers harboured a personal animus against him for what they considered his reactionary politics.

One comes to The Pit with certain expectations in view of the fact that it is stamped with the approval of The Post. To suit the tastes of Lorimer, a business novel must have a hero larger than life, leading an adventurous life. He should also be a self-made man who has come up in the world on the basis of his own enterprise. Curtis

Jadwin fits the bill remarkably, even though Norris had not set out with that intention. He was nevertheless blamed by several contemporary writers for glorifying and romanticizing Jadwin. Howells felt that Norris had forgotten the essential vulgarity of Jadwin's class.(29) Dreiser thought that <u>The Pit</u> was a cheap romance.(30)

The novel is the portrait of a man with an epic stature, performing mighty deeds and going down to defeat in a noble way. The business of buying futures in the commodity market is transformed through the alchemy of Norris' epic imagination into a deed as glorious and courageous as the ones described in the ancient sagas Norris was fond of quoting.

The comparison is by no means facetious. Norris' biographer describes how he developed a love for mediaeval lore as an art student in Paris. While his father thought that his son was learning painting, Norris spent his time reading Froissart and composing poems about mediaeval subjects. Later on he mourned that the American frontier had not given rise to such epic figures as Grettir, Roland, Hengist and Horsa, and the heroes of the <u>Magnusson Saga</u>.(31) So imbued was he with the world of romance that even the modern world was dyed in its hue. The modern trader became a crusader in his eyes:

> The desire for conquest - say what you will - was as big in the breast of the most fervid of the Crusaders as it is this very day in the most peacefully-disposed of American manufacturers. Had the Lion-Hearted Richard lived today he would have become a "leading representative of the Amalgamated Steel Companies," and doubt not for one moment that he would have underbid his Manchester rivals in the matter of bridge girders. Had Mr. Andrew Carnegie been alive at the time of the preachings of Peter the Hermit he would have raised a company of <u>gens d'armes</u> sooner than all of his brothers-in-arms, would have equipped his men better and more effectively, would have been first on the ground before Jerusalem, would have built the most ingenious siege engine and have hurled the first cask of Greek-fire over the walls.

The activities of American businessmen became for

him "our present commercial crusade". "The
difference", he wrote, "is hardly of kind and
scarcely of degree. It is a mere matter of names,
and the ghost of Saladin watching the present
engagement might easily fancy the old days back
again."(32)

Norris believed in America's ambition of
empire-building. He gloried over his country's
victories in the Philippines and Cuba in the
Spanish-American war which was vehemently opposed
by most intellectuals. The landing of U.S. marines
in China is for him "the steady march of
civilization".(33) The spirit of the age, in his
view, requires a different breed of men as compared
to what he would like to see them become in the
distant future. For the present, "The United
States in this year of grace of nineteen hundred
and two does not want and does not need Scholars
but Men, - Men made in the mould of the Leonard
Woods and the Theodore Roosevelts, Men such as
Colonel Waring, Men such as Booker Washington."(34)
In A Man's Woman, Lloyd says of Bennett, with
apparent authorial approval: "The world wants men,
great, strong, harsh, brutal men - men with
purposes, who let nothing, nothing, nothing stand
in their way."(35)

When the Spanish-American war broke out,
Norris was rather disappointed with the
unadventurousness of the modern battle:

> For him who smelleth the battle not very far
> off, Key West in war time is a great
> disappointment. . . . You ask more for your
> money than you actually get. You want to see
> excitement, turmoil, activity, the marching
> and counter-marching of troops, the excited
> going and coming of couriers a-horseback, the
> glint of epaulets and brass at street corners.
> . . . You want to see the correspondent in
> all his glory, leaping from a dispatch boat
> before she is even made fast to the docks,
> dashing ashore in all the panoply of pith
> helmet, Norfolk jacket, and field glasses, a
> bundle of dispatches in one hand, racing his
> fellows to the telegraph office, "getting in
> his stuff," beating his rivals, making a scoop
> . . .(36)

Naturally enough, he found Howells' novels
deficient in colour and excitement. They were

about people next door, living humdrum lives. "Why
should it be", he complained, "that so soon as the
novelist addresses himself - seriously - to the
consideration of contemporary life he must abandon
Romance and take up that harsh, loveless,
colorless, blunt tool called Realism?" The novel
Norris wanted to write would be the one "that takes
cognizance of variations from the type of normal
life."(37) It is interesting to note what he
considers "variations":

> We ourselves are Mr. Howells's characters, so
> long as we are well behaved and ordinary and
> bourgeois, so long as we are not adventurous
> or not rich or not unconventional. If we are
> otherwise, if things commence to happen to us,
> if we kill a man or two, or get mixed up in a
> tragic affair, or do something on a large
> scale, such as the amassing of enormous wealth
> or power or fame, Mr. Howells cuts our
> acquaintance at once. He will none of us if
> we are out of the usual.(38)

Leaving other variations aside, "adventurous",
"rich", and "not conventional" are used
synonymously. In the second sentence, doing
"something on a large scale" is explained as "the
amassing of enormous wealth or power or fame".
Norris would treat the accumulation of wealth on
the lines of romance, on "a large scale", just as
he had bought the biggest canvas possible for
painting the battle of Crécy in his Paris days.

The Pit, above all, is a large battle
canvas. It is Norris' attempt to portray the
romance of business life. He wrote:

> As much romance on Michigan Avenue [the street
> of wealthy Chicago merchants] as there is
> realism in King Arthur's court. It is as you
> choose to see it. . . . Romance and Realism
> are constant qualities of every age, day and
> hour. They are here today. They existed in
> the time of Job. They will continue to exist
> till the end of time, not so much in things as
> in the point of view of the people who see
> things.

If a novelist only tried, Norris continued in the
above passage, he could find "romance and adventure
in Wall Street or Bond Street".(39) True to these

sentiments, he filled <u>The Pit</u> with the clash and
roar of battle. And not the modern battle which he
had found so disappointing, but the battles of
mediaeval romance. As William Rose Benét commented
in 1942, "In writing that way, Frank Norris was
merely reflecting the American folk-legend of the
beginning of the century. In America, at that
time, the businessman was felt to be on a sort of
crusade - no one knew quite what it was all about,
but it was glorious!" The businessmen emerge from
the pages of the novel, according to Benet, as
"Nordic heroes in a lot of ironmongery, wielding
battle-axes!"(40)

The symbolic universe which Norris created
planting by romance in the Chicago of 1898, is
evident from the very beginning of the book. Laura
Dearborn, watching the opera, makes comparisons
between the ancient and the modern, the mediaeval
chivalry and the contemporary "Battle of the
Street".(41) At first, she imaginatively
transforms "the sordid, material modern life" [22]
by resorting to the mediaevalism of popular
historic fiction:

> Nobility, purity, courage, sacrifice seemed
> much more worth while now than a few moments
> ago. All things not positively unworthy
> became heroic, all things and all men. Landry
> Court was a young chevalier, pure as Galahad.
> Corthell was a beautiful artist-priest of the
> early Renaissance. Even Jadwin was a merchant
> prince, a great financial captain. [20-1]

This vision is evoked under the spell of an art
which, according to Norris, has no contact with
contemporary reality. Its "romance" is "an affair
of cloaks and daggers, or moonlight and golden
hair", the one which does "very well in the castles
of the Middle Ages and the Renaissance chateaux",
but which does not touch the modern reality.(42)

Norris objects to Laura's wish to obliterate
the present. The impossibility of doing so is
presented through the conversation between two
businessmen whose echoes "invaded the very
sanctuary of art" [40]. Initially, Laura is
irritated by the intrusion of the "discordant
element", this "hoarse, masculine whisper" [22].
She thinks, "Why could not men leave their business
outside, why must the jar of commerce spoil all the
Harmony of this moment" [23]. This is the Laura

who imagines herself to be "a maiden of a legend of chivalry" [24]. Sheldon Corthell's supplication to her is in this vein, in the style of the popular romance.

Jadwin figures at this juncture as the reality principle:

> She had had neither opportunity nor inclination to observe him closely during their interview in the vestibule, but now, as she sat and listened to him talk, she could not help being a little attracted. He was a heavy-built man, would have made two of Corthell, and his hands were large and broad, the hands of a man of affairs, who knew how to grip, and, above all, how to hang on. Those broad, strong hands, and keen, calm eyes would enfold and envelope a Purpose with tremendous strength, and they would persist and persist and persist, unswerving, unwavering, untiring, till the Purpose was driven home. And the two long, lean, fibrous arms of him; what a reach they could attain, and how wide and huge and even formidable would be their embrace of affairs. One of these great manoeuvres of a fellow money-captain had that very day been concluded, the Helmick failure, and between the chords and bars of a famous opera men talked in excited whispers, and one great leader lay at that very moment, broken and spent, fighting with his last breath for bare existence. . . . And abruptly, midway between two phases of that music-drama, of passion and romance, there came to Laura the swift and vivid impression of that other drama that simultaneously - even at that very moment - was working itself out close at hand, equally picturesque, equally romantic, equally passionate; but more than that, real, actual, modern, a thing in the very heart of the very life in which she moved. [33-4]

At the end of the chapter, when Laura's carriage is passing through the business district, comes another invocation of reality which once again proves how much more thrilling the world of modern commerce is than that of the courtly romances. Poor Corthell, the hot house artist dabbling in mediaeval stained glass art, cannot even explain it:

197

Here it was, then, that other drama, that
other tragedy, working on there furiously,
fiercely through the night, while she and all
those others had sat there in that atmosphere
of flowers and perfume, listening to music.
Suddenly it loomed portentous in the eye of
her mind, terrible, tremendous. Ah, this
drama of the "Provision Pits," where the rush
of millions of bushels of grain, and the
clatter of millions of dollars, and the
tramping and the wild shouting of thousands of
men filled all the air with the noise of
battle! Yes, here was drama in deadly earnest
- drama and tragedy and death, and the jar of
mortal fighting. And the echoes of it invaded
the very sanctuary of art, and cut athwart the
music of Italy and the cadence of polite
conversation, and the shock of it endured when
all the world should have slept, and
galvanised into vivid life all these sombre
piles of office buildings. It was dreadful,
this labour through the night. It had all the
significance of field hospitals after the
battle - hospitals and the tents of commanding
generals. The wounds of the day were being
bound up, the dead were being counted, while,
shut in their headquarters, the captains and
the commanders drew the plans for the grapple
of armies that was to recommence with
day-light. [40]

It could be said that this is the feminine
view of worldly affairs. The women, ignorant of
the actual details and eager to exalt the status of
their men folk, frequently translated their lives
into the metaphors of the historical romances they
were so fond of reading. It was an act of
imagination which at the same time glorified the
hitherto condemned commercial pursuits and
quietened moral qualms. As Duncan points out in
his study of the Chicago novel at the turn of the
century, many Chicago women novelists treated the
business world in this "epic" strain.(43) Henry
Blake Fuller provides a brilliant scene in The
Cliff Dwellers where a woman real-estate buyer
confers all kinds of heroic epithets on the
agent.(44) Similarly, Dreiser showed how Suzanne
in The "Genius", and Stephanie and Berenice in
The Titan see their lovers as Nietzschean

198

supermen. Both of these novelists, however,
satirize this inflated view of reality and present
the business pursuits in an unromantic light,
seeing the success of their protagonists in terms
of corruption and connections.

The presence of an ironic stance is nowhere
apparent in <u>The Pit</u>. In the light of Norris'
ideas, Laura's progression from the romance of
conventional art to the romance of real life has to
be considered seriously. Moreover, Laura's surname
endows her with an allegorical quality. By calling
her Laura Dearborn, Norris associates her with the
heroes of the American War of Independence and,
therefore, with the spirit of modern America
itself. She represents, perhaps, the new nation in
a state of transition, deeply attracted to the
heraldic past of European feudalism and yet unable
to resist the equally attractive song of the modern
era of industrialism. Norris' letter to Isaac
Marcosson seems to suggest such a conclusion:

> The story is told through Laura Dearborn.
> <u>She</u> <u>occupies</u> <u>the</u> <u>center</u> <u>of</u> <u>the</u> <u>stage</u>
> <u>all</u> <u>the</u> <u>time</u>, [Norris' emphasis] and I
> shall try to interest the reader more in the
> problems of her character and career than in
> any other human element in the book. The two
> main themes, consequently, are the story of
> Jadwin's corner of May wheat and the story of
> his wife's "affair" with Corthell.
>
> I shall try to show that all these are
> American issues, modern, typical and
> important.(45)

Seen from this allegorical point of view, the novel
presents Laura's ultimate renunciation of the old
world of romance in favour of the new world of
commerce which, paradoxically, is equally romantic.
In other words, she becomes, like Lloyd Searight,
"A Man's Woman". Till the era of international
brotherhood dawns - and his epochal view of history
postulates that it would not happen until the
Anglo-Saxons have circled the globe - men like
Jadwin are essential.

One is forced to draw such a conclusion
because Laura's point of view is never opposed.
Though we do see a glimpse of "a crowd of
miserables, shivering in rags and tattered
comforters" [7] in the first chapter, no attempt is

made to link their poverty to the wealth of the Dearborns or Jadwin. Later, when we hear about the starving multitudes of Italy who are suffering as a result of the high price of wheat, we also hear of the farmers who have benefitted from these same high prices. Similarly, while Cressler abhors speculation, he also admires the man who takes large risks. The moral issue regarding "cornering" the world supply of wheat is relegated to the bottom whereas its "danger" and the challenge it poses to the "smart man" are given precedence. The very impossibility of performing this feat would make the man who achieved it somewhat special if not heroic. The book opens with the Helmick failure and Jadwin's repeated statements about the virtual impossibility of maneuvering a corner.

There are other, more subtle preparations made in the first chapter. The world of art is associated with ease, femininity, warmth and enclosure, and the world of business with masculinity, reality and outdoors. Even if the battle imagery were attributed to Laura, this overt symbolism is certainly Norris' and, instead of under-cutting Laura's metaphors, seems to give them support. It would seem quite reasonable to suppose, then, that Laura's point of view is acceptable to Norris.

The business world is described again in the second chapter. Laura and her family have gone downtown and the rush of the city overwhelms her, just as it does Dreiser's characters. However, Laura is not looking for a job like them and therefore feels securely anchored:

> "There is something terrible about it," she murmured, half to herself, "something insensate. In a way, it doesn't seem human. It's like a great tidal wave. It's all very well for the individual just so long as he can keep afloat, but once fallen, how horribly quick it would crush him, annihilate him, how horribly quick, and with such horrible indifference!" . . . She was a little frightened - frightened of the vast, cruel machinery of the city's life, and of the men who could dare it, who conquered it. For a moment they seemed, in a sense, more terrible than the city itself - men for whom all this crash of conflict and commerce had no terrors. Those who could subdue it to their purposes,

must they not be themselves more terrible,
more pitiless, more brutal? She shrank a
little. What could women ever know of the
life of men, after all? Even Landry,
extravagant as he was, so young, so exuberant,
so seemingly innocent - she knew that he was
spoken of as a good business man. He, too,
then had his other side. For him the Battle of
the Street was an exhilaration. . . . The
gentle-mannered fellow, clean-minded, clean-
handed, of the breakfast or supper table was
one man. The other, who and what was he?
Down there in the murk and grime of the
business district raged the Battle of the
Street, and therein he was a being
transformed, case hardened, supremely selfish,
asking no quarter; no, nor giving any. Fouled
with the clutchings and grapplings of the
attack, besmirched with the elbowing of low
associates and obscure allies, he set his feet
toward conquest, and mingled with the
marchings of an army that surged forever
forward and back; now in merciless assault,
beating the fallen enemy under foot, now in
repulse, equally merciless, trampling down the
auxiliaries of the day before, in a panic dash
for safety; always cruel, always selfish,
always pitiless. [63-4]

Norris provides both facets of power here. The
grimness of the reality is first seen from the
point of view of the "weak" and it seems quite
similar to the annihilative vision of Dreiser's
characters who feel so threatened by the reality of
the modern city. However, a Dreiser novel does not
glorify the conqueror. In the Cowperwood trilogy,
Dreiser takes immense pains to demystify
Cowperwood's vast machinations. For Laura, on the
other hand, the "Battle of the Street" is in dead
earnest. It takes place in a mysterious,
terrifying realm where ordinary mortals fear to
tread:

To contrast these men with such as Corthell
was inevitable. She remembered him, to whom
the business district was an unexplored
country, who kept himself far from the
fighting, his hands unstained, his feet
unsullied. He passed his life gently, in the
calm, still atmosphere of art, in the cult of

> the beautiful, unperturbed, tranquil;
> painting, reading, or, piece by piece,
> developing his beautiful stained glass. . . .
> Of the two existences which did she prefer,
> that of the business man, or that of the
> artist? [64-5]

It is the businessman who wins, of course. Perhaps
no other American novel schematizes so clearly the
attitudes of late nineteenth century America. The
businessman's high estimate of himself is
contrasted with his correspondingly low estimate of
the artist. The terms of comparison are also
interesting. It is not because the artist is less
intelligent or less moral. The criterion of
judgement is what Theodore Roosevelt had called
"the strenuous life". The businessman is the
warrior-explorer whereas the artist is a recluse.
This denigration of the artist, John Kenneth
Galbraith believes, reflects the shaky self-image
of the businessman: "Scientists, writers,
professors, artists are also important competitors
of the businessman for public esteem." The battle
imagery, and the concomitant mental attitudes,
persist even today according to Galbraith: "There
is a surviving conviction, even on the part of the
executives of the largest business corporations,
that they live dangerously."(46)
    In this respect, The Pit is an extremely
relevant work in its portrayal of the mental life
of the business class. Its symbolic strategies
help us understand the hierarchal rivalries of
American society. It also helps explain why
Dreiser used the images of the frontier and the
explorer to bestow prestige on the philosopher and
the scientist. Unfortunately, The Pit does not
look at these images critically. The role of the
businessman as warrior-explorer is taken for
granted.
    Romance exists in the eyes of the beholder,
Norris believed, and it transforms the filthy,
muddy Chicago of Fuller's novels into a place that
echoes with the "thunder of battle" [80].
"Endlessly, ceaselessly the Pit, enormous,
thundering, sucked in and spewed out, sending the
swirl of its mighty central eddy far out through
the city's channels." Like the enchanted land of
romance, it is "gentle, insidious and persuasive"
at the circumference, though "terrible at the
centre" [79].

This is the unexplored territory into which
men like Sheldon Corthell never dare to come. The
"timid, innocent, feeble", "the Lambs", that is the
public, are daily "crushed to death" here [81].
Norris removes wheat, a product of man's labour,
from the realm of economics and transforms it into
a towering rival. He presents the issue as a
boxing-match of a celestial order, somewhat like
Prometheus against God. His terms free us from
worrying about injustice to the farmer or the
consumer as they present the cornering of the world
supply of wheat as a contest between two mighty
opponents.

We are told that such contests do not take
place every day. Hargus' corner was run twenty
years ago. The narrator describes it as
"legendary", "mammoth". It was lost only because
of "some chicanery on the part of his associate".
Since then, "Hargus had become a sort of creature
of legends, mythical, heroic, transfigured in the
glory of his millions" [84]. We are asked to
sympathize with him rather than rejoice that the
corner had been broken. Moreover, the corner broke
only because of "chicanery". We are somehow asked
to see Hargus as the betrayed King Arthur. Every
time we see these speculators, they are in the
"harness of the warrior" [65] battling against the
"uninterrupted thunder" of the Pit [98].

It is not that the reader does not see the
other side of the picture at all. Cressler
delivers a long speech on the evils of speculating.
He talks about "an average, legitimate value"
[129], which would keep both producer and consumer
happy. He points out the Pit's corrupting
influence on young men who lose "the very capacity
for legitimate business" [131]. However, the
problem of response stems from the overall effect
of the metaphors, the narrator's complicity in
establishing Jadwin's greatness, the contrast
between the artist and the businessman, and,
finally, an undercutting of Cressler's point of
view. For example, whereas Cressler had stripped
the speculator of his heroic aura, the narrator
reestablishes it by use of his usual, inflated
imagery:

But Jadwin was by now "blooded to the game."
He no longer needed Gretry's urging to spur
him. He had developed into a strategist,
bold, of inconceivable effrontery, delighting

in the shock of battle, never more jovial,
more daring than when under stress of the most
merciless attack. On this occasion, when the
"other side" resorted to the usual tactics to
drive him from the Pit, he led on his enemies
to make one single false step. Instantly -
disregarding Gretry's entreaties as to caution
- Jadwin had brought the vast bulk of his
entire fortune to bear, in the manner of a
general concentrating his heavy artillery, and
crushed the opposition with appalling
swiftness.
    He issued from the grapple triumphantly,
and it was not till long afterward that Laura
knew how near, for a few hours, he had been to
defeat. [190-1]

Such descriptions force the reader to believe that
the battle is risky and not just a whim of a
billionaire, as Cressler had pointed it out to be.
Jadwin believes that "the only ones who can
possibly win are the ones who take big chances"
[197].
    The information that we get from the novelist
proves his point. Jadwin takes the big decision to
become a "bull" against the bearish market of the
past three years. This step of his is presented as
an act of immense courage. No one else in the
market has thought of it. Here it is interesting
to note the facts Norris suppressed in order to
exalt Jadwin's stature. Joseph Leiter, whose
corner in the 1897 wheat crop is the basis of The
Pit, was the son of a multi-millionaire and not a
self-made man like Jadwin. At the time of the
corner, he was only twenty nine years old and was
"agent for his father's estate of more than
$30,000,000 and with large properties under his
direct control."(47) Moreover, the short supply of
wheat did not come as a great surprise as depicted
in the novel. "In fact, the years 1896 and 1897
were characterized by abnormally bad weather
throughout widely dispersed wheat producing areas.
. . . Thus there was drought in 1896 in India,
Australia, the winter-wheat belt of the United
States, and North Africa, while locusts and late
rains reduced Argentine yields."(48) Another
factor important for higher wheat prices was "the
certainty of war with Spain".(49) Norris does not
mention any of these facts. Nor does he mention
the collusion between Leiter and the Chicago meat-

packer Philip D. Armour.(50)

If Norris had included these aspects of the wheat trade, he would have found it hard to use the heroic paraphernalia. The Pit in that case would have to be seen as an economic institution and not as a kind of Grendel's den as it turns out to be. All these unpalatable facts are suppressed for the sake of creating "a single heroic protagonist". On the one hand, the reader is asked to admire the heroic warrior who ventures undaunted in dangerous territory and, on the other, he is also supposed to sympathize with his victims. The fact remains that Norris could not reconcile his sympathy for the poor with his deep admiration for the exploits of the entrepreneur and his indecision damages the novel. As Granville Hicks puts it, the reader is unable to decide whether to consider Jadwin as "hero, automaton, or villain": "[F]or the reader who wants to understand the mind of the businessman, and wants to see how speculative operations actually affect human lives, for the reader who asks that this novel should help him to understand the forces it deals with and to realize their expression in credible characters and events, for such a reader there is little but disappointment."(51)

Despite the problem of aesthetic response, The Pit remains an invaluable aid in the study of the role of business in America. Apart from its depiction of the romance of business, it also provides an insight into the process of linking the religious with the secular view of commerce. As seen earlier, Howells and Lorimer deal primarily with the religious view of the businessman. Norris, on the other hand, portrays the "rise" of the businessman in martial imagery. However, the religious view has not been entirely jettisoned. Jadwin, like the other famous businessmen of the period, is deeply religious. He runs a Sunday school which he wants to make "the biggest Sunday-school in Chicago" [73]. From Jadwin's point of view, religion and business seem complementary activities:

> I didn't 'get religion.' No, nothing like that. But I got a notion it was time to be up and doing, and I figured it out that business principles were as good in religion as they are - well, in La Salle Street, and that if the church people - the men I mean - put as

much energy, and shrewdness, and competitive
spirit into the saving of souls as they did
into the saving of dollars that we might get
somewhere. . . . I'll bet if D. L. Moody were
here today he'd say, 'Jadwin, well done, thou
good and faithful servant.' . . . The last
time I saw Moody I said, 'Moody, my motto is
"not slothful in business, fervent in spirit,
praising the Lord."' . . . [A]nd he said, 'J.,
good for you; you keep to that. There's no
better motto in the world for the American man
of business' [123-4].

Though Laura and the narrator usually present
his exploits in military terms, we are made to
realize that Jadwin himself sees his "rise" in
terms of his religious fervour. He is the steward
of the Lord, one of the men "who are doing the work
of the world, . . . the men who are making them
[the United States] the greatest nation of the
world" [125]. As Herrick perceived, the uniting
thread between the two spheres is the metaphor of
war. Since men visualize their religious pursuits
in terms of war, the next logical step is to see
the other spheres of their lives in the same
vocabulary. (52)
  It is a pity that Norris allowed his metaphors
to run away with the theme. If he had written the
novel in the same style as he used in his short
story, "A Deal in Wheat", it would have been a work
of remarkable merit. There is no doubt that if the
battle imagery had been curtailed and confined to
Laura's limited vision, Cressler's view allowed
more scope and the narrative voice made neutral,
the result would have been happier. In its present
shape, it has pleased few readers. Nevertheless,
with the disappearance of names like Harold
Frederic, Richard Harding Davis, E. W. Howe, George
Horace Lorimer, Edwin Lefèvere, and Merwin and
Webster, The Pit is our only source for
understanding that romantic vision which "brought
back in a humdrum business world the adventurous
swashbuckling life of another time."(53)
  This was the official version of the American
businessman, its justifications provided by the
Spencerian version of evolution and blessed by the
church. Its metaphors, culled from the popular
historical novels of the period, as well as from
the Darwinian jungle, allowed its propagators to
short-circuit the traditional ethical and religious

objections to the pursuit of wealth. It gave them a set of terms which allowed them to transform a hitherto ambiguous activity into a prestigious occupation. The feudal heroes were the ideal of the day and the businessman clung close to them to partake of their glory.

This self-estimation did not go unchallenged. Novelists like Howells and Twain attacked not only the romantic portrait of the businessman but the genre of romance as well. They insisted on presenting things as they looked in "the light of common day".(54) The novels of the realists are essentially involved in the process of unmasking and debunking. Mark Twain expressed his anger with the business class for its appropriation of the symbols associated with feudalism by satirizing its entire ethos in A Connecticut Yankee in King Arthur's Court. The novel presents the American inventor as a symbol of progress and civilization whereas the famous knights do nothing but manipulate stock. The addiction of the knights who do nothing but sit around round tables shuffling stocks reflects Twain's disgust with businessmen.

However Mark Twain's satire has become blunt with time. The general interpretation of the novel considers it to be Twain's indictment of European aristocracy and a tribute to the Yankee entrepreneur. My view, however, is corroborated by Howells' review in which he wrote: "There are passages in which we see that the noble of Arthur's day, who fattened on the blood and sweat of his bondmen, is one in essence with the capitalist of Mr. Harrison's day who grows rich on the labor of his underpaid wagemen. . . ."(55) Howells' remarks make absolutely clear that, for Mark Twain, Hank Morgan is not a Yankee entrepreneur but a scientist in the grip of profiteers. The knights of the Round Table are ridiculed not so much for their own sake but because of their appropriation by the business community in order to privilege itself.

Such meanings, however, cannot emerge unless more attention is paid to the public discourse of the period.

Perhaps no other novel reflects the ideological issues of the time as completely as A Life for a Life by Robert Herrick. The antipodal rhetorics of the two camps can be seen face to face in this novel. Disliked by the critics and the public alike, the novel is valuable for the purpose of this study as a compendium of the dominant symbols

of the age. The businessman's bulwark of rhetoric
is systematically examined and demolished under the
onslaught of Herrick's irony.

The novels that have been examined so far
present the world as it looks to their
protagonists. An American Tragedy, for example,
is constrained to examine life as it appears to the
unheroic outsider. Samuel Griffiths' estimate of
himself, though touched upon, is not examined in
detail, as the focus of the novel is on Clyde.
Likewise, in the Cowperwood novels, though we are
shown the inner motivations of Cowperwood, the
question of his impact on the character of the
unheroic outsider is not addressed. Herrick
attempted to break out of these restraints of what
he called the "single character" frame. He
considered such novels to be "simplification[s]".
The novel, he felt, is "a form that is peculiarly
adapted to the presentation of life broadly . . .
the wide expanse, the maze of life where
multitudinous forces act and interact."(56) Like
many other American novelists, he felt constricted
by "the harsh lines of Realism" and experimented in
allegorical modes.(57)

A Life for a Life is Herrick's "allegory of
the New World".(58) The novel, he was insisting at
this stage in his career, must go for a "freer,
more epic" breadth. It must become "social
history", a record of the total milieu rather than
a conventional probe into the mind of a single
individual.(59) However, though he thought his
novel contained "much of the best writing I have
ever done, or ever can hope to do",(60) the
critical response has been negative. The novel,
instead of being judged on its own ground, was
declared defective for its failure to depict
"minute human interplay"(61) among "genuine"
characters.(62)

Edwin Honig says that the very word "allegory"
is suspect to the modern sensibility. It connotes
to us "something obvious and old fashioned",
whereas symbolism, the fashionable word, stands for
"a superior literary practice". As a result, "the
question of technical skill, which should cover the
writer's management of all fictional materials, is
reduced to a question of his intention: the greater
explicitness or transparency of intention showing
allegory's inferiority to symbolism as literary
procedure."(63) Just this kind of a bias has
prevented A Life for a Life from receiving the

scrutiny it deserves. If our tastes were not so dominated by the realistic mode of fiction, we would, instead of condemning the novel outright, be asking why Herrick chose to write in what he himself called the "Hawthornesque" mode.(64) From my point of view, the novel is very interesting for its direct engagement with the symbols that mediated an American's view of reality at the turn of the century.

Even though Herrick had a rather low opinion of Dreiser's work, the thrust of their work points in the same direction. Like Dreiser, Herrick defined his work in terms of the economic aspect of reality: "I think the one subject, consciously or unconsciously, always to be found in my books is the competitive system - its influences upon men and women."(65) In his "allegory of the New World", Herrick attempted to look at both "the money-maker, his inner meaning and his self-explanation" as well as the "little people" who made him their ideal.(66) The plot concerns the quest of the hero, Hugh Grant, for a sustaining ideal in the welter of commercial life. Herrick examines the mysteries of social hierarchy and the rarefied upper levels of the social pyramid as they appear to a member of the lower orders.

When the novel opens, Hugh is about to leave his native town for the wide world of the city like a typical late nineteenth century hero. The symbolic nature of this journey is made explicit from the very beginning: "He quickened his steps as he reached the familiar stretch of road between dark willow trunks. The old trees made a tunnel for the road, and the memory of childhood fears at this forbidding passage seized him" [7]. Hugh is leaving "the shabby nest" to "take flight" to the city [8]. "The City! The lure of youth, the battle ground and the burial field, the tournament and the pageant - yes, it drew him as it was drawing all the strong youth of the land" [17-8].

A realistic novel would have proceeded with the journey. But Herrick inserts a chapter to contrive a meeting between Hugh and Alexandra who, true to her name and status, symbolizes the military nature of the undertaking. This symbolic woman, who appears regularly in late nineteenth century novels in a role similar to that of the mistress of the vassal knight in the mediaeval romances, representing both the cause and the reward of the quest, explains to Hugh the rules of

the "tournament" he is about to enter. This
millionaire's daughter tells him: "You have always
got to go in for things to win. . . . Father says
so. It's the men who fight hard who do things in
the City, just as in games. You've got to win if
you want to amount to anything" [30-1]. Alexandra's
values overpower Hugh. Thus far he had been led by
"the harmony and significance of that radiant inner
vision, in which there were deeds without strife,
triumph without defeat" [30]. He had believed in
"great deeds and beautiful living" [35], the "power
and peace that came with work well performed" [31].
The desire for Alexandra changes Hugh. "This was
not a world of abnegation", he realizes [35]. "Life
was a game for the prizes. 'The best man wins!' the
girl had said, smiling with suggestion in her eyes.
It was a word of truth. His heart leaped at the
thought of gathering his prize in the great arena.
At last the male will to prevail was roused in the
youth" [37]. The narrative comment alerts the
reader to the appropriation of the sport analogy by
the businessman: "Some day he would learn that to
play fair was a class ideal - in sport, and then he
would recall the phrase with ironical mirth,
knowing how little of this ideal there was in the
weightier matters of life" [27].

The city, always spelled with a capital C in
this novel, carries the same symbolic weight as in
Dreiser's, Fuller's or Norris' novels. It is a
place where the "deadly battle of existence" [29]
is fought daily. It also epitomizes a way of life
that is presented to the newcomer in many forms:
"And already it was sowing its seed in the heart of
the youth, this night. It was moulding him as it
moulds the millions, after its fashion, warming his
blood with desire, - the vast, resounding, gleaming
City . . ." [44].

During his wanderings in the city on his first
night, Hugh is attracted by "the bright light of an
immense sign, set upon the roof of a building. In
mammoth letters that stretched across the breadth
of the narrow roof, compact of soft fire, the
message burned itself upon the night

SUCCESS

The great sign shining in the dark night from the
roof drew the youth as the candle draws the moth"
[44]. "The glittering sign", placed above a ten
floor high building, "burned far into the night,

shooting its message into all quarters, printing itself in the radiance of the heavens. This was the text of the great City, its watch-word day and night, set high above in blazing letters, burning steadily, a brand to sink into the souls of men." It advertizes Benjamin Gossom's "The Success Correspondence School", and his weekly leaflets, "Gossom's Road to Success" [44-5].

This "fiery symbol" is the only source of lighting in the attic Hugh shares with a man called Anarch during his first days in the city. Benjamin Gossom, the novel makes clear, is Herrick's satire on Benjamin Franklin as well as the other apostles of the religion of success. Herrick blames him for having equated the desire for accumulation with the spirit of Christianity. "He, Benjamin Gossom, was accustomed to look upon himself as an agent of the Lord in the work of sowing broadcast the wealth of this His earth by enticing His children to desire whatsoever material things they did not possess" [56]. "In the Gossom faith, to be busy meant Prosperity, and Prosperity meant Happiness. And his good God blessed those who had attained Prosperity, and hence Happiness" [219].

Possessed by the spirit of this symbol, as well as literally "bathed in its beneficent beams" [57], Hugh goes out into the city "to find his way into the great arena" [58]. Hugh goes straight to Alexandra's father, appropriately named Alexander Arnold, who had once bought land from Hugh's adoptive grandfather. That transaction becomes Hugh's pass key to the magical inner sanctum. "The luxury of the place penetrated the ignorant youth like a fragrant perfume." The house awakens "new appetites" in Hugh. "The language was new, but it spoke powerfully to him." The next passage connects the religious and the heroic quests: "This was the secret of the great Symbol in whose beams of light he had slept. . . . And this was what Success meant, in exact terms!" [62-3].

Hugh is hired as a clerk in Arnold's bank, "that wonderful temple of marble and bronze erected in the heart of the City by its able president as a monument to himself" [66]. Here Arnold and his men play at "Credit, reorganization, receivership" which are but "the dull names of the modern powder and shot and shell" [68]. The papers in the vault, "deeds of trust, agreements of underwriting, prospectuses of bond issues", are poetry to these men: "Something of the poetry of these dumb

documents penetrated him. Deeds, they were, - deeds
of Ambition, Imagination, Daring, as well as of
Thrift, Opportunity, and Integrity" [328]. Hugh's
initiation in the bank is a moment of awe and
aspiration for him. However, his host in the attic
sees it ironically:

> "Found your place so quickly?" the bearded one
> commented jocularly. "and chosen Finance for
> your career? Good! It is the most promising
> ladder these days if you have nimble feet. Do
> you see yourself in the president's room or
> sitting behind a pile of currency at the
> cashier's desk?"
> "I've got a job, that's all." To tell
> the truth, he had been thinking in his few
> idle moments of that wonderful room in the
> rich man's house and the silvery tone of the
> woman's voice he had heard there.
> "No doubt," said his host, munching his
> food with good appetite, "you have read your
> Franklin, or at least my friend Gossom's
> imitation of him, and you are thinking that
> Thrift and Prudence and Purpose - with a few
> more capital-letter virtues - must lead to
> prosperity and fame _via_ the Bank." [75]

Anarch provides the commentary that links Hugh's
movements in the world of commerce to the
transcendental realm of religion. The first day
Hugh comes home in a new suit of clothes, he
remarks, "That's right; clothes count where you
aspire to climb. They are the first outward sign
of the inner grace of Success" [87].
However, Hugh soon realizes that the capital-
letter virtues will not take him where he wants to
go, to "the silvery voice in the silent room" [88].
Like Dreiser's heroes, Hugh finds himself separated
from his heart's desire by a wall:

> Between him and the field in which they seemed
> to move in a large freedom lay a thick wall,
> and he began to wonder if the Anarch were not
> right when he said that no faithful service,
> no mere fidelity to the virtues, would open a
> door in that wall. He believed that on the
> other side of the wall there was a wonderful
> land in which men achieved their wills, where
> there was beauty and splendor and pleasure to
> be had - where the silvery voice could be
> heard again! [92]

The "hard eyes" of the "Symbol" mock Hugh in his
despondent mood. "You will join the bread-line
around the corner", they say, "or sleep on the
public benches. For in the City no one waits for
the weak." "So the sign mocked, and the youth in
his fever began to know Fear - that terrible devil
the Anarch had predicted. . . . And with fear came
the sense of failure" [93].

Immediately afterwards, however, Herrick
causes the magic door to open and gets Hugh "the
chance" through an "accident", thus flying in the
face of the Franklinian philosophy:

> At last Fortune came tapping at the youth's
> door, but not in any expected guise.
>   "There are no accidents in a strong man's
> life," President Butterfield was wont to
> enunciate to the young men with their feet
> upon the threshold of life. "Chance is merely
> the marvelous pattern of destiny, working in
> terms of human character for failure or
> success!" [111]

President Butterfield - alongwith Gossom, the
scholarly arm of the banker's empire - paints his
deeds in the vocabulary of heroism, or what, to the
narrator, are "eloquent platitude[s]" [146]. These
platitudes are scattered throughout the novel,
providing a counterpoint to the narrator's ironic
voice. Butterfield picks his epithets from chosen
literary sources: "'The council of the gods still
continues,' replied the college president
homerically" [144], describing the meeting of the
industrialists. He provides moral and poetic
coatings to the deeds of the rich:

> "The world is full of heroes, . . . expectant
> of their hour. They say it is a material age,
> and yet nothing so stirs the blood of our
> people as the tale of some brave deed like
> this, some act of personal prowess. The love
> of deeds is keener than ever before in the
> history of the world. Our young men roam the
> earth in search of achievement, - the hunting
> of game, the taming of nature - fighting
> dragons wherever met." [147]

The deeds being described here are those of sea

captains and pilots. However, this is just the preamble of Butterfield's speech. As he continues, we realize that his earlier heroes are there just as analogies for the men of the business world:

> Business, I take it, has its fascination for most virile men because of the instinct for doing, - spur of accomplishment! It incites them to speculation, the conceiving of large enterprises, taking hazardous risks - the same love of deeds. [147]

The narrator comments: "The banker Whiting nodded approvingly, - it was a thought he often made use of in his dinner speeches" [147]. Butterfield skillfully removes all traces of money and market and dresses the act in the trappings of romance:

> "[D]oing is the proper function of men. The only men admired by real women are the doers - not for the money they possess, but for their power!"
> With this final touch of idealism he turned his handsome head toward Alexandra.
> "I like men who do things," she said simply.
> "We try to marry heroes," the broker's wife added.
> "Precisely; women demand heroes, - doers. And as long as the world is what it is and women are what they are, men will respond with deeds to lay at their feet - industrial triumphs, deeds of munificent charity, venturesome deeds, - ah, the world is full of deeds!"
> His modulated voice dropped into silence, and he lighted his cigar. The amiable man of learning had voiced the pagan creed of this world. [148]

Herrick had complained elsewhere of the romantic expectations of women, which they in turn got from reading the popular romantic fiction:

> For a democratic people, as we call ourselves, we have a singularly unreal and aristocratic literature. . . . American women must be held responsible for this aristocratic taste. . . . Their favorite epic still remains the old barbaric one of the triumphant male who

conquers the riches and the powers of this
earth, only to lay them at the feet of his
loved one, chivalrously surrounding her with
all the glories of his conquest, and rewarded
by her with faithfulness and love.(67)

Like Howells, Fuller, Norris and Dreiser,
Herrick felt that the American scene was somehow
being transformed into the semblance of chivalric
romance.   Herrick   traces   a   direct   connection
between social symbols and individual acts. Hugh,
the allegorical youth, comes to regard himself
through what Burke calls the "terministic screens"
of the dominant group.   "But now, with a leap of
hot pride, he said to himself that never again
should he be there, until he too was equipped with
deeds, and as an equal might cross the carpet
before her" [149].

Before Hugh considers himself worthy of
re-entering Paradise Valley, he must undergo an
initiation.   He   must   not   come   without   his
"certificate of deeds", if he wants to penetrate
this "warm centre of human destiny" [149-50]. The
deeds are obviously to be enacted in the battlefield of the business world.   The truth, on the
other hand, is that an "accident" has ensconced him
in Oliver Whiting's favour and Hugh climbs fast on
the ladder of power without much effort. Within a
matter of three years, telescoped in a short
paragraph, Hugh has become one of the "mighty".
There is, then, "a discrepancy between outward
seeming and inward truth" [114].   "Surely when
Oliver Whiting and his friends 'believed in a man,'
his path was paved with golden opportunities!"
[178].   While the pages of Ambition, the Gossom
magazine, record "weekly the stories of the heroes,
- with the tables of their possessions", and
Butterfield harps about "an era of great deeds"
[168], the rise of Hugh Grant has nothing in common
with their formula.

The realistic novels about the businessman
usually follow a biographical pattern. Dreiser's
Cowperwood novels, Abraham Cahan's The Rise of
David Levinsky, Will Payne's The Money Captain,
David Graham Phillips' The Master Rogue, and
Herrick's own The Memoirs of an American Citizen
concern themselves with the life of the hero and
its implications for the society. In A Life for a
Life, on the other hand, Herrick makes Hugh take
an about turn at the peak of success. Just when he

has been made a joint director of the newly formed
Universal Power Company, the germ of doubt enters
his mind. Like Howells, Herrick believed that man
could be the agent of his own regeneration. Just
as the natural goodness of Silas Lapham reasserts
itself after years of dormancy, Hugh's spiritual
nature rebels against the "domination of things"
[92]. This is in keeping with Herrick's
"idealistic" programme: "Literary art that presents
character and life under the influence of large,
uplifting, and ideal motives and impulses, apart
from reality, is idealistic. All great art has
something of the idealistic mood."(68)

Herrick ascribes Hugh's conversion to the
subtle influence of nature. "Distaste of the City
ways? He had lived good years in the wind-swept
places beneath the mountains, where men were men,
not jugglers of paper symbols. They built their
lives out of the ground, not in dizzy Babel towers
of cards" [178]. Now when Alexandra tells him
about the "law" of the survival of the fittest, he
informs her, "It is not so with men! . . . The
best may be eaten, and the worst be the eaters"
[191]. When he witnesses the casuistry of law as
practised by Arnold's lawyer in order to eat up a
smaller company, he thinks: "Is there not a vaster
realm, the realm of human justice, altogether
beyond the law?" [225]. Now he sees the likes of
Alexander Arnold shorn of their heroic mantle:

> Alexander Arnold had never created or imagined
> any thing. He had bought what was cheap and
> had sold it dear to the public. Others
> conceived, others dáred, others dreamed;
> Arnold bought and sold, like the huckster in
> the market, only on an enormous scale. [202]

The eulogistic rhetoric of Butterfield, Gossom
and his disciple Percy Todd had tried to exorcize
all the words connected with the marketplace. For
them, "Alexander Arnold is one of the most
effective forces of modern civilization, - a
supreme example of the application of imagination
to the economic world" [202]. "Hear President
Butterfield, phrasing the thought of the
contemplative observer, the guide of youth, 'Young
men should rejoice that it is their destiny to live
in such an era of great deeds as the present!' . .
. 'Achievement!' cries Gossom, 'is in the air. The
powers of men multiply'" [168]. Hugh is no longer

taken in by these eulogies even though the success
industry is touting him as the self-made man of the
hour. When a diplomat's wife remarks, "How you
Americans ennoble trade! . . . With you it is
statesmanship, war!", Hugh answers, "yes, . . . it
is hell" [243].

Eaten by doubt, Hugh goes away with Anarch on
"a little journey" to complete his "education"
[248]. "I will show you the process of
prosperity", Anarch tells him, "the waste of life"
[255] about which the Gossom faith keeps mum. The
novel, in this sense, is patterned on two opposing
journeys. The first has the elements of romance:
the trial, the deed, the beautiful woman waiting at
the end. The second is called a "pilgrimage", and
serves a purificatory purpose. "From this
pilgrimage there emerged a Man, - resolute, of
steadfast purpose" [253]. The journeys are
connected structurally as well as linguistically.
The first one had taken Hugh to "the lighted house
of mirth" [253], the second takes him away from it.
The first had introduced him to the men of "deeds".
The second is about deeds as well, but of a
different kind. These are the deeds of common men,
miners who had been trapped for eighteen days in
one of Arnold's mines. "There were heroic deeds in
the black hell those eighteen days, - deeds to make
tears come at the thought that men can rise so
high. And yet they say these miners are little
better than beasts!" [255].

The second journey questions all the smug
assumptions about the road to success. Hugh is
taken around small mining towns, factories,
warehouses and slums in order to see for himself
"what life means to the silent multitude upon whose
bent shoulders the fabric of society rests, - what
that 'life, liberty and the pursuit of happiness' .
. . has brought to the common man in this land of
destiny and desire" [268].

The regenerated Hugh, who has seen through the
mirage of "the shining way" leading to Alexandra
[316], goes back into the world with the hope of
changing it. He begins with his own family. His
cousins are as restless as he was at the beginning
of the novel. Their hearts are "brimming with
desires, soft pleasurable wishes, visions of
sensuous delights" [339]. The locus of these
desires is, again, the city. In them, life comes
full circle as they get ready to reenact the mythic
journey to the city. Hugh tries to change them and

succeeds moderately. He brings them to the city
and provides them with a home by taking up a bank
clerk's job himself. While their dreams of
material success are soon dashed to pieces, Hugh
gradually makes them at peace with their lot. One
of his cousins learns a new approach to life in the
university. His newly developed love of science
frees him from the anxiety to "make good".
    Hugh and his new family draw their strength
from an ideal community. "Here in Columbia Heights
there is a social solidarity lacking in more
privileged societies. We are all hanging on by the
same strap!" [367]. The community is made of
conscious men and women whose souls no longer dream
of the lures of wealth:

>   And slowly, imperceptibly, like the changing
>   seasons, as time sped, came that change which
>   the man desired in the lives about him. . . .
>   [T]he cycle of evil will in these beings was
>   being broken, new impulses taking the place of
>   old. . . . Thanks to the Venables, the
>   Professor, the organist's wife, a family at
>   the corner and another on the next block, the
>   household was drawn into simple human ties.
>   The drab streets of Columbia Heights became
>   thick with interwoven strands of friendly
>   meeting. Life, it seemed, was like some
>   silent place in the forest, carpeted with the
>   weaving tendrils of a common vine, and thus
>   made warm and soft for the feet of the
>   wayfarer. [368]

    Hugh and his friends achieve their modicum of
happiness in the midst of the noisy, polluted, ugly
and immoral city. Unlike classic American heroes,
Hugh does not abandon this fallen world but comes
back to begin "at the bottom" [361], with no desire
for climbing up. He has also acquired an
understanding of the historical tradition that has
given business its prestige and power:

>   My hatred somehow evaporated as I traced back
>   the strands of the web, and found how they
>   were woven out of tradition and false ideals -
>   out of the very aspirations of the fathers of
>   the country - so that each one feels justified
>   to himself in what he does to perpetuate the
>   chain of evil. [360-1]

Like Dreiser, Herrick felt that the novelist
had to penetrate to the bottom of things in order
to analyse how culture formed an individual's
identity. The need to excel in the marketplace, he
felt, was related to America's historical
experience. A Puritan himself, proud of his New
England ancestry, Herrick excoriated the pseudo-
Puritanism of the prophets of the gospel of wealth.
Property and the property-holders, he felt, were
being "sentimentalize[d]" in America: "One hears
much of the romantic quality of American life,
which when analyzed is found to consist for the
most part of our dazzling performances in
conquering wealth and the frequently bizarre
conduct of the successful rich." "Our novelists",
he complained, "still cling to the old
individualistic string, - the story of the
triumphant industrial pirate and his adventures
with the stock market and incidentally, womankind."
Herrick's own fiction parodies this romantic view.
Like Howells, he felt that realism was not just a
literary technique but a moral choice. The
romantic fiction, he charged, never questions the
status quo and therefore creates "morally flabby"
personalities.(69)
This preference for real life as opposed to
romance, for democratic values as opposed to
superman-worship, places Herrick in the company of
Howells, Twain and Dreiser. All of them fought
against what they considered the growing tide of
materialism. Their fiction satirized the heroic
pretensions of the parvenu dynasties and the values
they espoused. They portrayed them as sources of
corruption and misery for the common man while
masquerading under the cover of honorific symbols.
Hugh Dalziel Duncan wrote, "In the symbolic
life of the writer, there must be myths, legends,
heroes, utopias, ideologies. These images of the
past and the future supply the writer with themes,
plots, incidents and characters which give form to
the mind and soul of his community. Such symbols
must exist or the writer cannot write at all."(70)
The common symbolic strategies of the novelists
discussed in this study confirm Duncan's views
about the social origins of symbols. I have tried
to point out the relationship of these writers to
the symbolic environment of their society and the
necessity to include it in our analysis. When
literary works are studied from this perspective,
as a discourse addressed to an audience which is at

the same time listening to other discourses, they
provide deep insights into the cultural and
spiritual life of a society.

When formalists choose to disregard all traces
of rhetorical skirmish and linguistic appropriation
in literary texts, they forget that literature,
like all language, is, above all, communication.
Unless we recognize this, unless we agree to
explore the "why", "when", and "where" of literary
communication, instead of concentrating on only the
"how", we run the danger of playing esoteric and
socially irresponsible games.

NOTES

1. Quoted in introduction to William Dean
Howells, The Rise of Silas Lapham, with
Introduction and Notes by Walter J. Meserve, vol.
12 of A Selected Edition of William Dean Howells
(Indiana University Press, Bloomington, 1977) xxv.
2. Edwin H. Cady, The Road to Realism:
The Early Years of William Dean Howells (Syracuse
University Press, n.p., 1956) 231.
3. Howells, Atlantic Monthly 23 (February
1869) 260.
4. Howells, "Henrik Ibsen," Edwin H. Cady,
ed., W. D. Howells as Critic (Routledge & Kegan
Paul, London, 1973) 436.
5. These words of Jesus were freely adapted
to suit the needs of modern business, along with
other usable quotations from the Bible. See, for
example, Bruce Barton, The Man Nobody Knows.
6. From MSS Synopsis of "Rise of Silas
Needham," The Rise of Silas Lapham, 369. Howells'
emphasis.
7. Quoted in Edward Wagenknecht, William
Dean Howells: The Friendly Eye (Oxford University
Press, New York, 1969) 55.
8. Howells, Atlantic Monthly 24 (December
1869) 763.
9. Howells, "Glimpses of Central Park,"
Impressions and Experiences (Harper & Brothers
Publishers, New York, 1909) 180.
10. Howells, A Modern Instance, with
Introduction and Notes to the Text by George N.
Bennett, vol. 10 of A Selected Edition of William
Dean Howells (Indiana University Press,
Bloomington, 1977) 32.
11. Howells, "Puritanism in American
Fiction," in Literature and Life (Harper and

Brothers Publishers, New York, 1902) 281.
12.   Daniel Aaron, Men of Good Hope: A
Story of American Progressives (1951; Oxford
University Press, New York, 1969) 183.
13.   Howells, "Glimpses of Central Park,"
Impressions and Experiences, 174, 180.
14.   Henry B. Fuller, With the Procession
(1895; University of Chicago Press, Chicago, 1965)
17.
15.   Howells, "The New Historical Romances,"
W. D. Howells as Critic, 301, 304, 300.
16.   Marrion Wilcox, "The Works of William
Dean Howells," Harper's Weekly 40 (4 July 1896).
Quoted in Robert L. Hough, The Quiet Rebel:
William Dean Howells as Social Commentator (1959;
Archon Books, n.p., 1968) 29.
17.   From MSS Synopsis of "Rise of Silas
Needham," 369.
18.   Quoted in Cady, The Road to Realism,
236.
19.   Frank Luther Mott, A History of American
Magazines, vol.4, 1885-1905 (Harvard University
Press, Cambridge, Mass., 1957) 716.
20.   The New York Times (23 October 1937) 1.
21.   John Tebbel, The American Magazine: A
Compact History (Hawthorn Books, New York, 1969)
189.
22.   Mott, A History of American Magazines,
688.
23.   Tebbel, George Horace Lorimer and the
Saturday Evening Post (Doubleday, Garden City,
1948) 128.
24.   Upton Sinclair, Money Writes!: A
Study of American Literature (Published by the
Author, Long Beach, Calif., 1927) 69.
25.   George Horace Lorimer, Letters From a
Self-Made Merchant to His Son (William Briggs,
Toronto, 1902) and Old Gorgon Graham: More
Letters from a Self-Made Merchant to His Son
(William Briggs, Toronto, 1904).
26.   Tebbel, The American Magazine, 190-1.
27.   Henry Ward Beecher, Lectures to a Young
Man on Various Important Subjects (John B. Alden,
Publisher, New York, 1889) 45.
28.   Quoted in Richard M. Huber, The American
Idea of Success (McGraw-Hill Book Company, New
York, 1971) 77.
29.   Howells, "The Last Work of Frank Norris,"
Harper's Weekly 47 (14 March 1903) 433.
30.   Dreiser, Letters, 1: 329.

31.   Norris, "The Frontier Gone At Last,"
Donald Pizer, ed., The Literary Criticism of Frank
Norris (University of Texas Press, Austin, 1964)
113.
32.   Norris, "The Frontier Gone At Last,"
113-4, 114.
33.   Norris, "The Frontier Gone At Last," 111.
34.   Norris, "Salt and Sincerity," The
Literary Criticism of Frank Norris, 215.
35.   Norris, A Man's Woman (1900; AMS Press,
New York, 1970) 82.
36.   Quoted in Franklin Walker, Frank Norris :
A Biography (Doubleday, Doran and Company, Inc.,
New York, 1932) 176.
37.   Norris, "A Plea for Romantic Fiction,"
The Literary Criticism of Frank Norris, 76.
38.   Norris, "Zola As A Romantic Writer," The
Literary Criticism of Frank Norris, 71.
39.   Norris, "The True Reward of the
Novelist," The Literary Criticism of Frank
Norris, 86.
40.   William Rose Benét, "Rereading 'The
Pit,'" Saturday Review of Literature (25 July
1942) 17.
41.   Norris, The Pit, Introduced by James D.
Hart (Charles E. Merrill Publishing Company,
Columbus, Ohio, 1970) 64.
42.   Norris, "A Plea for Romantic Fiction,"
75, 77.
43.   Duncan, The Rise of Chicago as a Literary
Center from 1885 to 1920, 2.
44.   Henry Blake Fuller, The Cliff Dwellers,
146.
45.   Quoted in Don Graham, The Fiction of
Frank Norris: The Aesthetic Context (University
of Missouri Press, Columbia, 1978) 127.
46.   John Kenneth Galbraith, The Affluent
Society (1958; Andre Deutsch, London, 1977) 137,
86.
47.   Leonard D. Nesbitt, Tides in the West
(Modern Press, Saskatoon, 1962) 18.
48.   Wilfred Malenbaum, The World Wheat
Economy 1885-1939 (Harvard University Press,
Cambridge, Mass., 1953) 178.
49.   Charles Kaplan, "Norris's Use of Sources
in The Pit," American Literature, 25 (March
1953) 80.
50.   Kaplan, 79-80.
51.   Granville Hicks, The Great Tradition:
An Interpretation of American Literature Since the

Civil War (1933; The Macmillan Company, New York, 1935) 174-5.

52.   Cf. Robert Herrick, A Life for a Life (The Macmillan Company, New York, 1910) 420: "Of course they are happy! . . . A fine martial spirit,--that hymn. Even in our religious moods we have to fight. The sword in hand is the popular attitude for saint as well as sinner."

53.   Van Wyck Brooks, The Confident Years: 1885-1915 (E. P. Dutton & Co., New York, 1952) 103.

54.   This phrase of Howells' provides the title of Cady's The Light of Common Day: Realism in American Fiction (Indiana University Press, Bloomington, 1971).

55.   Howells, My Mark Twain: Reminiscences and Criticisms (Harper & Brothers Publishers, New York, 1910) 146.

56.   Quoted in Louis J. Budd, Robert Herrick (Twayne Publishers, Inc., New York, 1971) 64.

57.   Quoted in Blake Nevius, Robert Herrick: The Development of a Novelist (University of California Press, Berkeley, 1962) 200.

58.   Quoted in Nevius, 206.

59.   Quoted in Budd, 64, 65.

60.   Quoted in Budd, 78.

61.   Budd, 75.

62.   Nevius, 213.

63.   Edwin Honig, Dark Conceit: The Making of Allegory (Faber and Faber, London, 1959) 3, 4-5.

64.   Quoted in Budd, 80.

65.   Quoted in Edward Wagenknecht, Cavalcade of the American Novel: From the Birth of the Nation to the Middle of the Twentieth Century (Henry Holt & Company, New York, 1952) 235-6.

66.   Herrick, "The American Novel," Yale Review NS 3 (April 1914): 431.

67.   Herrick, "The American Novel," 430.

68.   Quoted in Nevius, 204.

69.   Herrick, "The American Novel," 419, 427, 426.

70.   Duncan, The Rise of Chicago as a Literary Center from 1885 to 1920, xiv.

Chapter Seven

CONCLUSION

The texts included in this study have been seen as part of a "symbolic interaction" which, according to Burke and Duncan, is an essential aspect of human society. Society, they propose, "arises in, and exists through, the communication of significant symbols".(1) This is a vastly enlarged conception of the power of symbols over the human mind than had been postulated before. Even though writers like Coleridge and Wallace Stevens had attempted to create a metaphysics of the imagination and to claim a higher role for metaphors than science and philosophy were willing to grant, it is Burke and Duncan who successfully proposed a systematic theory of symbols and metaphors in determining social reality.

Seen in the light of this theory, that is, as rhetorical utterances spoken in a context, works of literature become an invaluable aid to understanding the nature of social reality. They make us understand the source of the power of dominant groups in a society and the manner in which these groups seek legitimization by invoking the consecrated symbols of authority. Read this way, literature helps us to penetrate through the mystifications the social elite usually create around themselves. It gives rise to an enlightened citizenry, impervious to manipulation though not to reasonable persuasion. By demolishing the idols of power and by exposing their rhetorical arsenal, literature sets us free from our fears and anxieties concerning the need to perform according to a set of codes given by others and bids us examine our posture of supplication to the powers that be.

The American novelists studied in this work challenged the claims of the business community on

the sacred symbols of American society. For the
most part, they mocked the businessman's claims to
be a pilgrim or a knight and created strategies to
combat the world-view generated by this imagery of
quest. They felt that the canonization of the
businessman was destructive of the social fabric
because it created two classes of human beings: the
ordinary, dull mass of the unsuccessful ones and
the brilliant supermen of business. They refused
to accept the imagery of the battlefield as the
true representation of social reality and provided
their own model of community life.

However, most critical analyses of these
novels seem to attach secondary importance to these
issues. Though a considerable amount of pain is
taken to establish the recurrent symbolic, thematic
and structural patterns, little attempt is made to
relate them to the external reality. While the
smallest biographical detail is given careful
consideration, there seems little awareness of the
rhetorical nature of language, of the fact that
"each word relies for its meaning upon a social
context",(2) that words are "acts upon a scene".(3)
The need to paint the scene with appropriate
documentation is seldom acknowledged, history being
considered somehow irrelevant to examining the
artistic unity of a text.

By history I do not mean just the summary
background information which is considered
sufficient to orient the reader in the world of a
literary work. I mean the specific words and
utterances in which history is couched, and which
echo through a work of literature and are easily
understood by its first audience. They provide the
essential context for the literary work. It is the
role of the critic and the teacher to bring out
that context, to relate the words to their
particular "scene", lest it be lost in the passage
of time and the work lose much of its meaning. For,
as Burke points out, "effective literature could be
nothing else but rhetoric".(4)

It is, then, at their own peril that the
critic and the teacher cut off a work of literature
from this external world of other gestures and
other utterances which had provided the initial
artistic impetus. A study of a writer's private
symbolism can be meaningful only when supplemented
by an awareness of his existence as a social being.
Unless the symbolic environment of a writer's
society and the stock of public symbols circulating

Conclusion

in that society are taken into account, one is
bound to lose what Burke calls "perspective by
incongruity", the perspective a writer creates by
"violating the 'proprieties' of the word in its
previous linkages".(5)

NOTES

1.   Duncan, <u>Communication and Social Order</u>,
143.
2.   Burke, <u>Counter-Statement</u>, 164.
3.   Burke, <u>The Philosophy of Literary Form</u>,
xvii.
4.   Burke, <u>Counter-Statement</u>, 210.
5.   Burke, <u>Permanence and Change</u>: An
<u>Anatomy of Purpose</u>, introduction by Hugh Dalziel
Duncan (1935; Bobbs-Merrill, New York, 1965) 90.

Index

Herrick, Robert 2, 7,
20, 43, 163, 192,
206; A Life for
a Life 207-19

Hofstadter, Richard 29,
85
Howells, William Dean 2,
7, 23, 25, 74, 163,
193, 195, 207, 215,
219; The Rise of
Silas Lapham 168-
80, 181
Hubbard, Elbert 24, 26,
28, 159

James, Henry 2, 9, 26,
40, 74, 91

Kazin, Alfred 57, 58
Knight-errantry, imagery
of 4, 5, 25, 26,
27, 28, 29, 77, 194,
227; in Dreiser 39,
44, 62, 93, 122-3,
124

Legitimation, through
symbols 6, 12, 13,
15, 16, 18, 20, 21,
22, 28, 30
Lehan, Richard 45, 58,
150
Lorimer, George Horace
7, 24, 180, 205,
206; Letters from
a Self-Made Mer-
chant to His Son
and Old Gorgon
Graham 181-92

Masters, E. L. 2, 79,
133, 140, 149
Mather, Cotton 13, 14,
177
Matthiessen, F. O. 36,
76, 79, 99, 122
Mencken, H. L. 48, 71,
93, 132, 146
Mulqueen, James 122

Myers, Gustavus 76

Nietzsche, F. 71, 73,
79, 127, 160, 198
Norris, Frank 7, 25, 39,
88, 91, 123, 139,
149, 210, 215; The
Pit 192-206

Pilgrimage, imagery of
4, 5, 13-5, 16, 17,
18, 28-9, 46, 217;
in Dreiser 39, 120-
3, 154-5
Pizer, Donald 58, 92,
98, 122
Poverty, in gospel of
wealth 17-8, 24,
168, 175; Dreiser on
53, 64, 82, 126-7

Rockefeller, Sr., John D.
15, 21, 30, 63, 65,
85, 90, 125, 192
The romance genre and
gospel of wealth
23, 25-8, 168, 178,
181, 192, 196-8,
203, 214; in Dreiser
44, 77-8, 120, 122

Said, Edward 2
Scott, Sir Walter 25
Sherman, Stuart P. 38,
152
Shinn, Everett 139, 149-
50
Sinclair, Upton 2, 39,
76, 181, 192
Smiles, Samuel 41, 63
Social Darwinism, symbols
of 5, 17, 29, 46,
171, 185; in Dreiser
54, 84-5, 102
Success literature 15-8,
21-2, 24, 40-1, 43-
4, 90, 155, 169-70,
181, 211, 219; in
Dreiser 30, 39-40,
44, 56, 63-5, 77-8,

228